Mobile Bay and the Mobile Campaign

To my patient loving wife, Ann,
and her many lonely hours

Mobile Bay and the Mobile Campaign

The Last Great Battles of the Civil War

by CHESTER G. HEARN

McFarland & Company, Inc., Publishers
Jefferson, North Carolina, and London

British Library Cataloguing-in-Publication data are available

Library of Congress Cataloguing-in-Publication Data

Hearn, Chester G.
   Mobile Bay and the Mobile campaign : the last great battles of the
Civil War / by Chester G. Hearn.
      p.   cm.
   Includes bibliographical references and index.
   ISBN 0-89950-820-0 (lib. bdg. : 50# alk. paper) ∞
   1. Mobile (Ala.)–History–Civil War, 1861–1865.   2. Mobile Bay
(Ala.), Battle of, 1864.   I. Title.
   F334.M6H43   1993
   973.7'54–dc20   92-50891
                                                              CIP

Manufactured in the United States of America.

McFarland & Company, Inc., Publishers
  Box 611, Jefferson, North Carolina 28640

Contents

List of Illustrations

Introduction

In the early stages of America's Civil War, both governments recognized the importance of the South's seaports. Even ancient and ailing Gen. Winfield Scott, hero of the Mexican War and President Abraham Lincoln's chief military adviser, foresaw that closing Confederate ports would be the most effective means of preventing war materiels from entering the industrially weak Southern states. Designed to strangle the Confederacy, Scott's Anaconda plan called for the occupation of the Mississippi River and the blockade of every seaport from Norfolk, Virginia, to Galveston, Texas.[1]

Union Secretary of the Navy Gideon Welles opposed the Anaconda strategy for several reasons. He argued that Lincoln's formal proclamation establishing a blockade of Southern ports awarded the Confederate government status as a distinctly separate national entity. He did not believe that the United States could declare a blockade of its own ports without admitting to the world that the Union had been divided and two governments formed from one. Although Welles suspected that the Confederacy would eventually be granted belligerent rights by foreign powers – a step that fell short of full recognition – he continued to reject the Anaconda plan with his customary stubbornness.[2]

Welles probably had more in mind than political reasons when he first opposed the blockade. From Alexandria on the Potomac to Brownsville on the Rio Grande, the U.S. Navy faced the nearly impossible task of watching 3,549 miles of Southern coastline with only 90 vessels on the navy register. Much of the seacoast contained great stretches of double-lined shores with numberless bays and hundreds of small inlets along which shallow-draft coastal vessels traveled unmolested.[3] The principal ports of Wilmington, Charleston, Savannah, Mobile, New Orleans, and Galveston were well protected by large estuaries, narrow inlets, meandering sandbars, and land formations suitable for the development of protective forts. Although New Orleans surrendered to Adm. David G. Farragut on April 25, 1862, other important seaports, like Mobile, remained under Confederate control until the last year of the war. By then Welles had done his job well – the U.S. Navy had grown to 641 vessels.[4]

1

After capturing New Orleans, Farragut's orders from Welles stipu-
lated that he "also reduce the fortifications which defend Mobile Bay and
turn them over to the army to hold."[5] After several months of blockade
duty off Mobile Bay, the admiral admitted that his Gulf Squadron could
patrol the Alabama coast and prevent some blockade-runners from reaching their destination, but he did not believe his ships, which always needed
fuel and repairs, could eliminate the traffic. As an example he cited the ease
with which the undermanned and unarmed commerce raider *Oreto* (CSS
Florida) steamed through four Union gunboats posted off Fort Morgan in
daylight and escaped into Mobile Bay with minimal damage. Four months
later the same vessel ran back to sea without receiving a scratch.[6]

In August 1862 Farragut began developing plans for the capture of
Mobile Bay. He had just been promoted to rear admiral for forcing the surrender of New Orleans, and he wanted to duplicate that performance.
From refugees he learned that the three forts guarding the entrances to
Mobile Bay were being strengthened. Comdr. Robert B. Hitchcock, USN,
had picked up six deserters from Fort Morgan on July 31, questioned them,
and issued a detailed report on the strength of the forts and the small naval
squadron operating in the bay. At this time Farragut believed that the
forts could not withstand an attack by a strong naval force; their garrisons
were lightly manned, and many of the guns had not been mounted. Fort
Morgan carried the heaviest firepower, but most of the parapet guns were
32-pounder smoothbores with limited range and unreliable accuracy. The
smaller casemate guns, 24-pounders, were mostly smoothbores. Fort
Morgan, with 79 guns and 700 men under Col. William L. Powell, CSA,
could not match the firepower of Farragut's fleet if the admiral were able
to marshal all his ships for an immediate strike. Fort Gaines mounted
another 30 guns, but Fort Powell, still under construction, had not yet
become a factor in the defense of the bay. However, Farragut learned that
his old friend, Adm. Franklin Buchanan, had taken charge of the Confederate navy at Mobile, and he knew that "Buck," as he called him, would
eventually give him trouble.[7]

During the Civil War Buchanan's and Farragut's roles might easily
have been reversed. Born in Baltimore, Maryland, on September 17, 1800,
and after an impressive naval career, Buchanan became the first superin-
tendent of the U.S. Naval Academy. On April 21, 1861, he resigned his captain's commission after 46 years of service, believing that Maryland would
secede from the Union. When he discovered that the state intended to remain loyal, he wrote Navy Secretary Welles asking that his resignation be
withdrawn. Welles refused and dismissed Buchanan from the service, forcing him into retirement.[8] Although Welles might be criticized for discard-
ing an officer of Buchanan's high credentials, the navy secretary suspected
that Buchanan would never accept service against the South.[9]

U.S. Secretary of the Navy Gideon Welles (photo courtesy National Archives).

Buchanan, who hoped that sectional difficulties could be settled without war, returned to his home in Maryland and for several months looked after his estate, tended his crops, and tried to remain neutral. However, pressure from secessionists and friends in the South eventually added to his personal irritation over dismissal by Welles, and on August 31, 1861, he crossed the Chesapeake and made his way to Richmond. Five days later Navy Secretary Mallory accepted his application to join the Confederate navy and commissioned him a captain.[10]

Farragut, on the other hand, had been born on July 5, 1801, in the tiny hamlet of Campbell's Station, Tennessee, and, at the time Virginia seceded

CSS *Florida* running the blockade at Mobile (courtesy Century Publishing).

from the Union, resided comfortably with his family at Norfolk. By birth and residence Farragut was a Southerner. However, his well-known Union sympathies made his presence in Virginia unwelcome, and he moved north, only to be watched by some of his associates who doubted his fidelity to the Union. Navy Secretary Welles dispelled many doubts when he placed Farragut in charge of the West Gulf Blockading Squadron and ordered him to capture New Orleans. Four months later the South's greatest seaport surrendered, and Farragut became a national hero.[11]

Until then Buchanan's brief career in the Confederate navy had been equally impressive, earning him the grade of admiral. When Farragut heard of the promotion, he wrote his wife: "Frank Buchanan is at Mobile and is an Admiral. I suppose he was promoted for his conduct on board the *Merrimac[k]* [CSS *Virginia*]."[12] On March 8, 1862, Buchanan had demonstrated his fighting instincts by attacking the Union squadron at Hampton Roads in the converted *Merrimack* and destroying two wooden warships, *Congress* and *Cumberland,* and three steamers. A bullet wound in the thigh prevented him from commanding the *Virginia* in its famous battle with the USS *Monitor* the following day. The wound healed, and in August Navy Secretary Mallory wrote Buchanan of his promotion and gave him command of all naval forces at Mobile.[13]

As Buchanan began to build ironclads on the Alabama and Tombigbee rivers, Farragut nervously watched his plans for an early attack on Mobile Bay disintegrate. The Virginia campaign had turned out badly for the Army of the Potomac, and Welles could not send vessels from the James River Squadron to the gulf. Maj. Gen. Benjamin F. Butler, who ultimately proved to be one of Lincoln's most incompetent political generals, withheld troops Farragut needed to seize and occupy Forts Morgan, Gaines, and Powell.[14] Secretary Welles, worried that the Confederate army might mount an attack and recapture New Orleans, wrote Farragut "that an adequate naval force should be maintained in the Lower Mississippi, especially at New Orleans. That city must be held and our small army there must receive all necessary support from the Navy."[15]

Farragut refused to relent in his determination to convince Welles that Mobile Bay must be attacked and the forts occupied if blockade-running was to be eliminated. Fast, sleek runners dodged his gunboats and continued to slip into Mobile Bay with arms, ammunition, medicines, and blankets and then slipped back out again loaded to the gunwales with cotton and kegs of Confederate specie.[16]

During the war British consuls at Mobile kept fragmentary statistics on the number of successful blockade violations by runners entering the port. Their count of 208 did not include many of the smaller sailing vessels that plied their way into the bay by following safe, shallow coastal routes, nor did it include violations during slow periods, when the trade attracted less public attention. When Confederate finances abroad hit rock bottom, the government put agents into the field to requisition cotton throughout the Deep South and concentrate it for shipment to Europe in Mobile, Wilmington, Charleston, and a few smaller ports scattered around the Gulf of Mexico. Blockade-running sustained the South's war effort, and armaments entering the port of Mobile supplied Confederate forces in Mississippi, Alabama, Georgia, Louisiana, and Tennessee.[17]

A squadron of six well-armed Union vessels, stationed directly off Fort Morgan, could slow but not stop traffic between Havana and Mobile. Farragut also worried that more-heavily-armed cruisers built abroad and purchased by the South would continue to increase Confederate naval strength and threaten the blockade. He pointed to the unexpected arrival of the CSS *Florida,* writing: "They have now three 10-gun gunboats in Mobile, and [we] will require a large force to blockade them, and I think it will be cheaper to run the forts if I can secure an outlet through Grant's Pass. I will soon have my vessels in condition to try it."[18] Assistant Secretary of the Navy Gustavus Vasa Fox replied: "We have our navy yards filled with broken-down vessels, and we know your needs and will exert ourselves to help you." Somewhat casually Fox added: "I notice you speak of Mobile. We don't think you have force enough, and we do not expect you to run risks, crippled as you are. It would be a magnificent diversion for the country at this juncture, but act on your own judgment and do not give way to any unnecessary risks. We only expect a blockade now and the preservation of New Orleans."[19]

Farragut, remotivated by Fox's "magnificent diversion," again appealed to Butler for a commitment of troops, but the general temporized, ignored the request, and took refuge behind a profusion of self-imposed administrative duties.[20]

To keep Fox receptive to the project, the admiral warned that several ironclads were under construction that, when commissioned, would be very formidable in shoal water and that waiting for their completion before attacking Mobile made no sense. Farragut understood Welles' irritation over blockade-running, but privately he wanted to smash Buchanan's ironclad program before it developed into a serious menace.[21]

In the meantime Farragut's naval force captured Galveston and a large portion of the Texas coast. Applying again to Butler for troops to occupy and hold several captured forts, and again receiving no response, Farragut decided to go to New Orleans and find out directly from the general what military aid he could expect.[22]

Farragut found New Orleans in a state of disorder and Butler's military campaigns disconnected, badly organized, and on the verge of collapse. By now President Lincoln had become disenchanted with Butler's management of the department and sent Maj. Gen. Nathaniel P. Banks

Adm. David Glasgow Farragut (courtesy U.S. Naval Photo Center).

with a force of 20,000 men to relieve him.[23] Farragut greeted Banks with renewed hope and pressed for a combined operation against Mobile Bay, but he soon discovered that Lincoln had sent another political general who organized magnificent dinners and dances but equaled Butler in military incompetence. With operations muddled by a change of generals, new initiatives for the Upper Mississippi River, and chaos in Louisiana, Farragut finally realized that his plans for the occupation of Mobile Bay would have to wait. Unexpected disasters in the gulf and new orders from Welles kept most of his large wooden gunboats in the Mississippi. Mobile Bay got a badly needed respite that was to last nearly two years.

The year 1862 passed without Farragut getting beyond the planning stage. His plan of attack, developed that summer, remained on the shelf until the summer of 1864. Loyall Farragut, the admiral's son, joined his father at Pensacola in October 1862. He confidentially reviewed the plan and wrote:

> [I]t differed only in a few details from the one subsequently adopted. The admiral had made no provision for ironclads, as he did not expect any from Welles. He distinctly said that he should select a day when the tide was running flood, and a light breeze blowing from the west, so that the smoke from the rebel forts would be blown in upon their gunners and disconcert their aim.[24]

The delay gave Buchanan time to improve the defenses of Mobile Bay, although for the next two years he heard persistent rumors that Farragut was coming. At that time Buchanan's little naval squadron consisted of the wooden gunboats *Selma, Gaines* and *Morgan* and the small ram *Baltic*. During the latter part of 1862, the admiral spent most of his time getting the CSS *Florida* back to sea and expediting supplies for his ironclads.

Brig. Gen. John H. Forney, military commander at Mobile, worked well with Buchanan. They shared problems, discussed solutions, and behaved in a mutually supportive manner.[25] Forney, a professional soldier and West Point graduate, had received a wound in the right arm at Dranesville on December 20, 1861. His insistence on strict discipline made him unpopular among the men, although it earned him the respect of his peers. Buchanan, also a staunch disciplinarian, had confidence in Forney and spent much time with him inspecting land defenses and discussing better methods for improving and strengthening the forts, especially Morgan and Gaines.[26] Unfortunately for the admiral, Lt. Gen. John C. Pemberton also recognized Forney's ability, promoted him to major general, and ordered him to Vicksburg.[27]

Changes in army commanders made Buchanan's job more difficult; he considered the situation a crisis. Brig. Gen. William W. Mackall knew nothing of conditions at Mobile when he took command of the Department of the Gulf in December. About the time Mackall became familiar with his new post, he was succeeded by Maj. Gen. Simon B. Buckner. Buckner had specific orders from President Jefferson Davis to fortify Mobile, but he spent only four months in the area before receiving command of the Department of Eastern Tennessee.

No doubt Buchanan considered Buckner's new orders untimely. The small force at Mobile had no strong military commander for three months, and work on the fortifications languished. Maj. Gen. Dabney H. Maury reached Mobile in July 1863, and after a few weeks familiarizing himself with engineering plans, battery strength, the status of earthworks, the topography of the district, Buchanan's projects, and other problems in the Department of the Gulf, he gradually established priorities and issued orders.[28]

The Confederate army and navy shared a mutual cause but seldom acted with a spirit of cooperation. Maury and Buchanan worked together better than did most senior officers sharing responsibility for the same geographical area. However, Maury was more concerned with the immediate defense of Mobile, and Buchanan concentrated on naval requirements associated with the defense of the bay. To Forts Morgan, Gaines, and Powell Maury assigned commanders who had not distinguished themselves in battle; however, he did not always have a choice in their selection. He concentrated on the city's fortifications, and for almost two years watched Richmond siphon off his infantry and conscript his skilled workmen for service on other battlefields. Just before the Battle of Mobile Bay, Buchanan could not find enough experienced naval personnel to man his vessels. During the Mobile Campaign, Maury could not find enough men to defend the earthworks, and with Buchanan a prisoner and out of action, the admiral's lethargic predecessor, Ebenezer Farrand, gave Maury very little naval support.

Between August 1862, when Farragut first planned his attack, and August 1864, when it finally took place, Maury and Buchanan each had 24 months to prepare. Even after the Battle of Mobile Bay, Maury had another seven months to improve the city's defenses before Maj. Gen. Edward R. S. Canby mounted the Mobile Campaign. The scarcity of resources and supplies throughout the Confederacy condensed into a microcosm of agonies and frustrations faced by two competent commanders, one naval and the other military, at Mobile.

Conversely the two-year delay in attacking Mobile Bay cost the Union ten ships, several hundred men, and massive amounts of war materiel. Throughout this period blockade-running continued to keep the Confederacy supplied with necessities (and luxuries), and permitted cotton to finance the war by reaching Europe through Mobile.

The occupation of Mobile Bay was far more important to the Union than was the capture of the city. Whoever controlled the bay controlled blockade-running. Mobile never became a large industrial center and throughout the war remained principally a port. Once Farragut entered Mobile Bay, the capture of the city held more political allure than strategic importance. General Canby's Mobile Campaign concentrated on securing access to the Alabama and Tombigbee rivers, as he intended to march into central Alabama, from where grain, guns, and munitions still supplied the Confederate army. He needed a secure line of communications, and the Mobile defenses stood in his way.

Had Farragut and Butler occupied Mobile Bay in the summer of 1862, the engagement would have been fought very differently from the contest two years later. The same is true of the Mobile Campaign. Technology and battle experience drastically changed warfare during those years. New tactics, attitudes, and inventions all coalesced into new military concepts that continued to expand onto the oceans and into the trenches of World War I. Had Farragut made his attack in 1862, Mobile might have missed the opportunity to preview many of the future changes in warfare. Known as the Gem City of the Gulf, Mobile had its place in the Civil War. Though overshadowed by grander and bloodier battles, the two contests – one mainly naval and the other principally military – rise in stature as magnificent tactical examples of combined operations in which opposing commanders used the war's most advanced technology.

Chapter 1

Year of Transition

With United States Navy Admiral David G. Farragut busy on the Mississippi and the CSS *Florida* safely back at sea, his Confederate counterpart, Admiral Franklin Buchanan, concentrated on improving the strength of his small naval squadron and supporting the effort of the army to improve the impregnability of the forts. What began as a year of opportunity soon settled into months of frustration. Military priorities across the Confederacy took precedence over Mobile Bay. The Union navy seemed content to blockade the port, runners and coastal vessels continued their trade, and at times the war seemed far away. On rare occasions Fort Morgan exchanged a few shots with Farragut's blockaders, but only as a reminder that the war could not be completely forgotten.

At Mobile, Buchanan controlled the navy but exercised no influence over the regiments assigned to the district or to the fortifications guarding the entrances to the bay. Those belonged to the military. As long as no immediate threat existed, the numerous war secretaries concerned themselves with other military priorities. Work on the forts progressed at a snail's pace.

In November 1862 James A. Seddon became the Confederacy's fifth secretary of war.[1] In poor health but a staunch supporter of Jefferson Davis, Seddon acquiesced in presidential directives that a stronger administrator might have challenged. On important issues he seldom made decisions without first conferring with the president and obtaining his agreement. Because of military activity in Virginia, Tennessee, and Mississippi, he left the command of the District of the Gulf in confusion and without leadership until the spring of 1863.

At first Buchanan tried to overcome military inactivity by compensating with his usual untiring energy, but he had little patience for administrative hassles. Even at age 62, he would rather fight than quarrel with a bureaucracy. As a result Buchanan looked for more productive work, and defense projects continued to lag.

Seddon ordered Major General Maury to Mobile on April 27, 1863, but he did not take actual command until late May.[2] One month after his arrival he reported to the War Department: "I cannot perceive in any direction

hereabouts indications of an early attack upon Mobile. The blockading squadron have been more active recently, and no steamer has come in during this
'dark moon,' nor ha[s] the *Alabama* yet been able to venture out." Maury
optimistically added: "Were the two new iron-clads, the *Nashville* and the
Tennessee, now ready for service, we could not only break up the blockade,
but we could probably capture and hold New Orleans."[3] For the next 12
months Maury's messages to the War Office dwelt on the completion of the
ironclads and the much-heralded hope of dismantling the blockade.

Since the engagement between the *Virginia* and the *Monitor*, the Confederate program for building ironclads up inland rivers had become a well-
known fact. Through deserters and refugees, Farragut learned of four
ironclads under construction at Selma. He wanted to steam into Mobile
Bay, capture the forts, and eliminate the threat. Although restrained by
Welles from making the attack, the admiral was probably not overawed by
ironclads. Unlike some of his contemporaries, he considered them grossly
overrated "cowardly things," and he could not imagine a navy composed of
vessels that ugly.[4]

In February 1863 the commander of the Mobile blockade squadron,
Commodore Robert B. Hitchcock, captured a deserter, James Carr, from
the "rebel gunboat *Selma*." After questioning Carr, Hitchcock reported
that two rams were on their way down river and could be expected in
Mobile Bay any day. In a worried memorandum fraught with symptoms of
"ram fever," Hitchcock added: "So soon as they [rams] can be prepared for
service Admiral Buchanan intends to attack the blockading vessels . . . for
the purpose of raising the blockade. It is generally understood in Mobile
that this will occur about the 10th or 15th of March." From the same inter-
view, Hitchcock also learned that Buchanan was building two floating
ironclad batteries, one to be stationed at Grant's Pass and the other to be
anchored opposite Fort Morgan in the Main Shipping Channel.[5]

No record indicates whether James Carr willfully deserted or whether
Buchanan planted the information to create worry among Hitchcock's commanders. In the same report Hitchcock passed along estimates grossly ex-
aggerating the actual strength of Mobile Bay's defenses. It is difficult to
believe that a low-ranking deserter like Carr would have detailed knowledge
of the number of troops at Mobile, the exact strength of batteries surrounding the city, the number and size of the guns in each fort, and that three
more seagoing ironclad steamers were being built at Selma that were expected "to be finished and ready for service by the 1st of April." Hitchcock
did not report whether he believed Carr's statements, but at the close of
his memorandum, he added: "It was proposed [by Buchanan] to attack Ship's
Island by going down through the sound, but no volunteers could be obtained
for the purpose, and no thought of such a project has been entertained
since."[6]

While buying time to improve his naval force, Buchanan sought innovative ways to annoy the blockaders and keep Hitchcock's nervous squadron worried and rattled. In late January he organized an expedition consisting of the steamers *Crescent* and *Junior* and placed them under the command of some of his best officers. Each night one of the blockaders anchored in the Swash Channel to intercept inbound or outbound runners. Buchanan wanted the vessel captured. He discussed careful plans for a surprise night attack and instructed the men to carry only pistols and cutlasses. To distinguish between themselves and the enemy, each man wore a white cover on his cap and a white shirt. They planned to ease alongside the unsuspecting vessel, board it, overwhelm the crew, and bring it into port, thereby adding another gunboat to Buchanan's dismal squadron. Moments before the attack was due to be sprung, however the outbound runner *Alice*, with eight hundred bales of cotton, grounded under the guns of Fort Morgan. Though unaware of the planned attack, Hitchcock reacted by placing a second Union gunboat in the channel, thereby thwarting Buchanan's surprise.[7]

In late February Hitchcock learned that his squadron had been the target of an aborted attack by a submarine. "On or about the 14th," he wrote:

> an infernal machine, consisting of a submarine boat, propelled by a screw which is turned by hand, capable of holding five persons, and having a torpedo which was to be attached to the bottom of a vessel and exploded by means of clockwork, left Fort Morgan at 1 p.m. in charge of the Frenchman who invented it. The intention was to come up at Sand Island, get the bearing and distance of the nearest vessel, dive under again and operate on her; but on emerging found themselves so far outside of the island and in so strong a current that they were forced to cut the torpedo adrift and make the best way back. The attempt will be renewed as early as possible, and three or four others are being constructed for that purpose.[8]

The submarine attack Hitchcock reported was a second attempt at an experiment started at New Orleans by James R. McClintock and Baxter Watson, marine engineers and co-owners of a steam-gauge manufactory. The original project had been backed by well-to-do sugar broker Horace L. Hunley and investors H. J. Leovy, John K. Scott, and Robbin R. Barron. Early trials with the prototype submarine *Pioneer* encouraged the owners. Good businessmen that they were, they applied for a patent and received letters of marque from the Confederate government approving the vessel's private use to capture or destroy enemy shipping. Farragut attacked New Orleans before *Pioneer* could be perfected, causing McClintock to lament: "the evacuation of New Orleans lost this Boat before our Experiments were completed . . . this Boat demonstrated to us the fact that we could

Construck [*sic*] a Boat, that would move at will in any direction desired, and at any distance from the surface."[9]

The loss of the *Pioneer* did not discourage the inventors. Convinced that a profit could be turned from their enterprise, McClintock, Watson, and Hunley fled to Mobile and in the summer of 1862 engaged Thomas Parks and Thomas B. Lyons, owners of a local foundry and machine shop, to build a vessel similar to the one lost at New Orleans. The new contractors laid the keel on Water Street and moved the partially completed vessel to the foundry for final fitting.

Built of boiler iron, the sub was slightly larger than the *Pioneer* but similar in shape. Two sets of vanes at the bow controlled diving, and for steering a single rudder was placed aft. The inventors worked on an electromagnetic propulsion system, using the limited technology known at the time, but eventually abandoned the effort and reverted to the original crude method of using a crew of crankers. Two hatchways fitted with glass coamings (to keep out water) provided good vision and lighting. A mercury gauge indicated depth. Though the submarine handled easily in quiet water, it moved slowly. Limited space cramped the crankers, and once the vessel submerged the air quickly turned foul.

Eager to attack a Union gunboat, the owners attached a torpedo to *Pioneer II* and began towing the vessel to Fort Morgan. Five men squeezed into the shell—four crankers and the captain. Unlike the calm of inland waters, swells broke over coamings. Someone left the hatch open for ventilation, and wash from a passing ship filled the hull with seawater. The men bailed frantically, but the vessel rolled heavily, settled lower, and finally sank with all aboard.[10]

McClintock and Watson began work on a third submarine, named for their principal financier and fund-raiser, Hunley. The *Hunley* took a different form, elliptical in cross-section and lengthened to provide space for more crankers. A false keel of cast iron, easily detachable, provided the main ballast. Water compartments at each end gave the commander auxiliary ballast and the ability to trim. The ends were tapered, and hatches were placed on top. The result was a submarine that looked very much like a miniature of those used in World War I. The vessel was 30 feet long, 4 feet wide, and 5 feet deep. Between the two hatches on top was a conning tower with an air shaft rising above it. The shaft had a valve that could be closed when the ship submerged. Fins on the sides raised and lowered the ship as it moved underwater. The vessel carried an ordinary rudder and a propeller protected by a circular housing. The crew consisted of one officer, one petty officer, and seven seamen. Eight of the men provided the motive power by turning cranks geared to the propeller shaft. The ninth man stood with his head in the forward hatch and steered by looking through glass-panes set in the hatch coaming.[11]

Launched in the spring of 1863, the *Hunley* cruised around the inner harbor on numerous test runs. The vessel lacked longitudinal stability and had a bad way of nosing-down to the muddy bottom and sticking there until the crew suffocated. McClintock, however, claimed that all the accidents were caused by the crews' carelessness.

One successful trial almost ended in disaster. A copper torpedo containing 90 pounds of powder was connected by a towline to the *Hunley*'s aft. The captain closed the hatches, lighted the candles, and opened the seacocks. Water rushed into the tanks, and the sub settled until only the hatches remained above the surface. The captain peered through the coamings at his target, an old barge, and ordered the crankers to get the sub underway. Noting the compass bearing, he depressed the vanes and watched the green water close over the glass. When he reached the desired depth, he leveled off and slowly passed underneath the target's hull. Once clear he signaled the petty officer to pump the ballast, and the sub began a slow rise to the surface. A sudden deafening explosion rolled the sub over and made her hull ring loudly from the concussion. The *Hunley* steadied and triumphantly surfaced, her officers grinning from opened hatches, feeling resurrected from a watery tomb.[12]

More tests led to more modifications. Another near disaster occurred when the wind blew the trailing torpedo along at a faster rate than the submarine could travel. To avoid blowing the sub up with its own device, the pilot cut the line and barely got away from the drifting explosive.

Hunley, who now had taken charge of the operation, modified the vessel to carry a torpedo fixed to a 20-foot spar attached to the sub's bow. Instead of passing under the enemy, the sub would sink only to hatch depth and plunge the explosive into the target. This new method, when tried, resulted in a tremendous shock to the sub, but the *Hunley* and her badly shaken crew survived the test.

News of submarines continued to filter out to Commodore Hitchcock on the USS *Susquehanna*. He doubled watches, and any suspicious floating debris prompted a call to quarters. For numerous reasons Hitchcock showed signs of increasing demoralization. Criticized by superiors for not stopping blockade-runners and fretting over imaginary attacks on his squadron by Buchanan's feeble naval force, Hitchcock manifested early symptoms of command paranoia. Farragut relieved him but a few days later revoked the order. Hitchcock wrote an official friend: "I suppose that I deserved the castigation you gave me for growling.... As to the court of inquiry, it is all right; you will be my principal witness. If it will only take me out of this ship before something worse occurs I will be thankful."[13]

Hunley put an end to one of Hitchcock's worries when he received a proposal from John Frazer and Company of Charleston, South Carolina.

The banking firm offered anyone sinking the *New Ironsides* or the *Wabash* $100,000, and $50,000 for every monitor destroyed. After the last fatal trial on Mobile Bay, Buchanan's naval personnel had dubbed the *Hunley* "the Peripatetic Coffin." Although submarines of this type may have improved the odds against a fight with Farragut's fleet, Buchanan felt little regret when Hunley packed his drawings, loaded the sub on a pair of flatcars, and out of patriotism or the hope of financial gain, carried her away to Charleston. There four more crews gave their lives before a fifth, on the night of February 17, 1864, sank the USS *Housatonic* about five and one-half miles off Fort Sumter. The submarine never returned.[14]

Hitchcock continued to complain to the Department of the Navy about conditions affecting the efficiency of the West Gulf Blockading Squadron. He could not contact Farragut because the admiral had taken his fleet up the Mississippi and beyond Port Hudson. The terms of service for a large number of enlistees had expired, and replacements had not arrived. He wrote that off Mobile "some of our gunboats can not make seven knots, and all of them require repairs." He pleaded for reinforcements, warning: "There is strong evidence that an attack will be made by the rebel force at Mobile when they get their ironclads down from Selma and Montgomery. That our force should be strengthened to me is very evident."[15]

Two weeks later Welles responded unsympathetically, reminding Hitchcock that "schooners run the blockade from Havana every week, supplying the city of Mobile and the surrounding country with many of the necessities of life." Stung by the rebuff, a few days later Hitchcock chased and captured the schooner *Alabama* (Havana to Mobile), with a cargo of wine, brandy, coffee, cigars, and other dry goods. The skipper admitted running the blockade three weeks earlier.[16] But Hitchcock's problems were over, at least in the gulf. He headed for New York, leaving Capt. John R. Goldsborough in charge of the Mobile squadron.

Born in the District of Columbia on July 2, 1809, Goldsborough entered the U.S. Navy as a youngster, served under Capt. David D. Porter, and in 1855 was promoted to commander. Shortly after the outbreak of the Civil War, he received his captaincy and commanded the USS *Florida* as senior officer of the blockading squadron off Charleston. In March 1863 he moved his flag to the USS *Colorado* and took command of the Mobile squadron.[17]

Shortly after his arrival off Mobile Bay, Goldsborough reported the capture of the schooner *Clara*, caught trying to run under the protective guns of Fort Morgan. A month passed quietly before another schooner, the sloop *Elias Beckwith*, Havana to Mobile, with an assorted cargo, became a prize of the USS *Pembina*. Unlike Hitchcock, the new commander found Mobile Bay duty to be rather quiet and pleasant, at least for the moment.[18] Goldsborough appeared to be off to a good start.

When Lt. Comdr. James E. Jouett in the USS *R. R. Cuyler* overhauled another prize, the side-wheeler *Eugenie*, Goldsborough discovered an annoying fact. The steamer had been outfitted in New York and loaded with arms, ammunition, and powder, ostensibly for the port of Havana. Some arms merchant in New York was trading with the enemy. Before Jouett caught the vessel, the skipper had thrown the register, manifest, logbook, and all incriminating documents overboard. "She is a new side-wheel steamer," Goldsborough reported, "six months old, coppered, very fast, about one hundred tons, and would make a fine dispatch boat for Admiral Farragut."[19] Farragut, delighted with Goldsborough's suggestion, asked the judge at Key West "to have the prize steamer *Eugenie* sent to New Orleans for service in my squadron after she is adjudicated by the court."[20] On July 9, 1862, the Navy Department purchased the vessel from the prize court for $20,000, armed her with two small 12-pounders, and sent her to Farragut. Renamed the USS *Glasgow*, the vessel participated in the Battle of Mobile Bay as a dispatch boat.[21]

By May 18, 1863, Goldsborough's vessels had overhauled and captured ten prizes, including one steamer and the English brigantine *Comet*, whose master claimed innocence, complaining that currents had carried him off course. Another four vessels had been driven on shore and destroyed by fire from the gunboats. Outbound vessels carried cotton and inbound vessels carried cargoes varying from the luxuries of life to arms and ammunition. By the summer of 1863 the nefarious Mobile trade came to a near standstill.[22]

During this time a committee of Mobile citizens petitioned Admiral Buchanan to provide transportation for a number of Louisiana refugees who had been exiled from New Orleans. The refugees numbered "several thousand, including old men, women, and children," who in the opinion of the committee could not cover the distance by land without "great inconvenience and suffering." The committee suggested that under a flag of truce "permission could be obtained from the enemy's fleet off Mobile for the passage to and fro of a steamer . . . to bring away the refugees."[23]

Under a flag of truce, Comdr. Thomas T. Hunter, CSN, approached Goldsborough with the request and returned to Buchanan with an outright refusal. Nonetheless Goldsborough referred the matter to Farragut, who responded by writing: "You did right in refusing to accede to Admiral Buchanan's request . . . and you will not, upon any pretext whatever, allow a steamer to pass out of Mobile beyond your fleet." Farragut then added: "If the United States commanding general thinks proper to send a steamer or other vessel with refugees to you off Mobile, you will inform Admiral Buchanan that if he sends a steamer down to you they will be transferred by the officer in charge of the flag-of-truce boat from Mobile. But no boat will be permitted out of Mobile."[24]

Many brokers and agents converged on Mobile with schemes to obtain cotton. General Maury viewed their propositions with suspicion and believed that once the cotton had been delivered, payment would never be received. "Nothing was ever accomplished," Maury claimed, "except that I was ordered by our government to send 1000 bales of cotton to New York to be used to buy overcoats and blankets for our prisoners."[25]

Although it was early in the season, yellow fever ravaged the Caribbean, and cases were being reported in Havana, Galveston, Matamoras, and Key West. Farragut asked Welles to instruct all transports bringing supplies to his command to avoid contact with any of the contaminated ports.[26] As summer advanced the pestilence continued to sweep toward the mainland, ports were quarantined, and like the disease itself, fear spread among the squadron. Even before yellow fever struck the *Colorado*, Goldsborough's health had been weakened by the torturous summer heat off Mobile Bay. For more than four weeks the *Colorado* cruised under quarantine about 75 miles offshore, keeping the sick and their clothes separated from those who were still healthy.[27] On September 23, though still fearing that disease on the *Colorado* might reinfect the crew, Welles gave Goldsborough orders to return with the ship to Portland, Maine, as soon as Commodore Henry K. Thatcher arrived to replace him.[28] Thatcher relieved Goldsborough on September 24. He found no further evidence of the fever on the *Colorado* and retained the vessel for duty, but for several weeks the fever continued to claim lives on other vessels.[29]

Because of operations in the Mississippi, Farragut could not spare his gunboats for an attack on Mobile Bay. The capture of Port Hudson and Vicksburg dominated his attention well into the summer. At times he was out of communication with the West Gulf Blockading Squadron and forced to depend on his subordinates to maintain the blockade and defend themselves from attack.

After the fall of Vicksburg on July 4, 1863, Farragut started downriver to New Orleans in his shot-up flagship, USS *Hartford*. On July 15 he turned over the command of the Mississippi to Adm. David Porter. Two weeks later, he instructed Commodore Henry H. Bell to assume command of the West Gulf Blockading Squadron during his absence. Farragut planned to take a brief furlough while waiting for his ships to be repaired, but a quick assessment of his squadron's condition convinced him that at least three months of work lay ahead for the repair shops.[30]

As Farragut started home on August 2, the pestilent fever had just begun to invade his ships. By September deaths were being reported in New Orleans. The disease continued to disrupt the efficiency of the vessels, limiting naval activity in the gulf to blockade duty. Ice had formed in the rivers before Bell finally reported the end of the epidemic.[31]

For Admiral Buchanan and General Maury at Mobile, the year 1863 had passed quietly, giving them an opportunity to build ships and improve the defenses of Mobile Bay, but they accomplished very little, though not entirely to their own discredit. Military initiatives in Tennessee, Mississippi, Louisiana, and Virginia had dominated the attention of President Davis' War Office and siphoned off men and materiel. Shipbuilding plans at Selma had been delayed by the absence of men and metal. Guns needed to fortify the defenses of Mobile Bay went to Tennessee and Georgia. Submarine technology, a potentially effective defensive weapon, traveled by rail to Charleston.

Secretary of War Seddon and Secretary of the Navy Mallory usually submitted to the judgment of Jefferson Davis, a military man. With all the unexpected military reverses in 1863, however, Davis probably spent little time worrying about Mobile, especially with Farragut in the Mississippi. Even Buchanan worried less knowing that Farragut had taken his warships up the river, and he probably did not expect to see many of them return. When Farragut came back down the river with his patched-up fleet, Buchanan probably breathed another sigh of relief when he learned that his principal adversary had taken a furlough. All these factors led to a reduction of activity at Mobile. However, the makers of Confederate military policy placed too little significance on keeping ports like Mobile open to trade, and once they fell, the government would not be able to sustain its standing army.

Chapter 2
Rumors of Ironclads

As early as September 13, 1862, Farragut began to receive reports of ironclad construction far up the Alabama River at Selma. At that time J. W. Porter, a refugee claiming to be a Union man, evaded picket lines and crept into New Orleans at some peril "to avoid service under the rebel flag." Porter claimed to have traveled between Mobile and Selma on several occasions, which gave him an opportunity to evaluate potential Confederate naval strength. In Mobile Bay he had seen one ironclad, probably the *Baltic*, which he described as "heavily plated with iron," not railroad bars. He observed two eight-inch guns on her upper deck between the wheelhouses but could see no other guns inside. Porter believed that the vessel had been converted from a river steamboat with old engines, as the vessel went no faster than a man walking along the wharf.[1]

In considerable detail Porter described the activity taking place at Selma's small shipyard. He reported that two ironclads under construction appeared to be "nearly done." They had been laid with 12-inch-square timber to support plating on their sides and tops, and according to Porter, they were each 80 feet in length and designed to carry two guns. The informant sketched a diagram of a craft with pointed ends and a bulky shape. The vessels detailed by Porter never materialized, but what he probably observed were either hulls or casemates for the *Huntsville* and the *Tuscaloosa*.[2]

For the next 20 months reports of impregnable Confederate rams trickled into the Union naval office from all over the South. Deserters and informants muddled facts with fiction. "Ram fever," a pseudopsychological disorder that worked on the imagination of naval commanders and created symptoms of paranoia, spread from the chambers of the Secretary of the Navy to Farragut's blockaders off Mobile Bay. Wardrooms buzzed with rumors of ironclads. Commanders posted extra lookouts, expecting at any moment to be surprised and overpowered by Buchanan's unseen but invincible armored squadron.

Actual conditions at Alabama's shipbuilding sites hardly justified sleepless nights off Mobile Bay. Admiral Buchanan struggled with a multitude

Confederate Naval Secretary Stephen R. Mallory (photo courtesy National Archives).

of frustrating logistics and supply problems. Had Farragut known the severity of Buchanan's difficulties, he could have passed the forts at any time during 1863 and early 1864 without facing a single Confederate vessel capable of challenging any one of his heavy wooden gunboats.

Since the day Buchanan took charge of the naval squadron at Mobile, he had had nothing but trouble, and it all started when Secretary Mallory convinced the Confederate Congress that ironclads, and many of them,

could challenge the Union navy and successfully defend the South's important inland waterways. Riverboat shipbuilders stepped forward with elaborate plans and promises and received lucrative contracts with ambiguous
guarantees. Henry D. Bassett, a Mobile shipbuilder, made his pitch on
May 1, 1862, and signed a contract to produce two identical ironclad
floating batteries for $100,000 each. Somewhat incredibly he promised to
deliver the *Tuscaloosa* on July 1, 1862, and follow with the *Huntsville* 30
days later.[3] Bassett's optimism warranted closer evaluation, but Mallory
was desperate for ships.

Bassett chose the small city of Selma as an ideal site for establishing
a shipyard. Located about 160 miles up the winding Alabama River, the
town was situated far enough upriver to be protected from attack, and far
enough downriver to enable vessels to be floated to Mobile for final fitting.
He started the yard on a bluff one hundred feet above the river, where the
bank sloped at a desirable angle for launching heavy vessels. His construction equipment was incomplete and rudimentary, but he had the advantage
of nearby iron mines at Brierfield and rolling mills in Birmingham and
Atlanta to supply hundreds of heavy armor plates. Another important
reason for moving the project to Selma had been the influence of Colin
McRae. In 1861, McRae opened a brand new iron foundry on a bluff adjacent to the town, met Bassett, and promised to deliver guns, boilers, and
eventually, armor for the vessels.[4]

As the war escalated, demanding the entire industrial output of the
South, Mallory commandeered the foundry, added more capacity, and sent
Catesby ap R. Jones from the Charlotte ordnance works to run it. Jones
cast and machined Brooke rifles of unusually high quality. The foundry
produced calibers as large as ten inches. General Maury once declared,
"It must be the best gunmetal in the world," because he had never seen
a Selma-cast gun so much as strained by repeated firing of heavy charges.[5]

Not far from the gun foundry, the navy expanded the small but crude
Selma shipyard to support Secretary Mallory's growing ironclad program.
By mid–1862, three vessels had been started on the bluffs near the foundry,
and during their construction Buchanan made frequent visits to superin-
tend progress. Although he paid particular attention to the heavier *Tennessee*, he did not ignore the twin floating batteries. Buchanan relieved
Comdr. Charles H. McBlair from duties on the gunboat *Morgan* and transferred him to Selma, where he could concentrate full-time on the completion of the *Huntsville* and *Tuscaloosa*. While work on the *Tennessee* steadily
progressed, McBlair's projects faltered. Buchanan controlled the resources
and gave McBlair's requirements a lower priority.[6] In early 1864 Buchanan
started to build a fourth ironclad at Selma, similar to the *Tennessee*, but
scrapped the vessel after her hull was damaged during launching.

Mallory's plans for building ironclads in Alabama did not stop with the

Selma project. Commander Farrand, engaged in selecting defensive sites along the Alabama and Tombigbee rivers, received orders from Mallory to locate and acquire property suitable for more shipyards. On August 19, 1862, he contracted for one large side-wheel ironclad and two 150-foot propeller ironclads to be built at Oven Bluff on the Tombigbee River. The following month he issued contracts for another large side-wheeler, CSS *Nashville*, to be built at Montgomery.[7] By the time Buchanan arrived in Alabama, Farrand had approved contracts for seven ironclads, all either under construction or being laid down. When they were completed, Buchanan anticipated commanding a squadron of at least eight armored vessels, counting the *Baltic*, to defend Mobile Bay and challenge Union control of the gulf. For the next 18 months, both Farrand and Buchanan spent most of their time overcoming construction shortages, arming the vessels, and searching for qualified manpower.

For a rivercraft, the *Nashville* was a monster: 271 feet in length and 63 feet abeam, built with huge side-mounted paddle wheels that spanned 95 feet, 5 inches end to end. She drew 10 feet, 9 inches of water, slightly less than the *Tennessee*. Her side wheels, unlike those of any other Confederate ironclad, each had separate engines equipped with 30-inch-diameter cylinders and 9-foot piston strokes. Despite her 142-foot casemate, she carried only three 7-inch Brooke rifles and one 24-pounder howitzer mounted on a pivot. The immense size of the *Nashville* sounded frightful to the typical wooden-gunboat commander, but the finished product evolved into a perfect example of poor design and sloppy construction. At the end of the war Union officers inspected the vessel and discovered that her bottom had not been coppered, she had been hog-braced athwartships to compensate for a weakness in her hull, and she could never have withstood the weight of being fully armored.[8]

At Selma the *Huntsville* and the *Tuscaloosa* measured 150 feet in length. Armored with four inches of iron made up of 2-by-10-inch bolted plates, each vessel carried one six-inch Brooke rifle and four 32-pounders in broadside. Neither of these vessels could compare in strength, speed, or durability to the *Tennessee*. Under power they were very slow and carried a rating of "ironclad steam floating batteries."[9] At the end of September 1862, Farrand reported to Buchanan that the first vessel would be ready to come down the river in about six weeks. Two weeks later he grumbled: "I cannot write with the least encouragement with regard to the floating batteries here. They are at almost a dead stand still waiting for iron plating and machinery . . . not a particle of machinery for either and only the boiler for one has been received." Buchanan passed the report to Mallory, adding: "This deprives me of the use of these boats for at least two months, which I regret, as I relied principally upon them to prevent the passage of the enemy through the obstructions of the Bay."[10]

Farrand had ordered engines for the ironclads from the naval iron-works in Columbus, Georgia, but the factory had neither the capacity nor the capability to equip all the ships. In January 1863 the engines for the *Tuscaloosa* were installed at Selma, but the machinery for the *Huntsville* failed to arrive, and the vessel had to be towed to Mobile. The ironclads on the Tombigbee did not receive their power plants until late 1863 and early 1864.

In October 1862, McRae asked the Shelby Iron Company to hurry 25 tons of pig iron to Columbus, but two-thirds of the order failed to ship because transportation was unavailable. He then jumped channels and sent an urgent message to the army quartermaster imploring him to ship the iron immediately, explaining that "this iron . . . is required to complete the engines and machinery for the floating batteries at this place [Selma]."[11] Months passed before all the plates became available, and most of the installation had to be completed at Mobile.

Selma had been selected as a navy yard because iron was available nearby, and McRae had intended to produce armor plates in his own foundry. The Navy Department provided funds for McRae to erect a rolling mill, but most of the machinery had to be designed and produced on-site, and he could not obtain skilled master mechanics to build it. The Shelby Iron Works, about 60 miles away, had added a rolling mill to its facility, but when the mill started producing armor plate, pig iron could not be obtained. Plate to cover the *Tuscaloosa* arrived in December 1862 and January 1863 from the Scofield and Markham works in Atlanta. Months later Shelby delivered some of the armor for the *Huntsville* and *Tennessee*, but much of it still came from Atlanta. The three vessels started on the Tombigbee River were never finished because of iron shortages, and the *Nashville* received only a portion of her armor by utilizing plates removed from the *Baltic*.[12]

Unlike other vessels purchased by Farrand, the *Tennessee* was probably the finest ironclad ram built by the South inside the Confederacy.[13] Although first started at Selma, all the important work of fitting the engine, cladding the casemate, assembling the pivots, and installing the guns had to be completed at Mobile. When the vessel left Selma for her trip downriver, she was no more than a covered hull. Buchanan had forced her launching on February 8 to take advantage of high water. A few days later the Montgomery *Daily Advertiser* reported:

> The steamer *Southern Republic* passed down the river on Sunday last, having something in tow. What could be seen of it very much resembled the back of a whale, and yet looked something like a "terrapin," only its legs and head were not visible. . . . This was the ram *Tennessee*. The *Tuscaloosa* and the *Huntsville* came down the river about the middle of February, the former under her own steam, the latter . . . in tow.[14]

The trip down the snakelike Alabama with its steep banks and meandering bars took over a week. Because of snags and obstructions in the river, the towboats tied up at safe landings during the night. The captain of the magnificent steamer *Southern Republic* announced his arrival to each town by blaring several rounds of "Dixie" on the ship's elegant and boisterous calliope.[15]

Capt. James D. Johnston, who had been sent by Buchanan to bring the ram to Mobile, described the launching several years later to the Georgia Historical Society:

> About midday, there was heard the sound of a gun, and immediately afterward the *Tennessee* was shot into the swift current like an arrow, and the water had risen to such a height that she struck in her course the corner of a brick warehouse, situated on an adjoining bluff and demolishing it. This was her first and only experience as a ram.[16]

Buchanan spent most of 1863 and half of 1864 patiently completing work on the *Tennessee* and modifying defects in her design. Although smaller than the *Nashville*, the *Tennessee*, at 209 feet in length and 48 feet abeam, was heavier in construction and drew 14 feet of water. Twenty-five inches of solid oak and yellow pine planking formed the foundation for a casemate 79 feet in length, 29 feet wide at the roof, and eight feet high. The sides inclined at a 45-degree angle. Three layers of iron plates two inches thick by seven inches wide covered the front of the casemate. In a similar arrangement five inches of armor protected her broadsides and aftershield, running to a distance two feet below the water line where it formed a knuckle to buttress an attack from an enemy ram. Bolts one and one-quarter inches in diameter secured the plates to wooden beams 12 inches square. The portion of the deck not covered by the shield was overlaid with wrought-iron plates two inches thick.[17]

The battery, which did not get cast until December 1863, came from the Naval Gun Foundry at Selma. Shortages in the South and military demands elsewhere siphoned off men and metal. Jones, commanding the foundry, advised Buchanan that "I hope to have the two VII-inch [guns] for her ready by New Year [1864], and if they are not to be proved by me they can be shipped to Mobile.... I expect afterwards to turn out one a week."[18] Jones could never meet his schedules but he never stopped trying.

The foundry banded each gun to strengthen the breech, and on the seven-inch guns, mechanics installed nine bands, one over the other. Each band was first cast and then machined to close tolerances. When properly sized the band was expanded by heating, carefully inserted over the mouth of the gun, slid down the barrel and fitted over the powder chamber. In battle, or to increase the range of the projectile, gun crews rammed home double

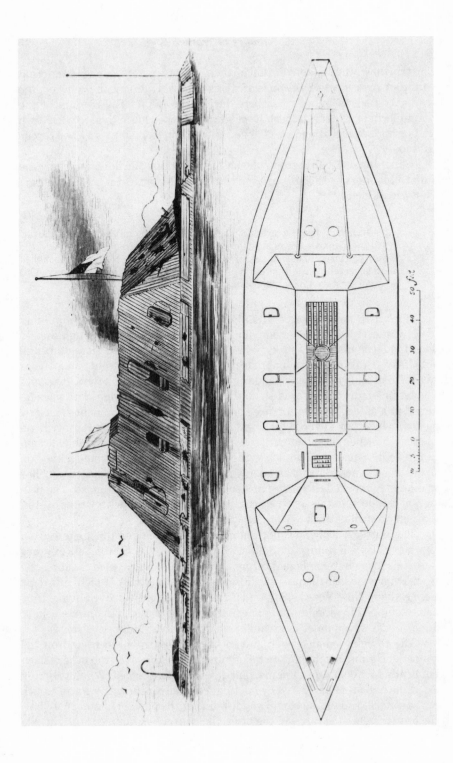

charges of powder and often double-shotted their guns. Without reinforcement powder chambers often shattered, killing or maiming members of the crew.

At times gunmaking at Selma suffered from delays other than iron shortages. Jones wrote Buchanan apologizing that the first two 7-inch Brooke guns would not be ready until mid–January and the 6.4-inch guns would not be completed for another month:

> We had an accident which may have been very serious. An explosion took place whilst attempting to cast the bottom section of a gun pit. The foundry took fire, but was promptly extinguished. Fortunately, but two of the molds were burned. I had a narrow escape; my hat, coat, and pants were burned. Quite a loss in these times, with our depreciated currency and fixed salaries. As a large casting is never made without my being present, I consider my life in greater danger here than if I were in command of the *Tennessee*.[19]

In the production of armor and guns, Jones encountered many problems just as serious as the fire in the foundry. The War Department conscripted skilled workers into the army to cover losses of Alabama regiments in the field. All machinery and equipment had to be designed and built by craftsmen at the Selma site; it could not be purchased or produced elsewhere in the South. Early in January Jones wrote Comdr. John M. Brooke, the chief gun designer in Richmond, beseeching him to solicit support from Mallory's Naval Office. "We are building ironclads," Jones complained, "whilst we have not iron to cover those now afloat, and if I had had the mechanics that I have applied for the mill would have been in operation before this."[20] But Mallory seldom took his problems to Davis, who usually did not want to be bothered by naval matters, and War Secretary Seddon continued to conscript skilled workers wherever he could.

Despite delays at the Selma foundry, the South was better equipped to arm than to plate its ironclads. Both Brooke and Jones were competent, dedicated officers whose individual efforts continued to improve the design, quality, and number of guns produced for the Confederate navy. With the introduction of Brooke guns, the 6.4- and the 7-inch rifles became standardized with interchangeable parts, eliminating the need to fit every gun with special handcrafted components. Brooke's concept of banding guns strengthened the powder chamber, eliminated fatal accidents, and led to improvements in both accuracy and range.[21] However, orders for guns took precedence over requisitions for armor plate, and limited supplies of iron were too often diverted to the production of artillery and ordnance. Consequently four Alabama ironclads never received their armor.

Opposite: CSS *Tennessee* (from *History of the Navy*, Edgar S. Maccay, D. Appleton, 1901).

On January 26, 1864, Buchanan reported the battery of the *Tennessee* complete. The 7-inch guns came from Selma, but the 6.4-inch broadside guns may have been removed from two stationary floating batteries in the harbor. Earlier in 1863 Buchanan had suggested this swap to the Navy Department, and there is no record showing the shipment of 6.4-inch guns from Selma for the *Tennessee*. Both Johnston and Buchanan superintended the final installation. Inside the casemate, both forward and aft, the officers mounted the two 7-inch Brooke guns on pivots opposite two slightly elongated ports. When firing, this enabled the crew to turn the guns in three different directions. Four 6.4-inch Brookes were placed in broadside on conventional mountings. Pierced for six guns and ten ports, each gunport had wrought-iron sliding shutters 5 inches thick that slid "on pivots at the side by means of pulleys or tackles passing through the shield so that as soon as each gun was discharged the port cover could be immediately drawn over the port and the gun reloaded."[22]

The bow of the ram carried a submerged beak or prow covered with wrought-iron plates that projected about two feet in length. Unfortunately ramming an enemy depended on speed and maneuverability, features all the rams constructed by the Confederate navy lacked.

No Confederate vessel took longer to build or cost more than the *Tennessee*. Despite the length of time in construction and an estimated cost of $595,800, she had many defects.[23] Her engines had been salvaged from the river steamer *Alonzo Child* on the Yazoo River, transported overland to the Tombigbee River, and then floated down to Selma. With insufficient horsepower, the power plant could not move such a great weight of wood and iron faster than six nautical miles per hour. Although a formidable vessel, she was too slow to function effectively as a ram.[24]

The design of the gunport shutters looked good on paper, but any steady hammering by heavy guns could deflect the metal and jam the pivots. The location of the rudder chains, on which the helmsman depended for steerage, seemed to be a design afterthought. They had been left partially exposed on the afterdeck, where any wayward shot could strike the chains and immobilize the vessel. Buchanan tried to conceal this defect by covering the channel containing the chains with one-inch sheet iron. The modification hid the problem, but any shot striking the thin plating could drive the metal into the chains, also jamming them.

Once the vessels reached Mobile, Buchanan took personal charge of the project, and with his characteristic energy tackled the job of getting each ship fitted out and ready for action. Shortages continued to cause delays, and personnel could not be found to man the vessels. About 150 infantry were detailed from a Tennessee unit to serve as seamen on the ironclads. Shortly after they reported for duty, Buchanan grumbled: "There are on board . . . some of the greatest vagabonds you will ever read of. . . . One or

Capt. Franklin Buchanan, CSN (USN 1815–1861), in Confederate uniform (courtesy of U.S. Naval Historical Center; donated by F. B. Owen, Cleveland, Ohio).

two such hung during this time would have a wonderful effect."[25] As late as May 7, 1864, Buchanan still complained to Jones that he had "but few officers, and many of them are inefficient, and all inexperienced.... I have neither flag-captain nor flag-lieutenant, nor midshipmen for aid[e]s: consequently, I have all the various duties to attend to from the grade of midshipman up." Buchanan tried to transfer Jones to his immediate command, intending that he captain the *Nashville*, but Mallory would not release him from Selma. The *Nashville* was still waiting for her iron. Had Mallory made the transfer, Jones would have commanded a shell.[26]

When the hull of the *Nashville* arrived from Montgomery in June 1863, her huge size made an impressive appearance. One officer commented that "the *Tennessee* is insignificant along side of her." Buchanan had hoped that the *Nashville* and the *Tennessee* would be ready before the fall of 1863, but the commissioning of the *Tennessee* waited until February 1864, and the *Nashville* barely made it into service before the end of the war. While the admiral concentrated on completing the *Tennessee*, the *Nashville* lay naked at the wharf, waiting for her armor.

Buchanan found that getting work done in Mobile was just as difficult as upriver at Selma. The location had changed but not the problems. He feared an attack before his squadron was prepared, and in his anxiety to get his vessels ready, he became very critical of any delay caused by anyone associated with progress on the vessels. He attempted to compensate for the lack of knowledgeable officers by trying to manage every detail himself, complaining: "The idleness of the workmen has caused remarks by citizens and others and I have been obliged to make a short speech but a 'strong one' to the men, and have also stirred up Mr. [Joseph] Pierce and Engineer [George W.] Fisher.... I spare no one if he is delinquent." A little later, referring to his chief naval constructor, Buchanan added: "Old Pierce ... can plan work, perhaps, but he cannot control men. He is a perfect old woman. I have gone on much further since he left here.... Pierce delayed the work [on the *Tennessee*] by putting on the wrong iron."[27]

The admiral took equally stong measures with civilians, both workers and contractors. When discontented carpenters struck at Selma and sought work in Mobile, marines met their boat, arrested them, and marched them to a guardhouse. Faced with the alternative of conscription, the strikers returned to work. When the admiral found their efforts on the job below his expectations, he had all of them conscripted and detailed to work under his orders.[28]

Contractors earned and received an equal share of criticism. When the *Nashville* reached Mobile, Buchanan could never find the contractors responsible for completing the work on the ironclad. He wrote Mallory: "Great delay on the *Nashville* is caused for want of material, which could be procured without difficulty if either of the contractors were here to attend to it; only one of them, Mr. Montgomery, has been here, and then only one day."[29]

The builders on the Tombigbee River also rankled the admiral. The poorly chosen site, located near a swamp, caused chronic sickness and dissension among the workmen. Buchanan observed that one of the contractors had earned the enmity of the workers while the other had distinguished himself as "a hard drinker ... [who] spends much of his time in Mobile." With Mallory's approval, Buchanan conscripted one of the contractors and fired the other, commissioning Sidney Porter as naval constructor and forcing him to take command of the yard. Porter had been the "hard drinker" who usually absented himself from the site, but the admiral felt that navy discipline would cure the problem. Like many military executives, Buchanan found working with civilians difficult and disagreeable. In January 1864 he wrote: "I have lost all confidence in *all* contractors."[30]

In early April 1863 the *Tuscaloosa* made her first trial run, followed two weeks later by the *Huntsville*. By summer both floating batteries were operational. With 125 pounds of steam pressure, the *Tuscaloosa* made only two and one-half knots. Dismayed by their performance, Buchanan chose not to send them into Mobile Bay.[31] Had they been anchored off the Main Shipping Channel on the morning of August 5, 1864, both vessels could have raked Farragut's fleet as it entered the bay.

Two years passed between the time Admiral Farragut first planned his attack on Mobile Bay and when he finally made it. All during this period, Buchanan knew that the Union navy would some day steam into the Main Shipping Channel with overpowering strength. He tried to build his squadron with every resource at his command, and when resources failed, he tried to keep the project alive by personal example. Trained in the U.S. Navy and accustomed to naval discipline, he received orders and gave them. At an early stage in building the Alabama rams, he probably realized better than Secretary Mallory that the navy had diluted its opportunity to create a small, effective squadron of ironclads by trying to build too many with the limited resources available. One of his deepest disappointments must have been the poor efficiency of the vessels he eventually commissioned and commanded. Had only three ironclads been built to the specifications of the *Tennessee*, Buchanan would have had a formidable squadron.

During 1863 and 1864 many of the reports gathered by Union naval officers from Southern informants contained inaccurate information. Some of the false statements probably emanated from local scuttlebutt, but Union Navy Secretary Welles listened, and his actions suggest that even if he did not believe everything he heard, he had decided not to take unnecessary risks. After Farragut came out of the Mississippi River in late 1863 to resume preparations for an attack on Mobile Bay, Welles promised him monitors. By then, both Farragut and Welles had misgivings about going against an unknown number of Confederate rams with a squadron composed of wooden warships.

By building inferior ironclads, and by starting so many, the Confederate Naval Office did the South a disservice. Although every effort was made at Selma and Mobile to comply with the government's wishes, shortages, lack of skilled workmen, and poor equipment made it impossible to produce, in good working order, more than one of the rams that had been ordered. Secretary Mallory grossly overestimated the South's shipbuilding capabilities, and he should have known better.

Mallory's ambitious ironclad program influenced naval policy at Washington. Instead of building more wooden gunboats, the Union navy fixed old ones and concentrated on producing heavily armed monitors to meet the threat. By the end of the Civil War, the U.S. Navy had built the strongest, most heavily armed, and most imposing fleet of ironclads on the planet. Farragut, still wedded to wooden gunboats, probably would have passed the forts with or without the four monitors sent to him by Welles. The admiral was not afraid to fight, but whether he could have remained in the bay without his monitors is questionable.

The *Tennessee* was a powerful warship, and one of the very few successful ironclad vessels built by the Confederate navy. Mallory deserves credit for starting it, but Buchanan deserves all the credit for shaping it into a fighting ship and, with it, engaging Farragut's entire fleet. The much-heralded battle between the *Monitor* and *Virginia* pales in comparison to the odds against which Buchanan fought in the Battle of Mobile Bay.

Chapter 3
Infernal Machines

Admiral Farragut returned to New Orleans in November 1862 and appealed to General Butler for troops to attack and hold Mobile Bay. Butler's military force had become disorganized, and the entire department was in a state of confusion. A short time later Major General Banks replaced Butler, and with the new commander came orders which failed to include Mobile Bay among his directives. The War Department wanted the entire Mississippi River under Federal control. Farragut's trip to New Orleans happened to place him where he was wanted, and nine months passed before he left the river.

In mid–December, Acting Rear Adm. David D. Porter, commanding the Mississippi Squadron, wrote Secretary Welles that the ironclad USS *Cairo* had been blown up by a torpedo in the Yazoo River. By way of explanation, he wrote: "These torpedoes have proved so harmless heretofore (not one exploding out of the many hundreds that have been planted by the rebels) that officers have not felt the respect for them to which they are entitled. The torpedo which blew up the *Cairo* was evidently fired by a galvanic battery . . . [and] officers followed the wires four hundred yards from the river banks."[1]

When Farragut learned of the loss of the *Cairo*, he may have wondered how long it would take before Buchanan and Maury anchored stationary torpedoes at the entrances to Mobile Bay. In Commodore Hitchcock's comprehensive report of February 25, 1863, he warned of a submarine with a spar torpedo, but up to that time there had been no evidence of mining activity in the channels.[2] As months passed sightings and accidents became more numerous, and worrisome reports of "infernal machines" began to trickle into Farragut's post on the Mississippi.[3]

Torpedoes were not an invention of the Civil War. During the American Revolution, David Bushnell had developed a keg torpedo. Later, both Robert Fulton and Samuel Colt had experimented with explosives and successfully destroyed their targets. Floating mines had been used at Canton, China, in 1857–58, and by the Russians in the Crimean War. Occasional experiments had been conducted by other inventors, but torpedoes violated chivalrous

33

notions of how warfare should fairly be conducted and failed to win pop-
ularity, especially during peacetime. When the Civil War heated up, Confederate military minds believed that torpedoes could help offset Union
naval superiority.

Although not an admirer of either Jefferson Davis or Stephen Mallory,
self-educated 54-year-old Matthew Fontaine Maury (Dabney Maury's cousin)
resigned his commission in the U.S. Navy on April 20, 1861, and after 35
years of service, cast his lot with his native Virginia because, he said, he
had been "raised in the school of states-rights."[4] Maury had become
America's most distinguished scientist of the sea. By charting the ocean's
winds and currents, he had acquired international recognition as "the Pathfinder of the Seas," but his inventive mind had also led him into many experiments with electricity and galvanic batteries.

On April 23, 1861, Maury traveled to Richmond, where Gov. John
Letcher asked him to make recommendations for the protection of the
state's waterways. Convinced that the South could never build a strong
navy, Maury suggested the development of torpedoes. Military authorities
differed, arguing that torpedoes were "ineffectual and unlawful warfare."
Undiscouraged by high-level opposition, which he had grown to expect,
Maury began experiments with small cans of powder in a large washtub
filled with water. Satisfied that he had solved some of the technical problems, he prepared for a full-scale test on the James River off Rocketts
Wharf. With a large oak cask built to his specifications by Talbott & Son
on Cary Street, and two barrels of gunpowder placed at his disposal by
Governor Letcher, Maury loaded his torpedo and with his son, Richard,
rowed into midstream. A host of dignitaries crowded the wharf, including
Secretary Mallory, the Congressional Committee on Naval Affairs, and the
governor. Maury set the percussion trigger, floated his torpedo, and carefully unrolled the lanyard rope. At a safe distance Richard yanked the rope.
"Up went a column of water fifteen or twenty feet!" Richard exclaimed.
"Many stunned or dead fish floated around; the officials on the wharf ap-
plauded and were convinced."[5] After the successful test, Maury received
promotion to Chief of the Sea-Coast, Harbor and River Defenses of the
South with the rank of commander, $50,000 in funds to develop torpedoes,
and a staff of eager assistants.

For a while all the navy's torpedoes were designed, manufactured, and
planted by Maury's small, secret organization, which had been attached to
the Office of Ordnance and Hydrography. Early weapons consisted of old
boilers filled with from 70 to three hundred pounds of powder and attached
to empty barrels that were anchored to float at varying depths beneath the
surface. Maury's technicians connected ignition devices to galvanic batteries ashore by using salvaged telegraph wire insulated with gutta-
percha. An operator detonated the charge by closing the circuit. Early in

Commander Matthew F. Maury, Confederate States Navy.

his experiments Maury observed that torpedoes could not be perfected without better wire and fuses. Properly insulated wire and reliable fuses could not be made in the South, and on October 1, 1862, he went abroad to purchase material for mine warfare.

On June 20, 1862, Lt. Hunter Davidson replaced Maury and took charge of the naval program. At the same time Col. Gabriel J. Rains received command of a new organization, the Army Torpedo Bureau. Records do not disclose whether the two services worked together and shared technology. Before leaving for Europe Maury spent three months instructing Hunter and Lt. Robert D. Minor in the construction and maintenance of mines. For several years after the war, Maury, Davidson, and Rains each took credit for developing the South's torpedoes and resolutely disclaimed any contribution by the others.[6] Regardless of the originator, torpedoes as a strategy for defending Confederate waterways had excellent merit. However, neither branch of the service was given the resources to develop the weapon's full potential. Those devices that worked created a sensation, but because of defective materials, most failed. Nonetheless Union skippers developed a growing awareness of "infernal machines" as sinkings increased.[7]

Where Maury had concentrated on galvanic batteries and wires to spark fuses, Colonel Rains developed a sensitive primer to explode on contact. Until he stabilized the trigger pressure to seven pounds, the device, when set and armed, endangered friend and foe equally. Unlike Maury's device Rains' torpedo worked on land or in water without dependence on electricity. The primer contained 50 percent potassium chlorate, 30 percent sulfuret of antimony, and 20 percent pulverized glass. A thin copper cap covered the mixture. When crushed the chemicals detonated and ignited a fuse that exploded the powder. For a fuse Rains used gunpowder dissolved in alcohol.[8]

Rains developed two types of water mines: the popular "keg" torpedo and the "shell," or "frame," torpedo. The "keg" device was notorious for its simplicity. The first design utilized small wooden kegs made for shipping lager beer. Rains modified the kegs by adding wooden cones to the ends, sealing them with pitch both inside and out, and inserting a sensitive fuse into the bung. Weights attached to the bottom floated the keg fuse-side up. Experts characterized the weapon as cheap, easy, quick to make, and deadly efficient. During the war the keg torpedo caused more damage than any other design.[9]

Rains' frame torpedo scored first, badly damaging the USS *Montauk* in water shallow enough to prevent it from sinking completely. This device was a modified four-hundred-pound artillery shell cast with a thin upper surface to direct the explosive force upward. Fuses were screwed into openings at the nose. Shells were mounted to the heads of a row of heavy timbers attached to weighted cribs anchored to the bottom of the waterway. The timbers were adjusted to the desired depth, leaving the armed shells, each with 27 pounds of powder, just beneath the surface of the water, poised and waiting for a heavy Union vessel to crush the soft copper fuses. This arrangement provided an effective barrier across rivers and bays. The depth of the charges could be regulated by simply adding or removing weights. Union naval specialists studied the devices and reported: "Our gunboats never attempted to force a passage through a channel known to have been defended by . . . them."[10]

In early 1863 Farragut began to receive reports of torpedoes sighted along the Mississippi River. Comdr. Charles H. B. Caldwell of the USS *Essex* described a device his men had observed hanging under buoys near

Port Hudson, Louisiana. His crew dragged it to the surface and discovered a pair of cylindrical mines, three feet long and about one foot in diameter, connected to shore by a network of wires. Caldwell wrote:

> This apparatus was skillfully made and carefully laid exactly in our track. . . . I had it taken on shore and secured in a hole in the levee, and a long line bent to the wire . . . and when it became taut the machine burst with a tremendous explosion, tearing away a large piece of the levee and throwing the pieces of iron in every direction; one piece weighing about 2 pounds fell on board this vessel, distant about three hundred yards.[11]

Although Caldwell did not know it, he had found a Brown-McDaniel-Ewing-Kennon torpedo, the design that had destroyed the *Cairo*.

A month later Caldwell found another torpedo, the first mine mechanically operated by a clock. He disassembled the device, weighed out 114 pounds of gunpowder, and discovered a clockwork mechanism connected to two hammers cocked over a pair of pistol-size percussion caps. The clock was ticking away in perfect running order when Caldwell raised the mine, but the time had not run out.[12]

Given a potential for rich rewards, the number of torpedo inventors continued to grow. E. C. Singer (a gunsmith) and Dr. J. R. Fretwell had been driven away from their experiments in Texas, migrated to Alabama, and developed a small torpedo factory in Mobile. Unlike Maury, whose devices depended on electric current, and Rains, whose torpedoes depended on crushing chemicals to ignite a fuse, Singer and Fretwell approached the problem of ignition by actuating a strong spring. Their design consisted of a floating tin cone two-thirds filled with powder. An iron rod with a spring and a plunger extended through the casing and an equal length below it. On impact the weight of an iron disk falling from the top of the cone pulled a pin, releasing a spring-driven plunger that smashed a percussion cap and exploded the powder. The inventors demonstrated a successful prototype before an examining board in July 1863 and received financing.[13]

Although the Rains "keg" torpedo remained popular throughout the war, once the Fretwell-Singer design reached production, clusters of the dull gray containers appeared in rivers and bays all over the South. With both Fretwell and Singer superintending the torpedo workshop in Mobile, the bay became the inventors' test site and a principal recipient of their product. Their drafting board contained a concept for building small, ironclad torpedo boats, but neither the time nor the resources were available to begin work on a prototype. Admiral Buchanan had enough problems as it was finding plate to complete his ironclads.

There is no evidence that torpedoes played a role in the defense of Mobile Bay prior to the spring of 1863. The army placed a dozen mines in the channel at Grant's Pass and a few near a battery on the Spanish River. After Fretwell and Singer went into production, boats scattered torpedoes in the channels of the Blakely and Apalachee rivers, and at Garrow's Bend, south of the city on the eastern shore. The Main Shipping Channel off Fort Morgan had not been mined, although Maj. Gen. Dabney Maury had developed plans to anchor torpedoes across three-fourths of the channel's width, leaving open only a narrow pathway directly under the guns of the fort. By the end of May Maury had 150 torpedoes, but a decision had not been made where to place them.[14]

By September 1863 30 torpedoes had been anchored in deep water about one-half mile west of Fort Morgan. Maury sent another 16 torpedoes to Grant's Pass, setting them in an area where Union gunboats sometimes anchored to lob shells at Fort Powell. Strong, shifting currents mixed with corrosive seawater deactivated most of the torpedoes within a week. By the time Farragut's fleet entered the bay on August 5, only a few torpedoes remained active, and most of those went into the water a few days before the attack.[15]

There is no record of the many different torpedo designs used in Mobile Bay, but the Fretwell-Singer device probably outnumbered all others combined. In 1864 several electric torpedoes went into the water after two miles of special submarine cable arrived from England.[16] After receiving the cable, General Maury dispatched several officers to nearby towns to gather up all the barrels suitable for torpedoes.

Before the battle of Mobile Bay, Rains – now promoted to brigadier general – made a visit to Mobile to assist in laying more torpedoes off Fort Morgan. Lt. Col. Victor von Sheliha, chief engineer at Mobile, did not want to place mines across the remaining three hundred yards of open channel. Sheliha wanted the passage to remain open for blockade-runners, although this traffic had reached a near standstill. Since electric mines were manually activated from shore, Rains argued that torpedoes could be placed in the open section of the channel without danger of explosion, but he could not cajole the stubborn engineer into issuing the orders. Maury also favored leaving the channel open, still nurturing hope that Buchanan would somehow get his squadron together and attack Farragut's ships. As a consequence Farragut's fleet had access to Mobile Bay as long as his ships stayed within the narrow open corridor a few hundred yards from Fort Morgan.[17] Both Maury and Sheliha still believed that the combination of Buchanan's naval force, Fort Morgan's heavy guns, and Fretwell-Singer torpedoes would keep Farragut out of the bay.

The first torpedo captured off Mobile Bay appeared in a report dated January 30, 1864. Acting Master Henry C. Wade spotted a suspicious raft just inside the bar off Fort Morgan. At dark he lowered a boat, went alongside the raft, cut the moorings and towed the object to Pensacola. Further investigation the following morning revealed a crude explosive device set to explode on impact.[18]

Although most torpedoes went into the water at night or during periods of low visibility, Union lookouts and picket boats studied the activity with constant interest. The Confederates, to protect themselves from their own weapons, marked the minefields in the Main Shipping Channel with buoys, thereby warning both friend and enemy. In the rivers and estuaries, local shipowners were warned away by guides and markers.

There is no count of the number of torpedoes distributed around Mobile Bay, but after Farragut's victory Maury intensified mining operations around Mobile and in the Apalachee and Blakely rivers. The city did not surrender until the following spring, and the local workshop continued to work diligently manufacturing more torpedoes.

Prior to and throughout the Mobile Campaign of 1865, Confederate pioneers planted hundreds of subterra shells, a name given to land mines, all along the approaches to Spanish Fort, Fort Blakely, and the fortifications surrounding the city. Union forces found these "devilish" devices buried along roads and fields, with large concentrations planted in front of breastworks and ditches dug outside earthworks. Mules and men lost their lives and limbs by walking on a torpedo and crushing the fuse. Most subterra shells followed the Rains design.

Just before the battle of Mobile Bay, Farragut had developed respect for the torpedo as a weapon. One afternoon the admiral and his staff stepped aboard the USS *Metacomet* and steamed inshore for a closer look at Buchanan's fleet. The *Tennessee* lay a short distance up the bay, and through his glass, Farragut thought he saw a torpedo fixture installed on her bow. He at once decided to add the feature to his vessels. After snubbing the weapon for nearly three years, the admiral wrote Welles: "I have always deemed it unworthy of a chivalrous nation; but it does not do to give your enemy such a decided superiority over you." During this reconnaissance, Farragut also observed a number of boats engaged in placing mines, and he issued orders for heavy iron cutters to be installed on the "bows of my vessels." For the first time Farragut acknowledged the destructive potential of torpedoes.[19]

During the war 43 Union vessels struck torpedoes, 29 went to the bottom, and ten of those sank in the environs of Mobile Bay. Farragut's dash through the minefields opposite Fort Morgan could have been disastrous if Confederate torpedo technology had reached a stage of perfection earlier. Farragut lost only one monitor that day, and another vessel went down a few days later while sweeping the Main Shipping Channel. Eight vessels sank during and after the Mobile Campaign, but unrecovered subterra shells continued to claim lives for decades after the war ended.[20]

Both Buchanan and Maury probably placed too much confidence in torpedoes as a defense against attack. On the other hand, Farragut probably did not give the weapon proper respect. As his squadron charged through the minefield on August 5, 1864, many commanders later reported listening in horror to the sound of torpedoes scraping against the hulls of their ships and praying that none would explode. One did, sending the USS *Tecumseh* to the bottom with its captain. After passing the minefield, Farragut's sailors probably shouted words of thanksgiving, while the defenders of Forts Morgan and Gaines groaned in disappointment as the other big Union warships steamed safely through the channel. Now the defense of Mobile Bay shifted to Buchanan and the *Tennessee*, and what little help the forts could provide.

Chapter 4
Fortifications at Mobile Bay

The city of Mobile is situated about 30 miles from the Gulf of Mexico at the head of Mobile Bay, whose width varies from 15 miles at the lower end and six miles at the upper. The principal entrance to the bay is by the Main Shipping Channel, which angles northeasterly from the gulf and closely skirts Mobile Point, a long, low sandy projection from the mainland on the east. West of the channel is Dauphin Island, the easternmost island of a chain that bounds Mississippi Sound. Grant's Pass, a shallower channel favored by coasting vessels, follows the north shore of Dauphin Island into the bay. Three nautical miles separate Mobile Point from the tip of Dauphin Island, but the Main Shipping Channel runs along the eastern edge of this opening, about three hundred yards from the Point.

Three forts protected Mobile Bay – Morgan on Mobile Point, Gaines on Dauphin Island, and Powell in Grant's Pass, but of the three, Morgan protected the Main Shipping Channel for deep-draft vessels and represented the greatest threat to the Union squadron. Named for Daniel Morgan, a Revolutionary War hero, Fort Morgan had been completed in 1834 after 15 years of work. Near the site a kiln had been built to cure bricks. Mortar came from pulverized seashells. The pentagonal structure consisted of a network of arches, seven on each side; some contained arches within arches, set at angles to support the roof of the fort and the heavy guns mounted above. Guns under the arches moved along a semicircular track and were fired upward and over a brick enclosure surrounding the fort. Originally designed to mount guns both in casemate and en barbette, the curtain embrasures facing the channel had been masked by the Confederates, who had also added an exterior water battery in front of the northwest curtain.[1]

Each side of the fort formed a separate bastion with its own battery of guns. Shot, shell, and gunpowder were stored in a bricked-over magazine seven feet thick. When soldiers began fortifying the structure, they occupied comfortable quarters in a large, narrow ten-sided building located in the center of the fort and known as the Citadel. Here four-feet-thick brick walls had been loopholed for muskets. Designed to withstand an assault

41

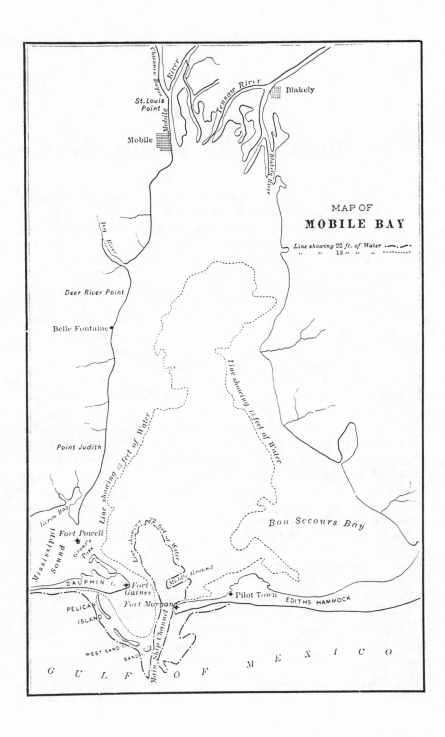

MAP OF
MOBILE BAY

from an enemy using early–19th-century weapons technology, Morgan was structurally strong but moderately armed with mostly 32-pounder shell guns and a few smaller-bore rifles.

The fort was situated at the tip of Mobile Point, a long neck of land ending at the eastern extremity of the Main Shipping Channel. French soldiers built the first fort on Mobile Point in 1699. Sandhills, scrub palmettos, and pine dotted this lonely strip, but the landward fields directly behind the fort had been cleared for better visibility, and smooth embankments had been sloped up to a series of outer brick walls covering the main ramparts. With Fort Gaines directly across the channel from Fort Morgan, and Fort Powell in Grant's Pass, the fortifications of Mobile Bay, on paper, looked formidable. The United States had spent huge sums of money fortifying Mobile against attack by an enemy. Morgan and Gaines had cost several million dollars, and at the outbreak of the Civil War, they were considered strong enough to prevent any fleet from entering the bay.[2]

Although Alabama did not secede from the Union until January 11, 1861, on January 4 Gov. Andrew B. Moore ordered state militia to seize and garrison the U.S. arsenal in Mobile and to occupy both Fort Gaines and Fort Morgan. Capt. Harry Maury entered Fort Morgan the following day and held it for two months before turning it over to Confederate troops. The small number of Federal regulars occupying the fort anticipated its capture, offered no resistance, and evacuated to two small sloops lying nearby.[3]

By May men crammed the fort, sleeping on the casements or squeezing their tents into designated niches around the parade ground. In 1861 the war still seemed far away, and soldiering became a pastime filled with a variety of amusements ranging from a pleasant sail around the bay to shooting at schools of porpoises. Even the arrival of the first blockaders that spring failed to interfere with the gathering of oysters or a jaunt along the beach to collect seashells. Blockade-runners continued to creep along the shore at night, run in under Fort Morgan's guns, and enter the bay safely. After a few days the runners headed back to sea, followed by cheers from the parapets. Soldiers found duty at the fort easy living, though filled with periods of loneliness during the chill of winter and tormented by fleas and mosquitoes during the heat of summer.

Between the time of Fort Morgan's occupation by Maury's militia and the bastion's final surrender in August 1864, the fort had several commanders. Brig. Gen. Edward Higgins took charge of Mobile's defenses in the fall of 1863, a crucial period for both Major General Maury and Admiral Buchanan, as much work remained to be done completing fortifications and finishing the ironclads. Captured and imprisoned twice, once at New Orleans and once at Vicksburg, Higgins had seen much of war without distinguishing

Opposite: Map of Mobile Bay (courtesy U.S. Naval History Collection).

Brig. Gen. Richard L. Page, CSA (photo courtesy Scribner's *Battles & Leaders of the Civil War–1888*).

himself. Higgins and Maury had fought together at Vicksburg, and Maury probably brought Higgins to Mobile because he knew the man and considered him competent and experienced. Higgins may have lost his taste for war or been demoralized by prison. Both officers and volunteers under his command considered him lax in discipline and slow to take action. Finally relieved of duty, Higgins awaited orders until the end of the war but never received reassignment.[4]

In May 1864 Brig. Gen. Richard L. Page took command of the forts and initiated crisp improvements in discipline and order. When the Civil War began, Page had 37 years in the U.S. Navy. He had served at stations all over the world, risen to the grade of commander, and for his staunch reputation to get things done had earned the nickname Ramrod. At Norfolk he had been a neighbor on friendly terms with Farragut. With gray hair and a medium-full beard, he closely resembled his first cousin Robert E. Lee. Promoted to captain in 1862, Page created the naval construction bureau at Charlotte, North Carolina, and commanded that post for two years. On March 1, 1864, he became a brigadier general in the Confederate army and took command of the outer defenses of Mobile Bay, establishing his headquarters at Fort Morgan. Much time had been lost, and Page approached the problems with vigor.[5]

By the summer of 1864, Fort Morgan mounted seven 10-inch, three 8-inch, and 22 32-pounder smoothbore guns, and two 6.5-inch and four 5.8-inch rifled cannons. Page completed the placement of 29 more guns in exterior batteries, the most formidable being a water battery armed mainly with 10-inch Columbiads, one 8-inch rifled gun, and two rifled 32-pounders.[6]

Earlier in the year Capt. Thornton A. Jenkins, senior officer off Mobile Bay, had interviewed a deserter who had worked as a mechanic at Mobile but escaped to the Union naval base at Pensacola. The informant claimed to be from New Hampshire and to avoid conscription had agreed to work for half wages. He reported that Fort Morgan mounted 48 guns and described their locations and calibers.[7] One year earlier Commodore Hitchcock had questioned another deserter who claimed that Fort Morgan mounted "from 120 to 125 guns," including five or six 11-inch guns.[8] Whether intentional or not, this exaggeration of Morgan's firepower nonetheless worried naval authorities. In the short time Page had to prepare Fort Morgan for battle, he finished much of the work started by others. When later captured, he surrendered some 60 pieces of artillery and several howitzers.[9]

On the eastern tip of Dauphin Island, about three nautical miles west-northwest of Fort Morgan, stood Fort Gaines—like Morgan, solidly constructed of brick. Because of its greater distance from the Main Shipping Channel, Gaines held a position of secondary importance in the defense of Mobile Bay. Although the fort mounted only 27 guns, its garrison consisted of 864 officers and men compared with 640 men in the larger and distinctly more important Morgan. With the exception of four rifled 32-pounders and three 10-inch Columbiads, the remainder of the Gaines guns were 32-pounder, 24-pounder, and 18-pounder smoothbores, good short-range shell guns but useless against armored vessels.

Col. Charles D. Anderson of the 21st Alabama commanded Fort Gaines, but unlike Page, he lacked the credentials for strong leadership. Failing to graduate from West Point, Anderson entered the regular army as a second lieutenant in the 4th U.S. Artillery where he served until joining the

Rear Adm. Thornton A. Jenkins, USN (photo courtesy Scribner's *Battles & Leaders of the Civil War–1888*).

Confederacy on April 1, 1861. When the war began, Anderson was a first lieutenant of artillery in Texas. He was appointed captain of artillery in the Confederate army on April 12, 1861. Promoted to major on December 9, he served with the 20th Alabama in Knoxville. On February 15, 1862, he was detached to serve on Brig. Gen. Adley Hogan Gladden's staff in Mobile and became his acting assistant adjutant general at Shiloh. When his regiment was reorganized, he was elected to command the 21st Alabama. There is little in the records to trace Anderson's contribution to the war prior to the Battle of Mobile Bay. His artillery experience should have provided him with excellent qualifications for commanding Fort Gaines.

Page considered his performance during the battle of Mobile Bay "disgraceful," and Major General Maury relieved him of duty.[10]

On Tower Island, a small, sand-covered shell bank at the mouth of Grant's Pass, Confederate engineers constructed an earthwork battery and named it Fort Powell. Although the fort never reached completion, 10- and 8-inch Columbiads and five rifled guns had been mounted around its outer perimeter. Only two long-range guns covered Mississippi Sound; the others faced toward the bay. The magazine was located in the center of a bombproof, approximately 12 feet thick, which could be entered from every mounted gun position through a network of passages framed with 24-inch pine and covered with 12 feet of sand. Five field howitzers of different calibers and a pivot gun completed the fort's firepower.[11] The fort occupied the entire island, and a breakwater four feet high had been added to prevent erosion. When under attack the men had quarters in the bombproof, but they normally lived in a building on a nearby wharf. The channel through Grant's Pass ran within 50 yards of the fort's guns.[12]

Lt. Col. James M. Williams, also of the 21st Alabama, commanded Fort Powell and about 140 men. He replaced Col. William L. Powell, who had started the fortification but never got much accomplished. Powell began to fall out of favor when he commanded Fort Morgan, failed to recover the grounded British blockade-runner *Ann*, and allowed Farragut's more resourceful officers to destroy an important cargo.[13] Williams hurried the work along, barging sand from the mainland to expand the earthworks, digging trenches, building bombproofs, and mounting guns. Union gunboats periodically harassed workmen by lobbing shells at the fort. Later, when Farragut's squadron steamed into Mobile Bay, work on the fort had not been completed, but the men fought the guns until further resistance seemed useless. Rather than surrender Williams blew up the fort and escaped with his troops. Major General Maury believed that Williams should have continued to fight his guns and relieved him of command.[14]

Brig. Gen. Danville Leadbetter designed, modified, or erected most of the smaller fortifications along the shores of upper Mobile Bay, including Spanish Fort, Fort Blakely, and Batteries Tracy, Huger, Choctaw Point, McIntosh, along with a series of shore batteries defending the waterway approaches to Mobile itself. Spanish Fort and Blakely, located at the head of the bay on the eastern shore, played no role in the Battle of Mobile Bay but became the focus of the Union army's attack on the city during the Mobile Campaign in March 1865. Clad with railroad iron, Old Spanish Fort, which lay about ten miles across the bay from Mobile, mounted six rifled 10-inch Columbiads that covered several island batteries and the Apalachee and Blakely rivers. The strong earthworks surrounding Old Spanish Fort and Blakely consisted of several redoubts placed at intervals along a line of defenses each more than two miles in length.

Leadbetter had started most of the work on the batteries built on the islands and peninsulas formed by the deltas of several rivers and estuaries flowing into the bay near Mobile. Armed mostly with 24-pounders and 32-pounders, both rifles and smoothbores, the island earthworks had been established upon piles driven into marshland and then covered over with sand and earth. They could not withstand a heavy attack and ultimately contributed little to the defense of Mobile.[15]

To the south and west of Mobile another series of fortifications guarded the landward approaches to the city. These entrenchments, designed by Sheliha, were very strong and consisted of a ditch 30 feet wide with a redoubt placed every four to five hundred yards. Thousands of slaves worked day and night for three years to build three lines of fortifications with 30 lunettes and redans, making the defenses of Mobile almost as impregnable as those surrounding Petersburg, Virginia. North of Mobile only one line of defense had been fortified, as an attack was not anticipated from that direction. Guns arrived months before emplacements could be prepared, and work to complete the fortifications continued up to the day of final surrender. In early 1864 only a few guns had been mounted along the entrenchments and the gateway into Mobile was still lightly defended.[16]

Opposite Fort Morgan and stretching into the Main Shipping Channel was a line of underwater obstructions that had been started in the shallow water off Fort Gaines. A string of closely driven piles stretched southeasterly along the sand reef in the direction of Fort Morgan, thereby preventing shallow-draft vessels from crossing the flats. Their heads protruded slightly above water at low tide. The piles terminated at the western edge of a bar that dropped off into the deeper water of the main channel. From that point to a distance less than eight hundred feet from the water battery at Fort Morgan, a network of buoys and tarred manila ropes one inch thick were anchored in deeper water to form a barrier designed to foul the paddles of side-wheelers or the propellers of screw steamers. The rope obstructions contained 24 segments 25 feet apart, with each section marked by eight hardwood buoys anchored by three or four pieces of railroad iron banded together. Each string of buoys stretched across 200 feet of water and trended with the tide, covering nearly a mile of channel end to end. Torpedoes made of sheet iron had been connected to the ropes, but Confederates tending the buoys discovered that many washed away or became fouled by seawater. New torpedoes, made of copper, had been held in reserve to plant if or when a Union attack threatened.[17]

With obstructions barring the western edge of the Main Shipping Channel and Fort Morgan's batteries covering the eastern shore from Mobile Point, any heavy gunboat entering the bay was forced through a narrow gateway about one hundred yards wide. This section of the channel had been left open to blockade-runners who depended upon signal lights from

Fort Morgan to guide them in and out of the bay. By 1864 this traffic had decreased, but the channel remained unobstructed and provided Farragut with a clear opening into Mobile Bay as long as he was willing to challenge the guns of Fort Morgan.

Union gunboats exchanged artillery fire with Fort Morgan on many occasions, but no attempt had been made to demolish any of the forts guarding the entrances to the bay until February 1864. At that time Farragut launched a bombardment upon diminutive Fort Powell in Grant's Pass by bringing up several mortar boats and light-draft vessels from the Mississippi River. He timed the attack to coincide with Gen. William Tecumseh Sherman's incursion into Mississippi, hoping to prevent the detachment of Confederate troops stationed at Mobile. For a week Union gunboats lobbed shells at Fort Powell from a distance of 4,000 yards, doing little damage beyond rearranging some sand and injuring one man. Gunboat skippers complained that the guns' recoil drove the ship's keel into the muddy bottom, where for several moments the vessel would remain stuck before breaking loose. Fire returned by the defenders was equally ineffective, often missing the target by three-quarters of a mile. Four shells struck the mortar schooner USS *John Griffiths* in succession but failed to explode. On February 28 Farragut recalled the gunboats on the eve of a norther, knowing that the wind would blow the water out of the sound and ground the deeper-draft vessels.[18]

Farragut's feint worried Maury, who was convinced that the long-expected attack would come within days. He expressed his fear to the War Department, asking for six or seven thousand more men and complaining that he had only 10,000 troops to garrison the forts and defend the entrenchments around the city.[19] After the storm passed Union gunboats returned to the sound and resumed a periodic bombardment of Powell until mid–March. With no troop ships in sight, Maury concluded that the shelling was no more than a demonstration, but he was probably grateful to Farragut for giving him a reason to hold on to his forces.[20]

During the shelling of Fort Powell, Farragut observed many weaknesses in the Confederate defenses, and he still felt confident that with his wooden ships and "two or three thousand troops" the forts could be captured. Major General Banks still refused to offer any help. However, the bombardment of little Fort Powell convinced Farragut that he could damage but not demolish Mobile Bay fortifications. Without Federal troops to garrison captured forts, local black crews could repair them in a few days. Farragut observed mostly inaccurate gunnery, at least from Fort Powell. Shells failed to explode because of defects or inexperienced gun crews.[21]

Farragut probably expected much better gunnery from Forts Morgan and Gaines. Both bastions had had ample time to exercise their guns and bracket them on the Main Shipping Channel. Shells could be fused to explode almost exactly on contact, especially since the width of the channel had been shrunk to about three hundred yards by obstructions. Farragut knew the risks of passing Morgan and Gaines, and he had been prepared to take those risks ever since the summer of 1862. He did not worry about the forts, but when the ram *Tennessee* finally made her debut, she took station off the Main Shipping Channel in a position to rake any enemy gunboat attempting to force an entrance. Buchanan's presence created a potent threat that induced Farragut to delay an attack until he could add ironclads to his own squadron.

The sudden appearance of the *Tennessee* created another worry for the Union blockading squadron – attack by a superior, heavily ironclad vessel, one capable of dismantling the blockade and reopening the port. No one knew the strength or seaworthiness of the vessel, although deserters had made worrisome claims that differed enough to keep everyone guessing and in a state of prepetual apprehension. Even Farragut, while reformulating his plans to conquer Mobile Bay, thought defensively and warned his commanders to be prepared for a sudden attack.

The emergence of the *Tennessee* bought the defenders a few more weeks to finish the forts, add guns, install more shore batteries, plant more torpedoes, and complete work on the other ironclads. Unfortunately shortages of men, materials and supplies, the perpetual nemesis of the Confederate government, would deprive the South of another port.

Chapter 5
Deeds of Daring –
Deeds Undone

While Buchanan and Maury exerted every effort to complete work on the ironclads and the fortifications, many junior officers hatched schemes for disrupting the blockade and annoying the Yankees. For the defenders of Mobile Bay, duty had been laborious, frustrating, and dull, the monotony broken only by periodic shelling or the arrival of an occasional blockade-runner. Younger officers grew impatient and looked for ways to earn recognition by drawing off the Union squadron or harassing their base of supply. Mississippi Sound to the west, banked by islands and shoals, provided ingress and egress to Mobile Bay for shallow-draft vessels, making it possible for small armed craft to attack commerce supplying Union commissaries at New Orleans. About 50 miles to the east, at the entrance to Pensacola Bay, lay federally controlled Fort Pickens, guarding a small naval repair and supply center used by Farragut's blockaders. Union controlled geographical areas east and west of Mobile were vulnerable to sorties launched by innovative commanders, but Buchanan could spare no vessels and Maury could spare no men.

On April 6, 1863, Acting Master George C. Andrews, CSN, organized a raiding party and left Mobile for the mouth of the Mississippi in a launch with 14 men. The Mobile *Tribune* reported that they were "so eager to take a prize that they resolved to board the first vessel they saw." The men changed their minds when the first vessel sighted turned out to be the USS *Illinois* "with six guns and a crew of 400."[1] After dodging the larger sloop-of-war, Andrews entered the Pass à l'Outre, the eastern outlet of the Mississippi River, and spotted the transport steamer *Fox* lying at a coal-yard. After nightfall Andrews' men boarded the *Fox* and quietly captured 23 prisoners, including the skipper, George W. Walker, who had formerly captained a Mobile boat. Without waiting for dawn, Andrews raised steam and with the Stars and Stripes flying at the masthead steered for Mobile Bay. When he entered by the Swash Channel at 3:00 A.M. on April 12, the blockaders fired 30 rounds but failed to do any damage. Once safely under the guns of Fort Morgan, the prize crew of the *Fox* cheered and tooted the steam whistle all the way to Mobile, where the *Tribune* clarioned the capture as "one of the most daring and well-managed exploits of the war."[2]

Andrews' success stimulated another venture into Mississippi Sound, this time by Acting Master James Duke. On May 28, 1863, Duke left Mobile with 18 volunteers in another launch and entered the mouth of the Mississippi. The men carried only small arms and had no specific objective in mind beyond reconnoitering the enemy's position and looking for an opportunity to cause some damage. After lying in ambush for three days in the swamps above the Pass à l'Outre lighthouse, on June 9 they sighted at dusk a steamer coming upriver with another vessel in tow. Duke chugged out of the swamp and in a few moments had his launch alongside the tug *Boston*, whose commander professed astonishment at finding Confederates operating in an area constantly patrolled by Union gunboats. With the *Boston* in his hands, Duke cut loose the *Jenny Lind*, the supply ship under tow, with her cargo of ice and headed back to sea. The next day he captured and burned the bark *Lenox*, New York to New Orleans, with a cargo of general merchandise. Standing out to sea, on June 14 the lookout sighted the bark *Texana*, also New York to New Orleans, with another assorted cargo and a quantity of arms. Duke captured the vessel and ordered it torched. He now had too many prisoners to guard and sent all ashore but the captain and the mate. After destroying cargoes valued at $200,000, he slipped through the Union blockade on June 17 and brought the *Boston* to the Mobile wharf.[3]

Duke's capture of the *Boston* had not been accomplished without risk. On several occasions Union gunboats had passed within gunshot of Duke's hiding place but failed to discover the Confederates. For several hours the USS *Portsmouth* had anchored within speaking distance. When Duke returned to Mobile Bay, he passed through the blockade without being seen. Farragut learned of the *Boston*'s unchallenged return and sharply criticized the senior officer of the blockading squadron.[4]

For several months the *Boston* lay in a small shipyard where workmen lengthened her by 25 feet and installed five light guns, fitting her out as a privateer. Before the converted tug could resume her career as a commerce raider, the Confederate government conscripted the crew and assigned the vessel to Buchanan for more noble service.[5]

In April 1864 another pair of resourceful officers, Lt. James M. Baker of the CSS *Huntsville*, and his brother, Master's Mate Page M. Baker of the CSS *Tuscaloosa*, worked on a scheme to capture Fort Pickens. Buchanan approved a reconnaissance and issued instructions to Lieutenant Baker to take his brother, a crew of ten men, and a cutter from the CSS *Morgan* to assess the practicality of launching an expedition by boat against the fort.[6] The admiral understood the strategic importance of capturing and holding Fort Pickens, although he probably doubted such a mission could be successful.

Situated on a narrow neck of sand jutting into the mouth of Pensacola Bay, Pickens guarded the entrance to the bay much like Fort Morgan commanded the entrance to Mobile Bay. About 40 nautical miles separated the two forts, allowing Union vessels the convenience of leaving the blockade, steaming to Pensacola for coal, and, if necessary, returning the same day. Without the navy yard at Pensacola, Farragut's ships had to travel to Key West or New Orleans. Why the Confederacy evacuated Pensacola and Fort Pickens without stronger resistance remains an unanswered question, especially with its close proximity to Mobile and its small but useful navy yard. It is equally curious why, before Lieutenant Baker presented the plan to his superiors, senior officers at Mobile had not considered a similar plan themselves, especially during the early months of 1863 when Farragut's ships and Banks' troops were occupied in the Mississippi River.

In March Baker had proposed not a reconnaissance but a surprise attack to capture Fort Pickens. His plan provided for a boat expedition to start from Mobile Bay with 150 men. After rowing along the beach 35 miles to the mouth of Perdido River, they would lie concealed during daylight. At nightfall they planned to row to the head of Grand Lagoon and haul the boats over the 30-yard strip of land that separated the lagoon from Pensacola Harbor. From there they could be observed by sentinels during the day, but Baker had learned from former Pickens prisoners that only one guard was placed outside the fort, another on the parapet, a third at the outer gate, and a fourth inside the gate in the guardroom.[7]

Baker possessed detailed knowledge of the approaches to Fort Pickens, and he had gathered intelligence about the fort's configuration and strength. He intended to enter the east face of the fort through embrasures normally left open. If he found them closed, he would carry enough ladders to mount the parapet and descend to the center of the fort by stairways inside. With his men ready to attack, he did not expect much resistance from the sleeping garrison, which he estimated at two hundred or less, and he seemed to know exactly where they stacked their weapons. Local citizens had informed him that about 20 vessels were anchored in the harbor. Since most of the men had been removed to man Farragut's squadron, the ships could become easy prizes once the fort fell.

Baker had one problem, however. At the navy yard across Pensacola Bay, there were about 3,500 men who could cooperate with Farragut's gunboats and recapture Fort Pickens. Baker suggested that a Confederate force of select volunteers, men who had been tried under fire, follow up the capture of Fort Pickens with an attack on Pensacola, and that a number of men accustomed to firing heavy artillery be assigned to hold Pickens if Farragut's gunboats, or Major General Canby's troops attempted to retake the fort. Involved with other problems related to the defenses of Mobile, Major General Maury would not commit land forces to the enterprise.

Consequently Buchanan issued orders for a reconnaissance rather than an attack.[8]

The reconnaissance followed a route similar to one suggested by Master's Mate Baker as an alternative to his brother's plan. The Bakers selected only eight seamen, and from the shore of Bon Secour Bay they carried a boat nearly a mile across land to the gulf and launched her through the breakers. Three men remained in the boat while the others, naked, shoved seaward until the breakers were passed and the boat bailed out. As they stepped their mast and set a course for Fort Pickens, the men could see the blockaders anchored off Fort Morgan, 16 miles to the west.

Baker intended to run directly into the mouth of the Perdido River, but a gale that had been blowing out of the southwest for several days tossed huge waves over the Perdido bar and threatened to swamp the heavily laden cutter. Unwilling to risk the loss of the boat, the men sailed slowly along the coast, just outside the breakers, and passed Fort Pickens in bright moonlight about 3:00 A.M. on April 26. Continuing eastward in search of a cove, the bow lookout sighted a sloop rocking gently at anchor. Baker's men glided over to the vessel, jumped aboard, and captured it. Benjamin Lancashire, master of the 90-ton New Orleans fishing smack *Creole*, expressed amazement at being boarded in waters considered to be the Union stronghold in the western gulf. Baker's men herded the prisoners below, concealed the cutter, arrayed themselves in the clothes of fishermen, and sailed into Pensacola Bay. As they passed Fort Pickens, Baker spoke to the guards, made a quick examination of the approaches to the fort from the gulf, noted the location of the sentries, and observed that there would be little difficulty landing a force of men on the beach. He noted that entrances could be made through the fort's unguarded sally ports or by means of simple scaling ladders. A moat that once existed on the sea face had been filled with sand. The observations confirmed the feasibility of the plan he had proposed, and the reconnaissance could not have been more thorough.[9]

Gale-force westerlies and a strong current running to the east prevented Baker from sailing back to Mobile. For a few days he remained in Pensacola Bay and made further observations, but when he returned to the gulf, winds and currents carried him eastward toward Santa Rosa Island. When the lookout reported a sail, Baker stood in chase, intent on capturing a supply ship headed for New Orleans. The men readied the boat, carefully concealing loaded pistols under their fishermen's garments. As the *Creole* took position to intercept the approaching vessel, Baker climbed the masthead and discovered that the intended prize was an armed Union steamer burning smokeless coal and bearing toward him like a greyhound. He ordered the *Creole* about and headed toward shore, resuming the masquerade of a peaceful fishing smack. The gunboat stopped alongside and several officers scanned the *Creole*'s deck. Numerous riflemen perched in the tops peered through their sights awaiting orders from the captain. Dinner had been prepared, and Baker had it served on deck, where the Union officers could observe his hungry fishermen enjoying their evening meal beneath the vessel's proudly displayed Stars and Stripes. After a prolonged scrutiny convinced the Federals that the *Creole* was a legitimate fishing vessel – although some distance from the usual fishing grounds – the captain ordered steam and the gunboat resumed its course. Captain Lancashire and the prisoners stowed below were deeply disappointed when the cruiser sailed away without sending the customary boarding party.

Lieutenant Baker sailed the *Creole* along the coast for nearly two weeks, hoping to catch favorable winds back to Mobile. With the sloop slow in any wind and provisions running low, he decided to destroy the vessel and lead the men back to Mobile overland. He burned the vessel in St. Andrew's Bay, Florida, and transported the cutter 80 miles to Marianna on ox wagons furnished by friendly coastal salt makers. From Marianna the men proceeded to Chattahoochee Landing and took a steamer to Columbus, Georgia. They caught a train to Montgomery, relaunched the cutter in the Alabama River, and finally sailed and rowed their way back to Mobile. Buchanan expressed surprise at seeing them safely back, especially with the cutter, since he had predicted they would lose it.[10]

Soon after Baker returned to Mobile, he drafted fresh plans to attack Fort Pickens and lobbied senior officers to solicit their cooperation and support. Before either Buchanan or Maury approved the project, Farragut attacked Mobile Bay, wounded the admiral, occupied forts, and controlled the lower bay. Baker continued to press for approval, all the way up the organization to Secretary Mallory, who referred the matter to President Davis and Gen. Braxton Bragg. On September 26, 1864, Mallory approved the mission and advised Commodore Farrand, Baker's immediate superior and chief adversary of the project, "to take all necessary measures for fitting out the expedition and securing its success."[11] Farrand obeyed his instructions, detached Baker from the *Huntsville*, and provided the junior officer with time and resources to prepare for the mission.[12]

On October 24, 1864, Baker notified Farrand that they would start that night for Blakely, transport the boats by wagon to Ross Point on the Perdido River, and prepare for the easy row over to Fort Pickens. Once in the fort, he would signal the land forces, which were standing by, to cooperate. By some delay Baker did not get away from Mobile until the following day. At nightfall on October 25, Baker had his boats and men encamped three miles from Blakely, the launching point for the mission. Rumors of Union reinforcements landing at Pensacola caused Maury temporarily to suspend the enterprise. Baker continued to wait at Blakely, keeping his force under cover. When the rumor of reinforcements proved false, Baker asked permission to go forward. Maury temporized another day before ordering that the men be returned to Mobile and report to their respective commands, thereby terminating the mission. Baker wrote a courteous protest to Mallory and rejoined the *Huntsville*.[13]

A few days later Mallory wrote the following reply, which clarified protocol but sounded like a senseless apology:

> Major-General Maury having withdrawn his men from the enterprise to the command of which you were assigned, its prosecution became impracticable. It was Captain Farrand's duty, therefore, to issue to you the order of which you protest, for the protection of either your men or the public interest, was unnecessary and irregular. I regret that circumstances beyond the control of the Department or yourself should have thus terminated an enterprise which seemed to promise good results.[14]

Six weeks later Maury received intelligence that Mobile was to be attacked by land and sea, and that extensive preparations were underway at Pensacola to forward troops by shallow-draft vessels to Mobile Bay. He also heard that another column was crossing the flats by land. Confronted with this new threat, he may have asked himself in the quiet of his chambers what Baker's small but determined force of volunteers might have accomplished if they had successfully snatched control of Fort Pickens away from the Federals. Without support Baker could not have held the fort indefinitely, but the damage and disruption he might have caused leave many possibilities to open speculation.[15] In early February Maj. Gen. Frederick Steele's U.S. Colored Regiments began debarking at Barrancas, a narrow peninsula directly west of Fort Pickens. Had both Pensacola and Pickens been under Confederate control, Union plans might have been upset or delayed until the naval center and the fort had been recaptured.

While waiting for a decision on their Fort Pickens expedition, the Baker brothers presented another scheme, also blocked by Farrand. After experimenting on their own, they believed that by carrying a spar torpedo in a small rowboat, they could circulate among the blockaders on a dark night without being detected. After selecting their target, Lieutenant Baker planned to edge the boat beside a Union vessel while his brother, a strong swimmer, carried the torpedo below the waterline and attached it to the underside of the ship. The men asked permission to attempt the task alone because of the risk. At first Farrand sanctioned the project, but a few days later he changed his mind and called "the whole scheme from beginning to end impracticable and attended with too great personal risk and danger to the person . . . using the torpedo. They will therefore dismiss all thought of it and return to their respective duties."[16]

Buchanan, Farrand, Maury, and other senior officers at Mobile probably considered and rejected many suggestions whose likelihood of failure far exceeded the prospects of success. However, preventing brave men from taking chances probably stifled creativity and led to the malaise that characterized the attitudes of many of the men assigned to defend the Mobile area. The few men who were able to break out of Mobile and demonstrate aggressiveness annoyed the enemy and could probably have caused more damage if given a little encouragement.

Not all young naval officers and seamen were willing to risk their lives out of patriotism to the Confederacy. In early 1863 Admiral Buchanan developed an interest in torpedo rams and promoted the project as an offensive weapon. He had the *Gunnison*, a small screw tug and messenger boat, modified with a 20-foot spar that could be raised and lowered by a windlass. Fitted with a torpedo equipped with three fuses, the steamer cruised the inland waters off Mobile Bay and was often observed by Union lookouts watching for outgoing runners. A deserter had informed Commodore Hitchcock that the *Gunnison* intended to blow up the USS *Colorado*.[17] Eight months later the *Gunnison* was still circulating around the bay, posing a threat but not attacking.

On November 9, 1863, Buchanan replaced Acting Master's Mate F. M. Tucker with Midshipman Edward A. Swain and issued instructions for him "to proceed off the harbor of Mobile and destroy, if possible, the USS *Colorado* or any other vessel of the blockading squadron."[18] Swain discovered that his crew had little appetite for the mission and replaced several of the men with more eager volunteers. After extensive drilling Swain announced that the new crew was ready, but at the very last moment his engineers recanted and refused to go. Since Buchanan had put the mission on a voluntary basis, he did not insist on trying another crew. The *Gunnison* spent the remainder of the war safely inside the harbor, engaged in laying torpedoes or serving as a dispatch boat.[19]

Admiral Buchanan suffered a similar disappointment but for a different reason. Soon after the *Tennessee* was floated over the mud flats of the Dog River bar, he prepared the vessel for an attack on the Union squadron. After moving into deeper water, the ram anchored and for four days reshipped provisions, coal, and ammunition. Finally on May 22, 1864, the admiral hoisted his flag and ordered the ship to prepare for action. Buchanan would have preferred to wait for the completion of the *Nashville* before challenging Farragut, but he had already been accused of foot-dragging and wanted to bloody the enemy. President Davis had been urging him to strike Farragut before Union infantry could gain a foothold on the beaches. The public applied additional pressure by conveying an exaggerated opinion of the ram's capabilities. Buchanan confided to Flag Officer James K. Mitchell of the James River Squadron: "Everybody has taken it into their heads that *one* ship can whip a dozen and if the trial is *not made*, we who are in her are damned for life, consequently the trial must be made."[20]

Buchanan planned to keep the ram out of sight, hoping that he could gain the advantage of surprise when he led the squadron outside the bay. At sundown on May 23, Lt. Comdr. James D. Johnston mustered the crew and read the admiral's fighting orders, followed by three cheers from the officers and the men. With enthusiasm for battle built to a high pitch, the pilots reported the sea too rough, and Buchanan called off the mission until the next day.[21]

On the following evening the admiral tried again, but when the anchor was raised, the vessel had grounded. Before the ram floated free, the Union squadron sighted the *Tennessee* positioned for attack, thereby eliminating Buchanan's planned surprise. Farragut came over from Pensacola with more gunboats and thereafter never left the Main Shipping Channel guarded by fewer than 13 vessels. Buchanan loitered around Fort Morgan and eventually gave up the idea of facing Farragut outside the bay. Brigadier General Page, commanding Fort Morgan, registered his opinion of the admiral's perceived apathy by writing: "Buchanan looks humbled and thoughtful. The movement[s] of his ship and squadron were, in my judgment, delayed and made unnecessarily public after she came down. She should have been kept alone, and the moment she was released from the camels she should have gone out.... The Secretary let B. [Buchanan] off easier than I expected."[22]

In Buchanan, Mallory had sent his most aggressive senior admiral to Mobile intending to raise the blockade and then cooperate in a combined effort to regain New Orleans and the Lower Mississippi River. Despite high hopes many of Mallory's plans for ironclads never fell into place, and for these failures Buchanan cannot be blamed. The *Tennessee* stood small chance of whipping all of Farragut's gunboats off Fort Morgan. Her weaknesses would manifest themselves during the Battle of Mobile Bay. It is doubtful whether the ram could have survived in rough weather without swamping. An experienced naval officer of Buchanan's stature certainly saw these deficiencies once the ram cleared the Dog River bar, and he justifiably hesitated to jeopardize the vessel by plunging her into the Union squadron for the sake of preserving his reputation as a fighter. Another opportunity would come for that.

If senior military officers at Mobile deserve criticism, they could probably be faulted for playing it safe and not encouraging younger officers to seek creative ways to harass the enemy. The scarcity of men and resources created great obstacles and enormous frustrations for the officers charged with the responsibility of recruiting manpower and building defenses. Over a period of time even Maury and Buchanan suffered demoralization and became conservative in their thinking and actions. They needed some successes to rebuild their confidence but failed to give men like the Baker brothers the opportunity to take risks and make a difference.

Buchanan, the relentless fighter, had little appetite for administrative

Comdr. James D. Johnston, CSN, at the time the CSS *Tennessee* surrendered (U.S. Naval Historical Center Photograph, courtesy the Harbeck Collection).

duties. Conversely many of his colleagues enjoyed administrative work but had little appetite for fighting. The mixture of personalities assigned to Mobile created a somewhat bureaucratic atmosphere of inaction that worked against the Confederacy's military interests and failed to create an inspired fighting force. Because Farragut did not attack Mobile Bay until August 1864, the command deficiencies and resource requirements at Mobile received little attention from the military policymakers in Richmond until too late. In the interim Union forces prepared their campaigns almost at their leisure.

Chapter 6
Union Preparations

In May 1863 Farragut came down the Mississippi River, turned the command of the USS *Hartford* over to Commodore James S. Palmer, and proceeded to New Orleans.[1] There he discovered that eight of his blockaders needed extensive repairs, three of them requiring new boilers – a condition he blamed on poor maintenance by the engineers.[2] Farragut disliked service on inland waters and confided to his wife: "I hope Port Hudson will soon fall, and that will finish my river work. As soon as Mobile and Galveston are away, I shall apply to be relieved."[3] Although Capt. Goldsborough had captured ten prizes and destroyed four others between March 25 and mid–May, Secretary Welles nonetheless reminded Farragut that blockade-running between Havana and Mobile had not been stopped. Eliminating this traffic required possession of Mobile Bay, and after an assessment of the condition of his vessels, Farragut did not believe an attack at this time would succeed.[4]

After Port Hudson fell on July 8, 1863, Farragut relinquished his command of the Lower Mississippi so he could devote all his time to preparing his squadron for the work ahead. After placing Acting Adm. David Porter in charge of the river squadron, he issued instructions for the *Richmond*, *Brooklyn*, and *Hartford* to return to New York for repairs. Other gunboats followed. The *Winoma* and *Kineo* headed for the Baltimore yard and the gunboat *Itasca* continued on to Philadelphia.[5] Then on August 1, 1863, Farragut climbed aboard the *Hartford* and started for his first visit home in more than 18 months.

By the time the admiral arrived in New York, West Gulf Blockading Squadron Commander Henry Haywood Bell reported seven gunboats lined up for repairs at New Orleans with others to come in when schedules permitted. The *Pinola*, still on station off Mobile, broke down, and Goldsborough began running out of vessels to maintain the blockade.[6] An unexpected outbreak of yellow fever kept ships scheduled for repair under extended quarantine. For several weeks Bell had his hands full trying to manipulate naval resources between Pensacola, Mobile, New Orleans, and Texas.

Damage to the heavy wooden gunboats had been severe. The *Hartford*,

Rear Adm. James S. Palmer, USN (photo courtesy Naval History).

after 19 months of active service, had been struck 240 times by shot and shell. Her masts, bowsprit, and lower rigging had all been injured by shot and needed to be replaced before the vessel would be fit for winter service. The *Brooklyn* and the *Richmond* were in worse shape, both having been shot up below the waterline, forcing them into dry dock.[7] Although Farragut's return to New York was celebrated by a huge welcome and a series of lavish banquets, the admiral regularly visited the yard to keep pressure on the workmen to finish repairs.

USS *Hartford* (1859–1956) in Mobile Bay in 1864 (photo courtesy U.S. Naval Historical Center).

On October 6 Farragut optimistically informed Welles that the *Richmond* would be ready in two or three days, but the *Hartford* would not be ready for another three weeks. "I can sail in the *Richmond*," he said, "if such is the wish of the Department." Welles advised him to remain in New York, press for the completion of work on the *Hartford*, and return to the gulf by the end of October.[8] By now, Farragut had grown restive. He wrote Bell that "I am run to death with the attention of the good people, but I am beginning to give out. . . . I have not been able to have a day at home in a week." Four days later he told Assistant Navy Secretary Fox: "I am very anxious to get to my station."[9] Had Farragut known in advance the extent of the *Hartford*'s repairs, he probably would have sailed on the *Richmond*. Work on both the *Hartford* and the *Brooklyn* continued to drag. Down in the gulf Bell pleaded for more gunboats. November passed and Farragut was still without a flagship.[10]

While marking time in New York, Farragut met Capt. Percival Drayton, and they soon became close friends. Drayton enjoyed duty at New York, but the admiral convinced him to give up the soft life and become his fleet captain. Of an old, respected South Carolina family, Drayton joined the navy as a midshipman on December 1, 1827, and thereafter considered Philadelphia his home. A staunch Union supporter, he believed that its preservation was worth sacrificing his family ties in the South. The legislature of South Carolina called his decision "infamous," but Farragut said of him: "Drayton does not know fear, and he would fight the devil himself; but he believes in acting as if the enemy can never be caught unprepared." In his first major action as commander of the USS *Pocahontas*, he had fought against his brother, Confederate Brig. Gen. Thomas F. Drayton, who commanded the military district at Port Royal. He then joined the South Atlantic Blockading Squadron under Capt. Samuel F. DuPont and in March 1863 rose in grade to captain. Although Drayton participated in a badly managed attack on Charleston, South Carolina, Farragut recognized and needed the captain's skill as an administrator and organizer. When Farragut finally put to sea in the midst of a heavy snowstorm, on January 5, 1864, Drayton took command of the USS *Hartford* and replaced Palmer as Captain of the Fleet.[11]

On the morning of January 17, the *Hartford* reached Pensacola Bay, where Farragut found the station buzzing with the rumor that Buchanan's *Tennessee*, "a ram more formidable than the *Merrimack*," would be ready for sea before the end of the month.[12] Earlier Bell had cautioned the squadron off Mobile: "Look out for a surprise," warning that the Confederates had five rams at Mobile.[13] Two days before Farragut reached Pensacola, Bell warned Porter of a Confederate plan to recapture New Orleans, cautioning that the Mobile rams would first dismantle the blockade and then, aided by troops in Louisiana and Mississippi and gunboats on the Red River,

descend on the city. Bell complained that he had no vessels to prevent the expected attack at New Orleans but the *Pensacola* and a few river steamboats, "all the gunboats here having their machinery apart and undergoing repairs."[14]

Farragut sailed over to Mobile to examine the situation himself and returned upset that only the *Richmond* was at her station; the other six gunboats were all at Pensacola for either coal or repairs.[15] Stunned by the weakened condition of his fleet, he wrote both Welles and Porter asking if two shallow-draft monitors could be spared for deployment off Mobile Bay.[16] Farragut later learned from deserters arriving at Pensacola daily that the *Tennessee* had not gotten over the Dog River bar and that only three small Confederate gunboats, *Morgan*, *Gaines*, and *Selma*, operated on the bay. The ironclads *Tuscaloosa* and *Huntsville* were not ready for battle, the *Baltic* was available but very slow, and the *Nashville* had been floated down from Montgomery but had not received her armor.[17]

After a close inspection of the forts, Farragut concluded that Buchanan could not raise the blockade and that the high state of alarm at Pensacola had been caused by the circulation of false rumors. However, he wanted to take no chances and steamed over to New Orleans to hurry along repairs on the USS *Lackawanna* and seven other gunboats. Aside from a series of obstructions between Forts Morgan and Gaines, the admiral did not find the defenses of Mobile Bay much changed from a year earlier. He wrote Welles "that if I had one ironclad at this time I could destroy their whole force in the bay and reduce the forts at my leisure." Referring to Buchanan's ironclads, Farragut added: "It would be unwise to take in our wooden vessels without the means of fighting the enemy on an equal footing." He had heard that three or four monitors were nearing completion at St. Louis and commented: "If I could get these I would attack ... at once."[18]

Farragut, who enjoyed rich food and an occasional bottle of wine, fell ill in February from an attack of rheumatism or gout or both. During this time a number of his gunboats shelled Fort Powell. Despite his illness he inspected the effects of the bombardment and concluded that his guns had merely rearranged tons of sand without causing injury to the fort. This demonstration reinforced his conviction that a cooperating land force was essential for the occupation of Mobile Bay. He wrote Welles: "I am ready the moment the army will act with me, but there is no doing anything with forts so long as their back doors are open."[19]

A few days later rumors spread that the *Tennessee* had come into the bay and taken position between the forts. From a distance Farragut scanned the vessel, estimated its length at three hundred feet, admitted it looked

Opposite: **Rear Adm. David G. Farragut, USN, and Capt. Percival Drayton, USN, aboard USS *Hartford* in Mobile Bay in 1864 (photo courtesy U.S. Navy).**

formidable, and dispatched a warning to the blockaders to "Look Out!" What Farragut actually saw that day is a mystery, however. The craft disappeared after a storm, and the admiral later learned that the real *Tennessee* was still up the Dog River. Farragut had notoriously poor eyesight, but a deserter who had worked on her pronounced that she was the *Tennessee* the moment he saw her. The admiral's reaction to the news indicated that he, too, suffered from the disorder known as ram fever.[20]

When Banks' Red River Campaign ended in disaster, Farragut interpreted the defeat as another reason for the general to withhold troops from Mobile. Later news arrived that Porter's supporting naval squadron had been stranded up the Red River by low water. To make matters worse Banks asked Farragut to send more ships and rescue Porter. Although Porter eventually recovered most of his vessels, Farragut doubted that his brother officer, after barely escaping a total disaster, would be willing to spare his coveted ironclads for an attack on Mobile Bay. Nonetheless the admiral continued to build his squadron and added nine more gunboats between the months of March and May, bringing the total number of warships at Pensacola and Mobile to 25 – but still no ironclads.[21]

Farragut wrote a long letter to Welles beseeching him to instruct Porter to release the Eads ironclads, named for their designer, engineer James Buchanan Eads. He had just spoken with a young lad who convinced him that pressure from Mobile citizens would compel Buchanan to get the ram over the bar and attack the Union fleet. In closing, he added: "If I saw any great importance that these vessels would be to Admiral Porter I would not ask for them, but I do not, nor do I see the least hope of my getting any from the North, as each of the admirals commanding the Atlantic squadrons have never yet thought they had force enough."[22] Had Porter lost his ten ironclads in the Red River, he would have had a strong case for refusing help. However, Farragut knew that when Porter started up the Red River, the Eads double-turreted monitors were not ready and were, in fact, still at Cairo, Illinois.

Correspondence between Farragut and Welles passed on a regular daily basis, but Welles consistently skirted the subject of ironclads. The admiral painstakingly hid his frustration but used every opportunity to elaborate on the risks by writing:

> The experience I had of the fight between the [CSS] *Arkansas* and Admiral Davis's vessel on the Mississippi showed plainly how unequal the contest is between ironclads and wooden vessels in loss of life, unless you succeed in destroying the ironclad. I, therefore, deeply regret that the Department has not been able to give us one of the many ironclads that are off Charleston and on the Mississippi.[23]

Capt. Percival Drayton, USN (photo courtesy Naval History).

Expecting an attack any day, Farragut commanded Capt. John B. Marchand to transfer his command off the Texas coast to a junior officer and come with the USS *Lackawanna* to Pensacola "so that I can have the use of your ship and your head in a case of great importance."[24]

Drayton shared Farragut's worry and passed his concern along to Jenkins: "They say some ironclads are coming out to us; if they don't soon, and 'Buch.' gets out, I doubt if we can, with all our ramming, do him much harm, and if he does us any, I believe the stampede in New Orleans will be such as to risk us the city."[25]

"Buch.," as Drayton called him, could not get his heavy ram over the Dog River bar. The vessel drew 13 feet, and to cross the bar the *Tennessee* had to be raised seven feet. Workmen cut timber and made large wooden tanks, or camels, which could be lashed to the ship, sunk, and then pumped full of air at high tide. Just as the first set of tanks were about to be fitted, they were destroyed by fire, and another set had to be made. Sometime between nightfall May 17 and daylight May 18, the *Tennessee*, buoyed by a series of floating camels, cleared the bar and moved into the bay, towed by two steamers. According to Buchanan's much-heralded plan, the ram was to proceed that night down the bay, break through the blockade, and then capture Fort Pickens and Pensacola. By the time the camels had been cut away, the tide had fallen and left the ram aground. She was observed in the bay the following morning by Union lookouts, thereby losing the element of surprise. Without realizing it, Buchanan may have lost an opportunity to make a successful daylight run at the blockade. Had he been accurately informed of the strength of the enemy the following morning, he would have realized that the *Richmond* and eight smaller gunboats could not have prevented the *Tennessee* from going out. That morning Farragut, with the *Hartford* and five gunboats, was at Pensacola; the *Monongahela* was being repaired at New Orleans; and the long-awaited *Brooklyn* had left New York but did not reach Pensacola until the end of May. Buchanan missed his best opportunity to take the offensive and strike the blockade.[26]

Word that the *Tennessee* had come down the bay did not reach Farragut at Pensacola until the evening of May 20. He sailed in the morning, leaving instructions to rush repairs on several gunboats and forward them to Mobile. Farragut braced for the attack and penned a brief note to his son: "I am lying off here, looking at Buchanan and awaiting his coming out. He has a force of four iron-clads and three wooden vessels. I have eight or nine wooden vessels. We'll try to amuse him if he comes."[27]

When no attack materialized, Farragut and his staff climbed aboard the gunboat *Metacomet* and steamed inshore to make closer observations of the enemy's strength. The *Tennessee*, flying the blue flag of Admiral Buchanan, bore close similarities to the reports given by refugees and informants. He observed several small boats planting torpedoes in the Main Shipping Channel and issued orders to have heavy wire cutters installed on the bows of his ships. Farragut's attitude toward "infernal machines" had changed. He wrote Welles: "Torpedoes are not so agreeable when used [by] both sides; therefore I have reluctantly brought myself to it."[28]

Back in Washington Navy Secretary Welles quietly rearranged his priorities and on June 7 ordered Comdr. James W. A. Nicholson to Mobile with the monitor USS *Manhattan*. Although Welles instructed Nicholson to "proceed with all possible dispatch," the monitor did not leave the

Delaware capes, in tow of the *Bienville*, until June 20. By then Welles had also decided to send Farragut the monitor *Tecumseh*.[29]

The 1,034-ton *Manhattan* had been launched at Jersey City on October 14, 1863, and was classed as a screw steamer, light-draft monitor, constructed of wood and iron. She was 190 feet long with a 37-foot, 9-inch beam and a draft of 11 feet, 10 inches. Similar in design to the USS *Monitor*, she traveled at a maximum speed of eight knots and carried two huge, 15-inch Dahlgren guns (invented by John A. Dahlgren, commander of the Washington, D.C., navy yard).[30]

Almost identical in design and weight, the *Tecumseh* had been launched from the New York shipyard of Secor & Company on September 12, 1863. When armed with two 15-inch guns, the requisite ammunition, and a full load of coal, her draft dipped to 14 feet. She had been ready for sea since early April, but Welles did not release her to Farragut until June 25. Each vessel cost the government about $650,000.[31]

Welles had been criticized by the press on many occasions for doing too little too late, and now he did not want to lose an important naval engagement because he had failed to support a national hero. Pursuing one of the admiral's earlier suggestions, Welles wrote Porter, asking: "It is of the greatest importance that some of the new ironclads building on the Mississippi should be sent without fail to Rear-Admiral Farragut. Are not some of them ready? If not, can you not hurry them forward?"[32]

Ill from exhaustion and emotionally drained by his near disaster on the Red River, Porter replied dourly:

> The only two iron vessels lately finished are the *Winnebago* and *Chickasaw*. They would break to pieces in the least swell, and they are not fitted to go anywhere but in the smoothest water, such as may be found in rivers. I would not take the responsibility of sending them to Admiral Farragut without express orders to that effect. They are very vulnerable and unfit to cope with anything carrying heavy guns, or to engage fortifications. They are all manned and fitted, though having been sent off in a hurry, will require some few ordnance stores. I doubt if they would ever reach Mobile.

However, Welles disregarded Porter's warnings and ordered the ironclads sent. After more foot-dragging, Porter finally complied on June 30, and the monitors headed down the Mississippi to New Orleans.[33] Porter's claims of unseaworthiness and structural weakness were eventually proved false, but the delays cost Farragut time he could not afford to lose.

Built at St. Louis, both the *Chickasaw* and the *Winnebago* were 970-ton double-turreted ironclad monitors carrying two 11-inch Dahlgrens in each turret. Both vessels followed the Eads design, although the *Chickasaw* was built under contract by T. G. Gaylord. The vessels were about 257 feet long, with a beam of 57 feet, well-balanced, and very steady in service.[34]

Unaware that Welles had sent him monitors, Farragut was equally unaware that General Sherman had written General Canby on June 4 suggesting that he make a "strong feint or a real attack on Mobile via Pascagoula in connection with Admiral Farragut's fleet." Anticipating Canby's request for troops, Sherman sent the following order to Brig. Gen. Andrew J. Smith:

> Make up a command of 6,000 to 10,000 men, including your division, out of the force that can be spared at Vicksburg.... Even if you make a landing, it will draw troops from Georgia; but I know there is little or nothing left at Mobile, and if you move rapidly you can take the city and hold it.... What is done should be done at once.[35]

Still certain that Buchanan had delayed his attack to wait for a dark night and smooth water, Farragut issued general orders to his commanders and divided the vessels into two wings. The right wing, composed of the gunboats to the east, were to attack the *Tennessee* from the flank and prevent her from getting back inside the bar. The *Brooklyn* and the heavy vessels to the west were to attack the other flank. The heaviest ships were to cooperate by closing together, concentrating fire on the *Tennessee*'s ports and waterline, then ramming the vessel just abaft the casemate, following with broadsides of grape whenever the ports opened. Had this plan been activated at night, with the entire squadron converging on a single vessel and with shot and shell ricocheting in every direction off the ram's casemate, Farragut would probably have cut up his own squadron without doing any significant harm to the *Tennessee*.[36] The admiral had no way of knowing that Buchanan had abandoned his plan to come out of the bay and face a Union squadron that had grown to 17 gunboats. Buchanan, conversely, expected an attack from Farragut.[37]

On June 17 General Canby arrived with his staff from New Orleans to confer with Farragut about operations against Mobile. After Banks' failed Red River Campaign, Canby took command of the Military Division of West Mississippi. The general had graduated from West Point in 1835 and had distinguished himself in the West as an Indian fighter and in the Mexican War by leading several major assaults. At the outbreak of the Civil War, Canby defeated Confederate forces in New Mexico. Afterward, he traveled to Washington, D.C., where he spent two years performing staff work as assistant adjutant general. Although Canby was untried in a major engagement in the Civil War, his stern, quiet, but businesslike approach to solving problems impressed Drayton as a significant improvement over "Dancing Master" Banks, whose penchant for fast women and lavish banquets had "finished him with all respectable people in that part of the world."[38] In their brief meeting on June 17, Canby and Farragut reached an agreement on combining forces for an attack on Mobile's outer defenses.[39]

Maj. Gen. Edward R. S. Canby, USA (*Photographic History of the Civil War— Review of Reviews*. U.S. Military History Institute).

Farragut now would not move until he received his monitors, and he passed his 63rd birthday on July 5, 1864, still waiting for them. Three days later the *Manhattan* arrived at Pensacola but needed repairs. Still fearful of an attack from Buchanan and unwilling to leave his post off Mobile, Farragut switched his flag to the USS *Tennessee* and sent Drayton on the *Hartford* to Pensacola to speed up work on the monitor.

Drayton reached Pensacola late in the evening, and as he prepared for a quiet night's sleep, the deck officer beat on his door and reported the *Manhattan* on fire. Horrified, Drayton rushed to the monitor but found the fire under control. A steamer had come into port that day with a steam pump and extinguished the fire before much damage was done. An investigation the following day revealed that the small fire had started in the engineer's storeroom but would not detain the *Manhattan* from sailing to Mobile. The loss of the monitor would have been a heavy blow to Farragut and to the morale of his men.[40]

Canby returned from New Orleans with Maj. Gen. Gordon Granger and his staff for a strategy conference. Plans were formulated for cooperation between land and sea forces, although it was agreed that no attack would be initiated until Farragut received his monitors. Canby could not provide enough troops to launch a full-scale attack on Mobile, but he committed enough force to capture or cut off communications in the rear of the forts.[41]

After waiting for this moment since the summer of 1862, Farragut composed General Order No. 10, forcefully detailing the preparations every ship must make. His first sentences reflected his mood:

> Strip your vessels and prepare for the conflict. Send down all your superfluous spars and rigging. Trice up or remove the whiskers. Put up the splinter nets on the starboard side, and barricade the wheel and steersman with sails and hammocks. Lay chains of sand bags on the deck over the machinery, to resist a plunging fire. Hang the sheet chains over the side, or make any other arrangements for security that your ingenuity may suggest. Land your starboard boats or lower and tow them on the port side, and lower the port boats down to the water's edge. Place a leadsman and the pilot in the port quarter boat, or the one most convenient to the commander.

Expanding on ideas developed two years earlier, the admiral explained exactly how the attack would be made:

> The vessels will run by the forts in couples, lashed side by side, as hereinafter designated. The flagship will steer and lead from Sand Island N. by E. by compass, until abreast of Fort Morgan: then N. W. half by N. until past the Middle Ground; then N. by W., and the others as designated in the drawing, will follow in due order until ordered to anchor; but the bow and quarter line must be preserved to give the chase guns a fair range, and each vessel must be kept astern of the broadside of the next ahead; each vessel will keep a very little on the starboard quarter of his next ahead, and when abreast of the fort, will keep directly astern, and as we pass the fort will take the same distance on the port quarter of the next ahead, to enable the stern gun to fire clear of the next vessel astern.

A painstaking planner, Farragut left nothing to chance, his orders covering every detail:

> It will be the object of the admiral to get as close to the fort as possible before opening fire. The ships, however, will open fire the moment the

Maj. Gen. Gordon Granger, USA (courtesy *Photographic History of the Civil War—Review of Reviews.* U.S. Military History Institute).

enemy opens upon us, with their chase and other guns, as fast as they can be brought to bear. Use short fuses for the shell and shrapnel, and as soon as within three hundred or four hundred yards give them grape. It is understood that heretofore we have fired too high, but with grapeshot it is necessary to elevate a little above the object, as grape will dribble from the muzzle of the gun.

Anticipating possible misfortune, Farragut added:

> If one or more of the vessels be disabled, their partners must carry them
> through ... but if they can not then the next astern must render the re-
> quired assistance; but as the admiral contemplates moving with the flood
> tide, it will only require sufficient power to keep the crippled vessels in the
> channel.

Then came a few brief instructions on the guns:

> Vessels that can must place guns upon the poop and topgallant forecastle
> and in the tops on the starboard side. Should the enemy fire grape, they will
> remove the men from the topgallant forecastle and poop to the guns below
> until out of grape range. The howitzers must keep up a constant fire from
> the time they can reach with shrapnel until out of its range.[42]

At the time Farragut issued General Order No. 10, the *Manhattan* had
not left Pensacola, the *Tecumseh* was somewhere in tow along the Atlantic
Coast, and the river monitors *Chickasaw* and *Winnebago* had just arrived
at New Orleans. His orders did not mention the monitors, but the admiral
had already decided how to deploy them. On July 18, he wrote Commodore
Palmer at New Orleans:

> I propose to go in according to programme – 14 vessels, two by two, as at
> Port Hudson; low steam; flood tide in the morning, with a light southwest
> wind; ironclads on the eastern side, to attack the *Tennessee*, and gunboats
> to attack rebel gunboats as soon as past the forts. Ships run up into deep
> water, seven vessels outside to assist the Army in landing on the beach and
> to flank the enemy; five or six in the [Mississippi] Sound to assist the Army
> to land on Dauphin Island. The signal to land will be the signal to form line,
> third order of steaming, and run in.[43]

Waiting for a light southwest breeze meant that Farragut counted on the
smoke from the fort's guns rolling back over the parapets and partially
obscuring his squadron from the sight of enemy gunners.

By July 25 Farragut grew impatient and urged Canby to land a force
in the rear of Fort Gaines, where it would be protected by his gunboats.
Fort Morgan had been receiving reinforcements from Gaines, which the
admiral interpreted as meaning that Gaines would fall easily and could be
held by fewer than 1,000 troops. Once inside the bay, Farragut needed a
base of communications, and Gaines provided the perfect location until
Fort Morgan fell. Canby had been forced to send troops to the Army of the
Potomac and now had fewer men to spare for the planned attack. At the
same time the Confederates sensed an offensive building against Mobile
and sent a force to the west bank of the Atchafalaya River to distract Canby.
Nevertheless he placed General Granger in charge of 1,500 infantry, two

light and two heavy batteries, and a battalion of engineer troops – 2,400 men in all – for operations against Fort Gaines and promised to send more troops a few days later to attack Fort Morgan. The men embarked on seagoing steamers and left New Orleans on July 29, followed by the monitors *Chickasaw* and *Winnebago*.[44]

In the meantime the *Manhattan* had taken station off Sand Island, and Farragut considered launching his attack as soon as the two river monitors arrived – with or without the *Tecumseh*. On the morning of July 28, officers on the *Hartford* observed the *Tennessee* cruising around the bay exercising her guns. That afternoon word reached Farragut that Comdr. Tunis A. M. Craven had just arrived at Pensacola with the *Tecumseh* and that the monitor would join the squadron in a few days. Unsure of the *Tennessee's* strength, Farragut decided to wait for Craven.[45]

Tunis Augustus MacDonough Craven had entered the navy in 1829 as a 16-year-old midshipman and eventually became one of the leading surveyors and hydrographers with the U.S. Coast Survey. In 1861, while commanding the USS *Crusader*, he helped save Key West, Florida, for the Union. In April 1864 he took command of the *Tecumseh*, and after a brisk exchange of fire with enemy batteries on Howlett's Bluff, Craven received orders from Welles to join Farragut's fleet. His arrival off Mobile on August 4 placed him at the ill-fated frontal position in the admiral's order of attack.[46]

Stepped-up reconnaissances by Union naval details disclosed more intelligence on the types of obstructions stretched between Forts Morgan and Gaines. On July 29 Farragut circulated contingency instructions and issued General Order No. 11:

> Should any vessel be disabled to such a degree that her consort is unable to keep her in her station, she will drop out to the westward and not embarrass the vessels next astern by attempting to regain her station. Should she repair damages, so as to be able to reenter the line of battle, she will take her station in the rear as close to the last vessel as possible.
>
> So soon as the vessels have passed the fort and kept away N.W., they can cast off the gunboats at the discretion of the senior officer of the two vessels, and allow them to proceed up the bay to cut off the enemy's gunboats that may be attempting to escape up to Mobile. There are certain black buoys placed by the enemy from the piles on the west side of the channel across it to Fort Morgan. It being understood that there are torpedoes and other obstructions between the buoys, the vessels will take care to pass to the eastward of the easternmost buoy, which is clear of all obstructions.
>
> So soon as the vessels arrive opposite the end of the piles, it will be best to stop the propeller of the ship and let her drift the distance past by her headway and the tide, and those having side-wheel gunboats will continue on by the aid of their paddle wheels, which are not likely to foul with the enemy's drag ropes.[47]

Both General Orders Nos. 10 and 11 showed remarkable knowledge of the enemy's defenses. Over a period of two years, most of the information had been collected from deserters and informants and then pieced together from personal observations. Farragut erred only once when he ordered the screw steamers to shut down their propellers as they passed the piles; the rope obstructions had been swept away by the current.[48]

Before issuing his orders the admiral had instructed his carpenter to make some miniature boat-shaped blocks of wood. Tracing the entrance to Mobile Bay on a large table, he carefully laid out compass points and experimented until he was satisfied that he had found the best method for entering the bay. Lt. John Crittenden Watson later wrote: "I used to help him maneuver the little blocks so as to concentrate and maintain as heavy a fire as possible upon Fort Morgan when we should be going in.... After these General Orders were issued, we played with the blocks preparatory to practicing the ships in keeping close order when under way, at varying speeds."[49]

When the *Manhattan* arrived Buchanan expected an attack at any moment, not aware that three more ironclads were on their way. From the gun works at Selma, Commander Jones wrote a letter of advice to his uncle, General Page, in command of Fort Morgan: "I think with their present force, including the monitor, that you would beat them off, notwithstanding your weak condition. Fire slowly and deliberately, taking care not to throw away a shot. Use hot shot and shell against the wooden vessels, aiming always at the water line, and at base of turret with precision. A simultaneous fire might, I think, be used against the ironclads, though I know it is difficult." Jones was less optimistic about retaining possession of the fort if Farragut gained entry to the bay:

> If the fleet run by you, you will then be beseiged [*sic*], it may be without being actively attacked, though I hardly think they would permit you to retain possession if they could prevent it, as your holding it would seriously incommode them. In the present temper of the people I am convinced that they would only be content with an obstinate resistance.

Aware that his uncle had been unable to obtain the resources he had requested to repulse an attack, Jones added a few words of consolation:

> When it will become known that your advice was unheeded, you will be relieved of the responsibility due to the proper want of preparation, and your character as an officer will not suffer.[50]

A few days before launching his attack, Farragut wrote his son a letter, apprehensive that it might be his last:

> The Confederates at Fort Morgan are making great preparations to receive us.... I know Buchanan and Page, who command the fort, will do all in their powers to destroy us, and we will reciprocate the compliment. I hope

Tunis August MacDonough Craven, Commander, USN (courtesy Naval Institute Photo Collection).

to give them a fair fight, if I once get inside. I expect nothing from them but that they will try to blow me up if they can.... With such a mother, you could not fail to have proper sentiments of religion and virtue. I feel that I have done my duty by you both, as far as the weakness of my nature would allow. I have been devoted to you both, and, when it pleases God to take me hence, I shall feel that I have done my duty. I am not conscious of having wronged any one, and have tried to do as much good as I could. Take care of your mother if I should go, and may God bless and preserve you both.[51]

As Farragut paced the deck of the *Hartford* and waited for his monitors, the month of August opened with a gale that could have swamped the *Manhattan* and the *Winnebago* had they not been snugly anchored to the leeward of Sand Island. The *Chickasaw* reached the protection of Petit Bois Pass in Mississippi Sound just before high winds struck. The *Tecumseh*, however, still delayed at Pensacola, taxed Farragut's patience. He dispatched Captain Jenkins in the *Richmond* to speed up work on the monitor and then sent the *Bienville* to tow her to Mobile. Two days passed without a word, and Farragut wrote Jenkins: "I have lost the finest day for my operations. I confidently supposed that the *Tecumseh* would be ready in four days, and here we are on the sixth and no signs of her, and I am told [the vessel] has just begun to coal. I have done very well without her, as I have three here . . . [but] every day is an irretrievable loss."[52]

In the meantime Farragut dined with Major General Granger and finalized details for the combined attack. Granger was one of many Union generals who had graduated from West Point, earned brevets for meritorious conduct in the Mexican War, and when the Civil War started, commanded regiments in the West, serving with distinction at Wilson's Creek, Corinth, Chickamauga, and Knoxville. A short, fiery, and profane disciplinarian, Granger was not well liked by his troops. He once wrote his superior, somewhat critically: "The battle is neither to the swift nor to the strong but to him that holds on to the end." His pugnacity suited Farragut, who described him as somewhat bald, black bearded and very soldierly in his bearing. Granger had his troops in position to force a landing, and Farragut did not appreciate being the cause of further delay.[53]

On August 3 all of Farragut's commanders came aboard the *Hartford* for a final conference before the attack, which had been planned for the following day. Signal officers, under Maj. Frank W. Marston, had been placed among the larger vessels to send messages to ground forces as the Union squadron entered the bay. When the *Tecumseh* failed to arrive, Farragut reluctantly postponed the attack another day. To the admiral's mortification, Granger had kept his schedule but the navy had not. He wrote Jenkins:

> The soldiers . . . are landing today back of Dauphin Island, and could I have gone in this morning, we would have taken them by surprise. Four deserters came off from Gaines last night, and they say they do not expect any landing there; but they are working like beavers on Morgan. I can lose no more days. I must go in day after to-morrow at daylight or a little after. . . . I have had the wind just right, and I expect it will change by the time I can go in.[54]

Late afternoon on August 4 the *Tecumseh*, towed by the *Bienville* and accompanied by the *Metacomet*, arrived at last and anchored near the *Hart-*

ford. Farragut now had his squadron assembled. He reissued a diagram of the line of battle, placing the *Tecumseh* at the head of the line of monitors, and distributed final instructions to his captains. To Comdr. Thomas H. Stevens of the *Winnebago* he outlined what he expected from the monitors:

> As the monitors are slower than the wooden vessels, I desire that as soon as a signal is made from this vessel in the morning, or if a signal cannot be seen, you perceive any movement which shows the fleet is about moving, you will get underway and proceed toward the fort, endeavoring to keep at about a mile distance until we are coming up and begin to fire, when you can move nearer, so as to make it certain that when abreast of the fort we have our ironclads as an offset to those of the enemy, which might otherwise run us down.
>
> The service that I look for from the ironclads is, first, to neutralize as much as possible the fire of the guns which rake our approach; next to look out for the ironclads when we are abreast of the forts, and, lastly, to occupy the attention of those batteries which would rake us while running up the bay.
>
> After the wooden vessels have passed the forts, the *Winnebago* and the *Chickasaw* will follow them. The commanding officers of the *Tecumseh* and the *Manhattan* will endeavor to destroy the *Tennessee*, exercising their own judgment to the time they shall remain behind for that purpose.[55]

In the privacy of his cabin, Farragut penned a farewell message to his wife.[56] The time had come for action. Two years of waiting and planning had ended. The admiral had gotten everything he had asked for – even the weather had cooperated. All that remained was to fight the battle – and to win.

Chapter 7

"Well, Drayton, We Might as Well Get Underway"

Admiral Farragut went to bed on the night of August 4, 1864, worrying whether his fleet could force an entrance to Mobile Bay in the morning. With much on his mind, he did not feel fit and slept poorly. A heavy rainstorm had passed at sundown, and he fretted that the perfect weather of the past few days would worsen and delay the attack. Granger's men had already landed, and he could not leave them unsupported on Dauphin Island. Unable to sleep Farragut sent his steward, John H. Brooks, topside at 3:00 A.M. to investigate the skies and to check the wind. Brooks reported that the storm had passed, leaving a few clouds overhead with a light breeze from the southwest that barely rippled the surface of the water. Farragut could not have hoped for better weather conditions. The southwest wind would blow the smoke of battle back into the eyes of Fort Morgan's gunners, spoiling their aim. Suddenly awake and full of fight, the admiral turned to his steward and said: "We will go in, this morning." When the orders reached the deck of the *Manhattan*, a member of the watch sighted a comet arcing across the heavens to the northeast and prophesied certain victory. The timely omen offset the sailors' dread of fighting on a Friday.[1]

Boatswains' pipes echoed down the line of ships, followed by the calls of "All hands!" and "Up the hammocks!" Before daybreak an early breakfast fortified the men as last-minute preparations were completed. Farragut ate with Drayton and Surgeon James C. Palmer, but as dawn crimsoned the eastern skies, rain threatened and then moved off to the north. At 4:00 A.M., according to plan, the wooden gunboats formed in a double column, lashed in pairs (and in the order shown below), with the first mentioned of each pair being the starboard vessel facing Fort Morgan. The gunboats tied to the three leading ships were shallow-draft side-wheelers, which were less likely to be fouled by obstructions or to strike submerged torpedoes. Although preferring to lead the attack himself in the *Hartford*, Farragut had assigned the lead to the *Brooklyn* because she mounted four chase guns and carried an ingenious apparatus attached to the jib boom for fishing up torpedoes. Her captain, James Alden, had assisted Supt. A. D. Bache in 1856 in the preparation of the chart of Mobile Bay. Although Farragut never mentioned this fact, he may have considered it important when placing Alden at the front. Several senior officers talked Farragut out of taking the lead, despite the admiral's insistence that "exposure is one of the penalties of rank in the navy." Later the admiral wished he had followed his own instincts.[2]

Brooklyn:	Captain James Alden
Octorara:	Lt. Comdr. Charles H. Green
Hartford (flagship):	Fleet Capt. Percival Drayton
Metacomet:	Lt. Comdr. James E. Jouett
Richmond:	Capt. Thornton A. Jenkins
Port Royal:	Lt. Comdr. Bancroft Gherardi
Lackawanna:	Capt. John B. Marchand
Seminole:	Comdr. Edward Donaldson
Monongahela:	Comdr. James H. Strong
Kennebec:	Lt. Comdr. William P. McCann
Ossipee:	Comdr. William E. Le Roy
Itasca:	Lt. Comdr. George Brown
Oneida:	Comdr. J. R. Madison Mullany
Galena:	Lt. Comdr. Clark H. Wells

Further to starboard, but directly opposite the four lead vessels, the monitors formed column in the following order:[3]

Tecumseh:	Comdr. Tunis A. M. Craven
Manhattan:	Comdr. James W. A. Nicholson
Winnebago:	Comdr. Thomas H. Stevens
Chickasaw:	Lt. Comdr. George H. Perkins

Farragut placed four small gunboats to the southeast of Fort Morgan: the *Sebago, Genesee, Pembina*, and *Bienville*, to harass the bastion from the rear. He sent five light gunboats into Grant's Pass: the *Stockdale, Estrella*,

Narcissus, J. P. Jackson, and *Conemaugh* to invest Fort Powell and keep their guns occupied while Granger's force attacked Fort Gaines.

Getting the fleet underway and into column took time. At 5:30 A.M. and still sipping coffee, the admiral turned to his captain and Fleet Surgeon Palmer and commented rather casually: "Well, Drayton, we might as well get underway." Drayton gave the order, and almost instantly answering signals came from the entire fleet. The wooden vessels filed into their respective positions and steered for Sand Island Channel. Pilots climbed the masts, and gun crews, stripped to the waist and waiting grimly, assembled at their posts. The four monitors, already inside the bar, filed into a single column to the right of the four leading wooden vessels and took their position to starboard. Because they moved slowly, the monitors advanced ahead of the main squadron.[4]

By 6:00 A.M. the fleet moved on a northerly course with the monitors flanked on the right to engage the water battery and the parapet guns of Fort Morgan. For observers at the fort, the fleet silently approached with a deadly magnificence, and a light westerly breeze carried in the distant voice of leadsmen as they called the soundings. As the fleet headed up the Main Shipping Channel, the men in the fort checked their primings and waited for the first ship to come into range. They could see the muzzles of huge guns protruding from banks of sandbags piled along the Union decks. Buchanan's small squadron took its position in single line of echelon across the channel with its port batteries bearing on the leading vessels. The *Tennessee* lay just off the red buoy that marked the edge of the inner line of torpedoes. As the Union vessels closed, daylight flooded the scene and disclosed a panorama "worthy of the brush of an Angelo or Raphael." From every peak, staff, and masthead fluttered flags and banners in colorful splendor. The admiral's blue pennant streamed from the *Hartford's* mizzenmast, tempting the enemy with the choicest target for their gunners.[5]

At 6:47 A.M. the monitors *Tecumseh* and *Manhattan* engaged Fort Morgan at long range, and shortly afterward the fort replied. The first shell, fired by the *Tecumseh,* burst high over the fort. As the wooden vessels came within range, Farragut signaled to the squadron for "closer order," and in a few minutes each pair of vessels had closed to within a few yards of the one ahead, but slightly to the starboard quarter to enable the chase guns to be fired without endangering the next ship in line. At one-half mile, Fort Morgan opened on the *Brooklyn.* Shot and shell ripped through the top hamper, splintering spars and tearing up rigging. The Union fleet had reached its most vulnerable position, exposed to a raking fire from Buchanan's gunboats and Fort Morgan's heavy shore batteries. Farragut could not return the fire with his broadsides without steering the squadron into the minefield, so he pressed slowly forward using only his chase guns. Shortly after 7:00 A.M. the *Brooklyn* and the *Hartford* moved far enough

Capt. James Alden, USN (courtesy *Photographic History of the Civil War—Review of Reviews*. U.S. Military History Institute).

into the channel to open with their broadsides. The first gun to fire on Fort Morgan from the *Hartford* was the starboard one-hundred-pounder Parrott on the topgallant forecastle. When opposite the fort, the flagship opened with all 12 of her nine-inch guns, firing shells with fuses set at ten seconds. As the wooden warships came abreast the fort, gunners cut their fuses back to five-second shells and two-second shrapnel. Before the *Brooklyn* and the *Hartford* had passed Morgan, both the water battery and enemy gunners in the barbette had been driven back into the fort. The engagement

became general as more ships came within range.[6] Under a steady bombardment from the fort, the ships pressed forward, partially hidden behind a screen of dense smoke that rolled over the bay toward the fort.

About this time the Union gunboats stationed off the South East shoal behind Fort Morgan opened, but through some misunderstanding on the part of Lt. Comdr. Edward C. Grafton, the senior officer, the vessels had anchored at too respectful a distance from shore and their shots fell short. By placing the smaller gunboats under Grafton, Farragut had hoped they would draw off some of Fort Morgan's firepower. Grafton may have created a small diversion, but he did no damage and suffered no damage.[7]

After the *Hartford* discharged her first broadside, smoke from the guns obliterated Farragut's view of Fort Morgan. Unable to see the effect of the firing, the admiral climbed the port main rigging, ascending step by step "until he found himself partly above the futtock bands and holding on to the futtock shrouds." Martin Freeman, the pilot, had preceded the admiral up the rigging and had stopped just beneath the top. At Freeman's suggestion Farragut steadied himself by grasping the pilot's foot. When Drayton discovered Farragut perilously perched aloft, he sent Quartermaster John H. Knowles up the rigging to secure him. Knowles wrote:

> I went up with a piece of lead-line, and made it fast to one of the forward shrouds, and then took it around the Admiral to the after shroud, making it fast there. The Admiral said, "Never mind, I am all right," but I went ahead and obeyed orders, for I feared he would fall overboard if anything should carry away or he should be struck.[8]

From his elevated position on the mainmast, Farragut had a splendid but dangerous view of the battle. Through a speaking tube, he could communicate with Drayton, who remained below on the poop with his staff. Captain Jouett, shielded by the *Hartford*, stood on the starboard wheelhouse of the *Metacomet*, lashed alongside, where the admiral could communicate with him. Freeman, the pilot, passed Farragut's directions down to steerage where three old sailors, McFarland, Wood, and Jassin, who had been with the *Hartford* in all her engagements, were at the wheel and proud in their knowledge that on their coolness depended the safety of the ship. Grasping the rigging in one hand and a marine glass in the other, Farragut remained in the rigging and swung around in the tops until the fleet entered the bay.[9]

Other vessels in the fleet had smaller, less complicated, and less experienced organizations than the admiral's flagship. Young officers and sailors found themselves under fire for the first time. The *Lackawanna*

Opposite: **U.S. fleet entering Mobile Bay (courtesy Scribner's *Battles & Leaders of the Civil War–1888*).**

carried a number of officers recently out of the Naval Academy who, when firing started, left their stations to dodge incoming shells, bumping into each other in their rush to safety. Veteran officers steadied their nerves by shaming them back to their guns.[10]

On the other hand, some of the experienced officers demonstrated unheralded bravery. When Commander Stevens of the *Winnebago* came within range of Fort Morgan, he remained on the deck of the monitor and paced between his two turrets, issuing orders to one and then to the other. Shells exploded and shots splashed seawater onto the deck, but Stevens remained outside the turret and guided the vessel into the bay. On the *Galena* a black seaman coolly promenaded the poop, seemingly unconscious of the roar of battle, and with his hands uplifted to heaven, loudly sang a gospel hymn.[11] Twenty-seven-year-old Lt. Comdr. George H. Perkins of the *Chickasaw* stood on top of one of the turrets, waved his cap tauntingly at the fort's gunners, and directed the fire of the monitor as it passed by.[12]

Farragut, from his elevated view of the battle near the top of the main-mast, must have led a charmed life, as an officer on the *Hartford* later noted in his private journal:

> At twenty minutes past seven we had come within range of the enemy's gun-boats, which opened their fire upon the *Hartford*, and, as the Admiral told me afterward, made her their special target. First they struck our foremast, and then lodged a shot of 120 pounds in our mainmast. By degrees they got better elevation; and I have saved a splinter from the hammock netting to show how they felt their way lower. Splinters after that came by cords, and in size were sometimes like logs of wood. No longer came the cheering cry, "Nobody hurt yet." The *Hartford*, by some unavoidable chance, fought the enemy's fleet and fort together for twenty minutes by herself, timbers crashing, and wounded pouring down – cries never to be forgotten.[13]

Five minutes later, the battle suddenly took an unexpected turn that might have led to disaster had Farragut not been aloft where he could clearly see what had happened and take decisive action. The *Brooklyn*, ahead of the *Hartford*, started to slow. An army flagman, who had come aboard Farragut's ships to communicate with General Granger's land forces after Fort Morgan had been passed, appeared to be sending a message to the *Hartford*. No one on the flagship could interpret the signals coming from the *Brooklyn*, and Farragut could not understand why Captain Alden did not use navy signalmen if he wished to communicate with naval officers on the *Hartford*. At the commencement of the battle, Farragut had sent two of Granger's officers and five flagmen below to assist the surgeons. They returned to the deck, read the signal, and translated the following message from the *Brooklyn*: "The monitors are right ahead. We cannot go on without passing them. What shall we do?" From his perch on the mast, Farragut replied that Alden should be signaled: "Go ahead."[14]

In his eagerness to engage the *Tennessee*, Captain Craven had begun to edge the *Tecumseh* to port and into the path of the *Brooklyn*. Farragut's general orders specified that all vessels pass "inside the buoys," and though the space was narrow, if every vessel held the line, there was sufficient room to maneuver and still avoid the minefield. When the *Tecumseh* moved off the bow of the *Brooklyn*, Alden could not hold his position without running into the monitor. Uncertain what to do, he stopped, but the tide continued to carry him toward the torpedoes. With all the trailing gunboats unaware of the problem, Farragut's entire fleet began to close on itself.[15]

About the time the *Hartford* signaled the *Brooklyn* to go ahead, Lt. John C. Kinney climbed into the foretopgallant crosstrees to get above the smoke of the flagship's bow guns, where he could see the signals from the *Brooklyn* more clearly. He reached his position just in time to see the *Tecumseh* career to one side and sink. About the same time word passed along the fleet that the *Tecumseh* had sunk the *Tennessee*, and men began cheering without realizing that they cheered the loss of their own monitor. Five minutes later Alden signaled Farragut: "Our best monitor has been sunk."[16]

The sinking of the *Tecumseh* came as a shock to Farragut, as he had purposely placed the monitor at the head of the line and counted on it to engage the *Tennessee*. By 7:30 A.M. the *Tecumseh* had just passed the fort and was bearing toward the *Tennessee*, which stood off her port beam. At this time both the *Brooklyn* and the *Hartford* were heavily engaged with Fort Morgan and shrouded in smoke. Craven, who had thirsted for the opportunity to engage the *Tennessee* singly, gave the fatal order to change course to westward. The *Tecumseh*'s pilot, who survived the sinking, claimed that as the monitor approached the buoy marking the eastern edge of the minefield, Craven had commented: "The Admiral ordered me to go inside that buoy, but it must be a mistake."[17] At that moment Craven was probably less concerned about torpedoes and much more anxious to engage Buchanan's turtle-backed flagship. When the pilot announced that there was plenty of water inside the buoy, Craven ran just the breadth of his beam too far to westward and struck a torpedo. The monitor sank in two minutes. Alden then saw the buoys ahead and stopped the *Brooklyn*. It was at this point, 7:35 A.M., that Alden signaled the *Hartford* that the *Tecumseh* had been sunk. Moments later Farragut signaled back: "Tell the monitors to go ahead and then take your place."[18]

The sudden sinking of the *Tecumseh* created a moment of jubilation for the *Tennessee*'s gunners. The ram's bow gun, which they kept trained on the approaching monitor, had been loaded with a steel bolt weighing 140 pounds. Captain Johnston of the *Tennessee* cautioned his lieutenant: "Do not fire, Mr. Wharton [Lt. Arthur D.], until the vessels are in actual combat." The words were hardly said before the underwater explosion was felt and the *Tecumseh* reeled over on its port side. Several of the crew scrambled

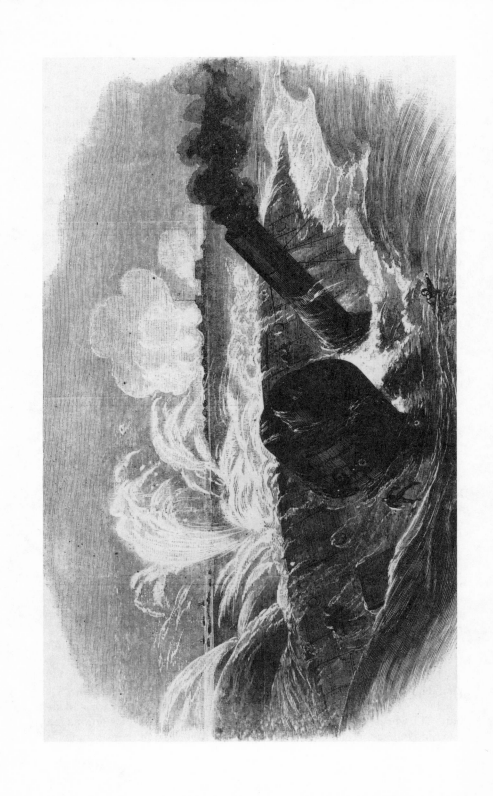

from the turret, and for a brief moment, her screw came out of the water and rotated in the air. Then the vessel plunged bow foremost into the deep.[19]

In a final act of courtesy just before the *Tecumseh* sank, Craven and his pilot, John Collins, met at a small hatchway in the floor of the pilothouse leading down into the turret. Only one man could pass through at a time, and there was no other exit from the pilothouse to the outside but through the turret. The pilot stepped aside and said: "Go ahead, captain!" "No, sir!" replied Craven. "After you, pilot! I leave my ship last." Collins reached the turret and escaped through one of the sliding hatches in the top. "There was nothing after me," Collins related later. "When I reached the upmost round of the ladder, the vessel seemed to drop from under me." When rescued by the *Metacomet*, he learned that the captain had gone down with the ship.[20] Acting Masters Charles F. Langley and Gardner Cottrell of the *Tecumseh* reported seeing Craven on the turret, wearing a life preserver, just before the vessel sank. Whether Craven went down with the ship or was sucked into the vortex as the vessel sank will never be known. Of 114 officers and men, only 21 escaped death. Four swam ashore and were captured, seven escaped in one of the *Tecumseh*'s boats, and ten were rescued by Acting Master Henry Clay Nields in a boat sent from the *Metacomet* by Farragut.[21]

Jouett, anticipating Farragut's order, had already lowered a rescue boat. Nields started from the port quarter of the *Metacomet* and, steering the boat himself, pulled directly under the battery of the *Hartford* around the *Brooklyn* to within a few hundred yards of Fort Morgan. Exposed to fire from both friend and foe, he suddenly realized that he had no flag flying. He dropped the yoke ropes, picked up a small ensign from the bottom of the boat, unfurled it from its staff, and slipped it into a socket by the stern sheets. In an act of mercy General Page in Fort Morgan spotted Nield's boat attempting to save the *Tecumseh*'s survivors and issued the following instructions: "Pass the order not to fire on that boat; she is saving drowning men." The men on the *Tennessee* also withheld their fire. "I can scarcely describe," wrote Lt. Arthur D. Wharton, CSN, how I felt at witnessing this most gallant act. The muzzle of our gun was slowly raised, and the bolt intended for the *Tecumseh* swept harmlessly over the heads of that glorious boat's crew and far down in the line of foes." After saving Ensign John P. Zettick, eight men, and the pilot, Nields was picked up by the *Oneida*, where he remained until the action ended.[22]

From the lofty heights of the *Hartford*'s rigging, Farragut witnessed

Opposite: **"Destruction of the Monitor *Tecumseh* by a Rebel Torpedo" in the Battle of Mobile Bay, Aug. 5, 1864 (engraving from *Harper's Weekly*, Sept. 10, 1864; courtesy Naval History).**

the fleet's formation deteriorate after the unexpected sinking of the lead monitor. At 7:40 A.M. he had signaled Alden: "Tell the monitors to go ahead and then take your place," but the captain of the *Brooklyn* seemed to be paralyzed into inaction by the prospect of encountering a similar fate. Alden demonstrated no appetite for achieving the same "immortal fame" as Craven, and by failing to go forward, he forced all the wooden ships to slow their engines and stack up behind the *Brooklyn*.[23] As the tide continued to carry the *Brooklyn* slowly through the channel, Alden received reports of shoal water. Then, as the smoke cleared, a lookout reported "a row of suspicious-looking buoys" directly under the bows. Instead of moving forward, he reversed his engines and started backing off the buoys and into the approaching fleet. Alden had gotten off course, and he believed that he was leading the entire Union fleet into the minefield Farragut's orders had expressly directed him to evade. After entering the channel, the slower *Tecumseh* had veered to port, and to maintain the required interval, Alden had followed, steered too far to the west, and entered the edge of the minefield. When the *Tecumseh* sank Alden probably had visions of creating a greater catastrophe by leading Farragut's entire fleet off course and into waiting disaster. He had just cast off the smaller *Octorara*, which was to engage Buchanan's smaller gunboats, when he found himself in the minefield. The position of the *Octorara* made it difficult to turn the *Brooklyn* without colliding with her consort, and for this reason, Alden decided not to turn away from the buoys but to reverse his engines.

All this confusion made for tense moments on the *Hartford*, as Farragut could not understand Alden's problems, and the vessels in the rear continued to close upon those in the van. Certain of some unseen disaster, the captains of the trailing vessels slackened their fire to clear away enough smoke to see what problem lay ahead. At the same time Fort Morgan's gunners accelerated their rate of fire, and with less smoke to obscure their aim, started pouring shot and shell into visible targets. Fires broke out on several Union vessels, and blood started to stain their decks.[24]

The *Hartford*, forced slightly out of position by the *Brooklyn*, could only fire a few of her bow guns at Fort Morgan, but a deadly rain of shot and shell from the fort began cutting down her men by the scores. From his station in the tops, Signal Officer Kinney described the deadly scene below:

> The sight on deck was sickening beyond the power of words to portray. Shot after shot came through the side, mowing down the men, deluging the decks with blood, and scattering mangled fragments of humanity so thickly that it was difficult to stand on deck.... The bodies of the dead were placed in a long row on the port side, while the wounded were sent below until the surgeon's quarters would hold no more. A solid shot coming through the bow struck a gunner in the neck, completely severing head from body. One poor fellow lost both legs by a cannon-ball; as he fell [he] threw up both arms, just in time to have them also carried away by another shot. At one gun, all the crew

on one side were swept down by a shot which came crashing through the bulwarks. A shell burst between the two forward guns in charge of Lieutenant [Herbert B.] Tyson, killing and wounding 15 men. The mast upon which the writer was perched was twice struck, once slightly, and again just below the foretop by a heavy shell, by a rifle on the Confederate gunboat *Selma*. Fortunately the shell came tumbling end over end, and buried itself in the mast, butt-end first, leaving the percussion cap protruding.[25]

On the brink of colossal disaster, Farragut had little time to think, and from his perch aloft, from which he might topple at any moment, he had no senior officers at hand with whom to confer. He felt that with the sinking of the *Tecumseh* and the backing of the *Brooklyn*, all his plans had been thwarted, and he could not decide whether to advance or retreat. In times of indecision, his natural impulse was to seek guidance from above. For a precious moment, he looked to the sky and silently prayed: "O God, who created man and gave him reason, direct me what to do. Shall I go on?" Farragut claimed later that a spiritual response commanded that he go on![26] Without further hesitation the admiral decided to take the lead, as he had wished to do from the beginning. He asked the pilot if there was sufficient depth of water for the *Hartford* to pass to the left of the *Brooklyn*. Receiving an affirmative reply, he said: "I will take the lead," and called down orders for full speed ahead. In order to clear the *Brooklyn's* stern, the *Metacomet* had to back engines before the *Hartford* was clear to change course. As Farragut passed the *Brooklyn* on his starboard, Alden warned that there was "a heavy line of torpedoes across the channel." At this moment Farragut is reported to have shouted, "Damn the torpedoes!" and then turned to Drayton and ordered: "Four bells! Captain Drayton, go ahead!" and to the captain of the *Metacomet*, still lashed alongside, "Jouett, full speed!"[27] Exactly what Farragut said from the port rigging is open to speculation, as the din of battle probably made it impossible to communicate between ships. Chief Engineer Thom Williamson claimed to be on deck and standing near Farragut when he gave the order: "Go ahead!" Williamson asked: "Shall I ring four bells, sir?" Farragut responded sharply: "Four bells – eight bells – sixteen bells – damn it, I don't care how many bells you ring!"[28]

As the *Hartford* steamed past the *Brooklyn*, Ordinary Seaman Bartholomew Diggins reported that sailors on the flagship ran to the rail and hooted at Alden: "Coward! Take him out! He ran away at Vicksburg!" Most of the men had fought with Farragut at Vicksburg, and when the admiral made his first attack on the stronghold, the *Richmond*, then commanded by Alden, failed to follow the flagship past the Confederate batteries.[29]

After the *Hartford* passed to the front, the *Brooklyn*, *Richmond*, *Lackawanna*, and other gunboats followed behind. Each captain saw that Farragut was cutting across the minefield and believed "that they were going to their death with their commander in chief." Earlier rumors that the torpedoes had been rendered useless by exposure to seawater were dispelled when the *Tecumseh* sank. The specter of imminent doom pervaded each vessel as it moved across the string of mines anchored west of the red buoy. Officers of the *Hartford* and the *Richmond* could distinctly hear the snapping of Singer torpedo primers as they scraped against the hull, but every one failed to explode. Farragut might not have been so eager to cross the minefield had he known that 90 torpedoes had been planted as recently as August 3 and 4. When the minefield was swept later that month, one torpedo out of ten was still dry. Farragut had probably been lucky to lose only one vessel to mines. Another theory explaining the admiral's mysterious safe passage through the minefield involved the unexpected change of course to the northwest. The torpedoes had been arranged in quincunx, echelon order, and the point Farragut chose to change course carried him into an open space between three rows of torpedoes.[30]

As the *Hartford* moved through the "middle ground," a narrow section of channel banked on both sides by shallow water, the *Selma* kept directly in front of the flagship and raked her fore and aft, causing more damage during this brief exchange than done later by the entire enemy fleet. The other Confederate gunboats, *Gaines* and *Morgan*, remained in shallow water off the *Hartford*'s starboard bow and suffered considerable damage from Farragut's broadsides. Up to this point Buchanan and the *Tennessee* had remained at some distance, content to let the fort engage the Union fleet and cripple as many vessels as possible. When the *Hartford* crossed the middle ground and started into the bay, Buchanan ordered the throttle opened and initiated a vigorous attempt to ram the flagship. At about one hundred yards, the *Hartford* maneuvered to avoid being struck, and the *Tennessee* pulled up and veered to the left. After firing a broadside at the ram, which bounded harmlessly off her plating, the *Hartford* advanced toward the three Confederate wooden gunboats, and the *Tennessee* started toward the *Richmond* and the *Brooklyn*.[31]

Lieutenant Wharton, in command of the *Tennessee*'s forward guns, related that he was quite sure that his 7-inch bow gun would sink Farragut's flagship:

> I took the lock-string from the captain of the gun myself, took a long deliberate aim, and gave the commands: "Raise," "Steady," "Raise a little more," "Ready, Fire!" I was as confident that our shell would tear a hole in the *Hartford*'s side big enough to sink her in a few minutes as I was that I had fired it. It did tear the hole expected, but it was above the water-line.[32]

It is not understood why the *Tennessee* abandoned her attack on the *Hartford*, unless Buchanan felt that by bottling up the rest of the squadron in the middle ground and within range of Fort Morgan's guns, he could return and finish off the flagship later. The *Brooklyn*, next in line, now became Buchanan's target, but again the slowness of the ram allowed Alden just enough time to slip aside. "She missed us," he reported, "and passed clear of our stern, only a few yards distant . . . at the same time throwing shot and shell at us which inflicted considerable damage at and above the water-line forward."[33]

Frustrated but not finished, Buchanan steamed by the *Brooklyn* and went first after the *Richmond* and then after the *Lackawanna*. Each time the slowness of the rams allowed the enemy gunboats just enough time to move aside, but her broadsides never failed to tear up planking and "laid many a brave fellow low."[34]

When the *Tennessee* started her run at the *Brooklyn,* Captain Jenkins, commanding the *Richmond,* prepared his own strategy. Fully expecting to see the ram strike the *Brooklyn* amidships, Jenkins thought that this "would be our opportunity, for if she struck the *Brooklyn* the concussion would throw her port side across our path, and being so near to us, she would not have time to 'straighten up,' and we would strike her fairly and squarely, and most likely sink her."[35] Jenkins maneuvered for the strike, assuming that Alden could not avoid the collision:

> The guns were loaded with solid shot and the heaviest powder charge; the forecastle gun's crew were ordered to get their small-arms and fire into her gun-ports; and as previously determined, if we came in collision at any time, the orders were to throw gun charges of powder in bags from the fore and main yard-arms down her smoke stack. To our great surprise, she sheered off from the *Brooklyn,* and at about one hundred yards put two shot or shells through and through the *Brooklyn*'s sides, doing much damage.[36]

The *Brooklyn*'s gunners scattered several shots from their one-hundred-pounder Parrotts as the ram closed, and when the *Tennessee* crossed a few yards off the stern, Alden followed with the 60-pounders mounted on the poop. All the shots bounded off the ram's casemate and splashed harmlessly in the bay. The *Brooklyn* followed the *Hartford* into the bay, and Buchanan continued down the line as more Union vessels crossed through the middle ground.[37]

For some reason Buchanan decided not to attack the *Richmond,* but when he passed and headed for the *Lackawanna,* Jenkins poured three full broadsides of 9-inch shot from all 11 guns into the side of the ram. Every shot caromed off the casemate, leaving nothing but scratches on the plating. Musketry fired into the ram's two ports prevented Buchanan's gunners from leveling their guns, and two of the shots passed high, one cutting a ratline in the port main shroud, just under the feet of the pilot, and the other whistling dangerously close to Lt. Comdr. Edward Terry's head.[38]

Buchanan then steamed past the *Lackawanna,* received another harmless broadside, and headed for the *Monongahela,* which steered out of line and attempted to run over the *Tennessee*. The two vessels came together at an acute angle, nudged each other slightly, but failed to do any damage. Buchanan swung around the *Monongahela* and worked into position alongside her lashed-together consort, the *Kennebec*, bumped the bow, dislodging the *Kennebec's* quarter boat, and fired a shell through her hull that wounded five men and filled the vessel with smoke.[39]

The *Tennessee* turned, passed between the *Monongahela* and the *Ossipee*, and delivered a broadside into each vessel before steaming toward the *Oneida*, the last of Farragut's heavy wooden gunboats. The vessel had already been shot up by shells from Fort Morgan; one pierced her chain armor, exploded in one of the boilers, and killed or scalded all her firemen and coal heavers. Other shells had damaged her steering gear and set the vessel on fire. She had been saved by the *Galena*, lashed to her port side, which had remained undamaged and pulled her through the channel.

With the *Oneida* and her consort, Buchanan had a pair of Union gunboats ripe for destruction. As he passed alongside with his broadsides leveled at the *Oneida's* waterline, "primers failed to explode the charges in the guns three times." Buchanan had to content himself with delivering two raking broadsides from astern, which resulted in the amputation of Comdr. J. R. Madison Mullany's arm and an increase of the wreckage already on board the vessel. Eight men were killed and another 30 wounded, but Buchanan could not deliver a mortal blow. As he maneuvered for a ramming run, the monitors, which had been covering the passage of the wooden vessels, came up, opened fire on the *Tennessee* and placed themselves between the *Oneida* and the ram. With three monitors positioned on his front and flank, Buchanan pulled away from the *Oneida*, steamed over to Fort Morgan, and anchored under her guns.[40]

Back up the line the CSS *Selma* had been delivering an accurate raking fire at each Union vessel as it passed through the middle ground. Both the *Gaines* and the *Morgan* were positioned near her, but their gunners had failed to get the range. Because of the position of the Confederate gunboats, Union vessels entering the bay could not bring their guns to bear. At about 8:00 A.M. Farragut ordered Lt. Cmdr. Jouett to unlash the *Metacomet* and engage the *Selma*. The side-wheeler had already been hit when a shell from the *Selma* pierced the forward storeroom, killing one man, wounding another, and setting the ship on fire near the powder room. Jouett got the fire extinguished and at 8:05 A.M. headed for all three rebel gunboats.[41]

After the *Tennessee* passed the *Brooklyn* and the *Richmond*, the other side-wheelers were cut loose and followed the *Metacomet*. When the engagement opened, the *Gaines* retreated to shoal water in sinking condition, and during a rainsquall beached about five hundred yards from Fort Morgan. Lt. John W. Bennett, CSN, commanding the *Gaines*, had not been able to deliver an effective fire because of damage to the vessel:

FRONTIER AND PIONEER LIFE—TEXAS.

HUNTER, John Marvin, 1880-
    Pioneer history of Bandera County, seventy-five years
of intrepid history ...   Bandera, Tex., Hunter's printing house [c1922]
1 p.ℓ., 5-287, [4] p.   illus. (incl. ports.)   23.5 cm.

    Howes, U.S.IANA, no. H.815.

    Micropublished in "Western Americana: Frontier History
of the Trans-Mississippi West, 1550-1900".   New Haven, Conn.:
Research Publications, Inc., 1975.

    1. Bandera county, Texas—History.   2. Frontier and pioneer
life—Texas.   I. Title.

9492 M 741

973.757

#436

Early in the action a shell exploded near the steering wheel, wounding the two men stationed at it and cutting the wheel rope.... Shortly after this, it was reported that the forward magazine was filled with smoke and thought to be on fire.... An XI-inch shot had entered the starboard bow, striking the deck above the magazine, [and] had broken it in.... About this time the ship was subjected to a very heavy concentrated fire from the *Hartford*, *Richmond*, and others at short range as the enemy passed by me. Nearly their whole fire for a time seemed directed at the *Gaines*. The after magazine was now discovered filling with water.... Finding the magazine filled, also the afterhold and shell room . . . the stern had settled some and the steering became difficult. Under these circumstances I determined to withdraw from the action . . . and thinking I might be able to reach the shore, now about two or three miles distant, I made the best of my way toward the fort . . . and placed her bow upon the beach within five hundred yards of Fort Morgan, about 9:30 A.M.[42]

The withdrawal of the CSS *Morgan* by Comdr. George W. Harrison is open to question, especially since the vessel sustained little damage and only one man had been slightly injured. Harrison had positioned the *Morgan* on the far left of the three Confederate gunboats, and as the flagship came up the channel, he kept off the starboard bow and away from the *Hartford*'s heavy broadsides. To hold her raking position on the flagship, the *Selma* passed the *Morgan*, firing as rapidly as the gunners could reload. At this point, the *Metacomet*, detached from the flagship and supported by the USS *Port Royal*, approached to engage the smaller Confederate gunboats. The crippled *Gaines* headed for the beach, and the *Morgan* did not wait to be attacked. Harrison exchanged a few distant shots with the *Metacomet* and began withdrawing from the action. Chased next by the *Kennebec* and the *Itasca*, the *Morgan* grounded in the shallows of the Spit, backed off, and fled to the fort, coming to anchor on the north side of Mobile Point and just off the starboard beam of the *Tennessee*. The USS *Philippi*, a supply vessel, had grounded on a shoal west of Fort Morgan at high tide and could not get refloated. Harrison spotted the stranded vessel and sent an officer in a boat to burn her. He explained the light damage to the *Morgan* by writing: "I owe this exemption from injury and loss, doubtless, in a great measure, to the excellent position I was enabled to keep, generally on the *Hartford*'s bow." However, once the *Hartford* passed and Harrison could no longer hold his position, it did not take him long to seek refuge by the Fort Morgan wharf. The *Morgan* was struck superficially six times before Harrison decided to disengage. The same providential rainsquall shielded the *Morgan* during her race to the fort.[43]

The withdrawal of the Confederate fleet to temporary safety left the four-gun *Selma* facing the ten-gun *Metacomet*, with three other Union gunboats on the way. Lt. Peter U. Murphey, CSN, commanding the *Selma*, had been running with full steam to hold his position off the starboard bow of

Lt. Comdr. James E. Jouett, USN (photo courtesy Naval History).

the *Hartford*. His stern guns had been scoring direct hits on both the flag-ship and the *Metacomet*, but as he maneuvered off the *Hartford*'s port bow, Jouett cut the *Metacomet* loose and stood in chase. Murphey changed course and headed east across the middle ground, pursued by Jouett in one of the fastest vessels in the Union squadron. Murphey's best gunner had just

Opposite: Metacomet capturing Selma (courtesy Scribner's Battles & Leaders of the Civil War–1888).

fallen from a shot by the *Hartford,* and during the chase his next best gunner fell. Jouett attempted to get into position for a raking shot, which would rip through the *Selma* end to end, but Murphey steered out of position just in time. With the *Metacomet's* superior speed, Jouett gradually overhauled the *Selma* and at close range, fired her nine-inch guns. One shell killed six men and wounded seven others, disabling the gun they served. At this point Murphey could use only two of his four guns, he had a badly wounded left arm, his first lieutenant was killed, and his master's mate had fallen. The *Metacomet,* her guns recharged with grape and shrapnel, had moved into a raking position, and the *Port Royal,* with broadsides ready, had come up to enter the fight. Murphey emptied his guns one more time and surrendered before Jouett could fire the lethal broadside. Outgunned, outclassed, badly wounded, and his deck "a perfect slaughter pen," Murphey had fought well.[44]

Before the war Jouett and Murphey had been close friends, and when the latter came on board the *Metacomet* with his wounded arm draped in a sling and his sword clutched in the other, he drew himself erect and said, "Captain Jouett, the fortunes of war compel me to tender you my sword." With warmth and generosity, Jouett kindly replied: "Pat, don't make a damned fool of yourself; I have had a bottle on ice for you for the last half hour!" But before drinking the promised refreshment, Murphey went below to have his arm dressed.[45]

At the opening of the battle at 6:30 A.M., Buchanan had ordered his small squadron to stand off the channel, just inside Fort Morgan, and meet Farragut's ships as they approached. The monitors, which were to engage the *Tennessee* and keep her attention diverted away from the wooden gunboats, failed to maintain their designated position and disrupted Farragut's order of battle. When the *Selma, Gaines*, and *Morgan* peeled out of line to hold their position off the *Hartford's* starboard bow, the *Tennessee* followed up the line, firing her port broadsides at the flagship. Buchanan realized too late that the *Hartford* was outrunning the *Tennessee,* and by the time he moved his sluggish ship into position for a ramming run, Farragut was through the channel and eluded Buchanan's attack. "Old Buck" then wheeled to port and attacked each Union gunboat as it came into the bay, but the great weight of the *Tennessee* so reduced her speed that even the *Oneida,* crippled by fire from Fort Morgan, had time to parry a potentially fatal blow into a glancing one. Buchanan's starboard battery hulled several Union vessels as they passed into the bay, but by 8:30 A.M. most of the Union force was four miles inside and in good fighting condition. Farragut anchored and ordered breakfast for the fleet. Buchanan returned to Fort Morgan to assess his damage. The ram's surgeon, Daniel B. Conrad, reported that fire from the Union vessels "was so destructive, continuous, and severe that after we emerged from it there was nothing left standing as large as your little finger. Everything had been shot away, smokestacks, stanchions, boat davits, and in fact, fore and aft, our deck had been swept absolutely clean."[46] Nonetheless the *Tennessee* had suffered no vital damage to her machinery or armor, none of her crew had been injured, and Buchanan was determined to renew the fight.

Brigadier General Page, commanding Fort Morgan, at first believed that the guns of the fort had sunk the *Tecumseh*. Since the *Tecumseh* was one of the first vessels under fire from the fort, the sinking of the monitor must have given Page's gunners much encouragement as they faced the rest of the Union squadron, although the fort received a severe bombardment that at times chased many gunners into bombproofs. As the gunboats progressed up the channel, Page reported that "shot after shot was distinctly seen to enter the wooden ships, but, as was evident, their machinery being protected by chains, no vital blow could be given them there.... Four hundred and ninety-one projectiles were delivered from this fort during the passage of the fleet. Our naval forces under Admiral Buchanan fought most gallantly against odds before unknown to history."[47]

Page reported only "slight" loss at the fort, claiming that Union guns were too much elevated. Although his men fought their guns bravely, the general must have been disappointed that so many vessels passed the fort without showing any evidence of serious damage. Perhaps to excuse poor marksmanship, General Maury, who was not there, claimed that none of Farragut's vessels passed nearer than eight hundred yards from the fort. Most other records place the range at three- to four hundred yards. Farragut's natural smokescreen befuddled the gunners, not the distance.[48]

Although Farragut had gained an advantage, all the forts, the dreaded *Tennessee*, and an unknown number of land forces in the environs of Mobile city still remained in Confederate control. The admiral could not determine whether Fort Morgan had been materially damaged. Shot and shell from every Union gunboat had struck the *Tennessee* and bounded off without causing any apparant damage to the ram's thick plating. The *Selma* had been captured, the *Gaines* grounded and the *Morgan* chased out of the action. Farragut knew the *Nashville* was at Mobile, but did not believe that the vessel would become a factor in the next phase of the battle.

Between 8:30 and 9:00 A.M., Farragut and Buchanan enjoyed a brief breathing spell as both naval commanders steeled themselves for the battle each had expected and planned. Buchanan took advantage of the respite to order breakfast. Farragut assessed his damages and commented to one of the junior officers of the *Hartford* during the lull: "You may pass through a long career and see many an action without seeing the bloodshed as you have this day witnessed."[49] The statement was premature. The admiral did not then know it, but before the morning would end, much more blood would be spilled in a desperate fight with "Old Buck" and the *Tennessee*.

Chapter 8
Battle on the Bay

About four miles separated the *Tennessee*, which stood under Fort Morgan's guns, and the Union fleet, which had converged up the bay and was anchoring well out of range. While Buchanan paused to consider his alternatives, the cook distributed biscuits and coffee to the men as they flocked topside for air. Second Assistant Engineer John C. O'Connell, CSN, wrote, "It was very warm in the engine room. The Thermomiter [*sic*] was at 140 to 145. It was almost impossible for the engineers and firemen to stay below."[1] Between the heat and the humidity, universal thirst had nearly debilitated the men.

Old Buck, grim and pensive over the prospect of further fighting, stumped up and down the deck, still lame from the wound sustained two years earlier at Hampton Roads. He inspected the vessel and found no serious damage to either her armor or machinery, but perforations through her smokestack had decreased her speed. Although the men were hot and tired from the morning's exertions, no one had been injured, giving substance to the claim that the *Tennessee* was impregnable. Someone advised the admiral not to make a second attack, implying that the men of the ram were already prisoners and further bloodshed would not alter the ultimate outcome of the fight. Buchanan turned to the spokesman and replied sharply: "No, I will be killed or taken prisoner, and now I am in the humor I will have it out at once."[2] Piqued by the suggestion of a cheap surrender, he turned to the captain of the ram and issued a sharp command: "Follow them up, Johnston; we can't let them off that way," and the *Tennessee*, instead of remaining under the protection of Fort Morgan's guns, turned up the bay and headed for the enemy.[3]

At first most of the men on the *Tennessee* failed to comprehend that Buchanan had decided to engage the entire Union squadron. Surgeon Conrad, who was never far from the admiral wrote:

> In about 15 minutes we observed that instead of heading for the safe lee of the fort, our iron prow was pointed to the enemy's fleet. Suppressed exclamations were beginning to be heard from the officers and crew: "The old

admiral has not had his fight out yet; he is heading for that big fleet; he will get his fill of it up there!" Slowly and gradually this fact became apparant to us, and I, being on his staff and in close association with him, ventured to ask . . . "Are you going into that fleet, Admiral?" "I am, sir!" was his reply. Without intending to be heard by him, I said to an officer standing near me, "Well, we'll never come out of there whole!" But Buchanan heard my remark, and turning around said sharply, "That's my lookout, sir!"[4]

Contrary to the opinions of some of his officers, Buchanan believed that his decision to attack the Union fleet was justified and not a reckless or vainglorious act to quell his anger. He did not believe the *Tennessee* could be shattered and sunk by Union guns, although he worried over the impact of Farragut's big 15-inchers at close range. In summing up his decision, Buchanan stated:

> Having the example before me of the blowing up of the *Merrimac* in the James River by our own officers, without a fight, and by being caught in such a trap, I determined, by an unexpected dash into the fleet, to attack and do it all the damage in my power; to expend all my ammunition and what little coal I had on board, only six hours steaming, and then, having done all I could with what resources I had, to retire under the guns of the fort, and being without motive power, thus to lay and assist in repulsing the attacks and assaults on the fort.[5]

During the lull in the fighting, crews of the Union vessels washed the decks and cleared away splinters while officers examined damage and carpenters hurried repairs. The cooks prepared another breakfast, joining their Confederate counterparts in an interregnum that took on the character of a modern morning coffee break. For the less fortunate men, surgeons bent to their task of amputating limbs and binding arteries, while other rows of men lay deadly silent, covered by sheets of canvas, waiting in a ghastly line on the port side of each vessel for a sailor's burial. As time permitted, officers converged on the wardroom to ascertain who of their mates were missing, but as the shock and excitement of the morning's battle began to settle, the boatswain piped a sudden call to quarters and word passed around: "The ram is coming."[6]

At first the movement of the *Tennessee* puzzled the officers on the *Hartford*. Farragut had just descended from the main port rigging and rejoined the captain on the poop when Drayton remarked: "What we have done has been well done, sir; but it all counts for nothing so long as the *Tennessee* is there under the guns of Fort Morgan." Farragut replied: "I know it and as soon as it is dark enough for the smoke to prevent Page from distinguishing friend from foe, I intend to go in with the three monitors, myself on board the *Manhattan*."[7] When the lookout reported that the *Tennessee* was moving, Drayton believed that Buchanan was headed outside the bay to attack the outer fleet. "Then we must follow him out!" ordered Farragut. A few moments later it became clear that the ram was moving up the bay – not out – and Farragut exclaimed: "No! Buck's coming here. Get under way at once; we must be ready for him." Still unconvinced, Drayton hesitated, and despite the admiral's impatience, was a little slow in getting up anchor.[8]

Drayton ordered the call to quarters around 8:45 A.M., cutting short the "coffee break." Signals from the flagship alerted the fleet: "Rebel ram coming up the bay towards us." Army signalmen passed the admiral's instructions to the *Brooklyn*: "Hail the monitor [*Manhattan*] and tell her to run alongside of us. Prepare to ram." Surgeon Palmer had just stepped on board the dispatch boat *Loyall* to visit the other ships and assist their surgeons when he heard the call to quarters. Just before he shoved off on his mission of mercy, Palmer saw Farragut beckoning and paused while the admiral instructed him to "go to all the monitors, and tell them to attack that *Tennessee*."[9] The *Loyall*, a swift little steamer named for Farragut's son, had followed the gunboats into the bay by sheltering under the port side of the *Seminole*. Palmer consumed precious time circulating Farragut's instructions to the three monitors scattered about the fleet. More time was lost while they slowly maneuvered into position. On the *Chickasaw* Lt. Cmdr. Perkins received his orders as an excuse to celebrate. "Happy as my friend Perkins habitually is," wrote Palmer, "I thought he would turn a somersault overboard with joy when I told him 'The Admiral wants you to go at once and fight that *Tennessee*,'" but each minute lost brought the dreaded ram closer to the Union fleet and the vulnerable wooden gunboats.[10]

Buchanan, hoping for a surprise attack, saw his opportunity diminish as the Union fleet prepared to receive him. The Union commanders had orders to meet him with every gun they could bring to bear and with bows on at full speed. As 12 Union warships swung into position to assail the *Tennessee* in an unequal battle, hundreds of Confederate soldiers crowded the ramparts of the forts to witness a contest of unparalleled importance to their lives and their futures. Better ringside seats could not be obtained at any price. At this time many authorities considered the *Tennessee* the strongest vessel afloat. Buchanan had his doubts, but the preservation of Mobile, the reopening of Mobile Bay to trade, and the flow of arms and munitions to continue the war all depended upon one Confederate ram and a limping 63-year-old admiral who could not pass up a good fight. Farragut said it best when he later wrote Welles: "Then began one of the fiercest naval combats on record."[11]

The *Tennessee* had one advantage in the forthcoming battle: So many ships were arrayed to attack her that she could fire in almost any direction and hit the enemy. Also, in the earlier engagement the guns of Farragut's wooden vessels had caused no damage to her casemate.

As the *Tennessee* approached, the 1,378-ton *Monongahela* under Comdr. James Hooker Strong attacked at full speed, attempting to run her down by overriding her partially submerged deck. With throttles wide open and a full press of steam, the *Monongahela* struck with tremendous impact, whirling the *Tennessee* around and upsetting everyone inside her. For a moment the ram sagged in the water and then bounced away unharmed.

Buchanan had been so intent on engaging and destroying the *Hartford* that he had paid little attention to the approach of the *Monongahela*. Because the ram's helm had been ordered hard aport a few moments before the collision, the *Monongahela* struck at a slightly oblique angle, but hard enough to knock almost all the men off their feet. "The *Tennessee*," wrote Lieutenant Wharton, "yielded to the impact, and spun swiftly around as upon a pivot. I felt as if I were going through the air. 'What is the matter, Captain Johnston?' I asked. 'We've been rammed, sir,' was the response from the pilot house where he stood."[12]

Strong backed off and discovered that the *Monongahela's* iron prow had been snapped off and carried away with the cutwater. Just before impact the *Tennessee* had fired two six-inch shells into the enemy's starboard bow, one exploding in the berth deck, wounding three men and tearing up the vessel's interior. At ten yards Strong opened with 150-pounder shot and shell, and then followed with his 11-inch guns – shot, shell, and shrapnel – all rebounding off the shield with no telling effect. Two more six-inch projectiles from the ram pierced the *Monongahela's* hull, one exploding under the no. 2 pivot port. A ten-inch shot or shell entered the port side and plunged back out the starboard side, driving pieces of the headboard through the fire-room ventilators.[13]

As soon as the *Monongahela* sheered off, Captain Marchand surged forward with the 1,533-ton *Lackawanna* and struck the ram at right angles near the after end of her casemate. The impact caused the *Tennessee* to list slightly, but the *Lackawanna's* stem buckled, crushing the ends of several planks to a length of five feet below the waterline and causing heavy leakage in the bow. Marchand wrote: "Fortunately our yards and topmasts were down, otherwise they, in all probability, would have been carried away by the concussion, which caused the ship to rebound and the stern of the *Tennessee* to recede." Reeling from the impact, the ram's gunners fired only two guns through the *Lackawanna's* bows. After the shock the two vessels swung head and stern alongside each other. Marchand could only bring one nine-inch gun to bear on the ram; he had pivoted his broadsides to the opposite side of the vessel. At a distance of 12 feet, a shell from the *Lackawanna's* nine-inch gun smashed into one of the enemy's port shutters, damaging it and driving some of the fragments into the casemate. Marchand reported that "a few of the enemy were seen through their ports, who, using opprobrious language, our marines opened upon them with muskets;

Battle of Mobile Bay, August 5, 1864. Adm. David Glasgow Farragut directing the battle from the rigging of USS *Hartford* (courtesy U.S. Naval Historical Center).

even a spittoon and a holystone were thrown at them from our deck, which drove them away."[14] Marchand separated the *Lackawanna* from the *Tennessee* and, with seawater seeping into his mangled bow, put the helm hard over to circle for another attack.

As the *Hartford* built momentum for her first run at the *Tennessee*, the admiral leapt into the port mizzen rigging above the poop for a firsthand observation of the collision. Lieutenant Watson seized the tails of his frock coat but failed to hold him back. He then grabbed an end of rope and, climbing up behind the admiral, said: "If you will stand there, you had better secure yourself against falling." Farragut thanked him, took the rope, looped it around and over the shrouds, and then around his body. Watson remained in the rigging, revolver in hand, ready to fire at anybody on the *Tennessee* who attempted to shoot the admiral.[15]

From the beginning of the engagement, Buchanan had set a course to strike the *Hartford*, and after being jostled around by the *Monongahela* and the *Lackawanna*, he readjusted the *Tennessee's* heading and resumed the attack. Although Drayton would have preferred to circle around and strike the ram on her side, he did not have the time. At full speed the 1,273-ton Confederate ram steamed toward the huge, 2,900-ton Union flagship, bows on, iron against oak, with Farragut lashed to the mizzen rigging. Had Buchanan remained head-on and not eased to starboard at the last moment, the impact might have snapped the masts and brought everything down from aloft, including the admiral. For a few minutes, the Union squadron remained out of the action for fear of hitting the *Hartford*. Drayton, annoyed that Buchanan had avoided a square bows-on blow, ran to the bow of the flagship and shook his lorgnette at the ram, shouting: "The cowardly rascal; he's afraid of a wooden ship."[16]

Although Drayton believed that Buchanan had sheered off to avoid a head-on collision, had the two vessels met bows-on, they would probably have destroyed each other. The ram would have plunged so deeply into the wooden ship that as the *Hartford* filled and sank, the *Tennessee* would have been pulled down with her. Farragut had more to gain by taking that risk than Buchanan, who was down to his last ship. By colliding just off their port bows, the two vessels scraped along each other's sides. An uncatted port anchor on the *Hartford* buffered the collision when it caught on the *Tennessee's* gunwale. The shank bent in such a way that the flukes were squeezed parallel with the shaft.[17]

As the port sides of the two vessels grated against each other, Farragut was only a few feet above the ram when the guns, which almost touched each other, exchanged broadsides. The *Hartford's* nine-inch solid shot made little dents in the *Tennessee's* armor and bounded into the air. Buchanan tried to return the fire, but defective primers prevented all but one gun from discharging. That one shell ripped through the berth deck and exploded, killing five men and wounding eight. Fragments continued plunging through the spar and berth decks, smashing a launch and bounding into a hold where wounded men lay in misery. When fired, the gun's muzzle was so close to the side of the *Hartford* that powder blackened her side. Captain Drayton saw Buchanan's head and shoulders at an open port. Taking off the binoculars hanging from his neck, he hurled them at the admiral, shouting as he did so: "You infernal traitor!"[18]

The smoke and heat in the *Tennessee* had become stifling, and as the ram passed the *Hartford*, Engineer William Rodgers stood near a gunport to get a breath of fresh air. One of the *Hartford's* men spotted Rodgers and cursed him soundly. Rodgers grabbed a musket and jabbed at him with the bayonet, but for his aggression he received a ball in his shoulder from another Union marine.[19]

The two vessels passed in opposite directions, but Farragut wanted another crack at the *Tennessee* and turned on a wide circuit, intent upon building enough momentum to override the ram. The *Lackawanna*, attempting a similar maneuver, crashed into the flagship a little forward of the mizzenmast, cut her down to within two feet of the water, bashed in two quarterdeck ports, and dismounted one of the Dahlgren guns.[20]

When the *Lackawanna* struck the *Hartford*, Farragut was standing aft on the poop deck. Bewildered by the collision, he climbed over the side to assess the damage. Fear spread among the men. Some thought the ship would sink. Drayton wrote:

> Immediately there was a general cry all around "Get the Admiral out of the ship!" and the whole interest of everyone near was, that he should be in a place of safety.... The Admiral jumped outside to see what injury had been done, and finding that we should float, ordered me to keep on with all the speed and strike the enemy's ram again.[21]

The collision between the two Union vessels was caused mainly by the *Hartford*. The *Lackawanna* had made her circle and was moving at full speed toward the ram when the *Hartford* turned into her path. When the cry rang out: "Save the Admiral! Save the Admiral!" someone ordered the port boats lowered, and in their haste the sailors cut the "falls," and two of the cutters dropped into the water wrong side up and floated astern.[22]

Drayton slowed to inspect the damage, but the *Lackawanna* continued her run at the *Tennessee*, struck another blow, sheered off, and started to circle for a third try. By then, the officers and crew of the *Hartford* had just gathered themselves together and were about to resume the attack when the *Lackawanna* again appeared off their starboard and another collision seemed imminent. Lieutenant Kinney, the signal officer assigned to the flagship, wrote the following account:

And now the admiral became a trifle excited. He had no idea of whipping the rebels to be himself sunk by a friend, nor did he realize at the moment that the *Hartford* was as much to blame as the *Lackawanna*. Turning to [me] he inquired. "Can you say 'For God's sake' by signal?" "Yes, sir," was the reply. "Then say to the *Lackawanna*, 'For God's sake get out of our way and anchor!' In my own haste to send the message, I brought the end of my signal flag-staff down with considerable violence upon the head of the admiral, who was standing nearer than I thought, causing him to wince perceptibly . . . It was a hasty message . . . and by a fortunate accident. . . . Captain Marchand never received it. The army signal officer on the *Lackawanna* . . . had taken his station in the foretop, and just as he received the first five words, "For God's sake get out" – the wind flirted the large United States flag at the mast-head around him, so that he was unable to read the conclusion of the message.[23]

Whenever the three monitors found an opening to engage the ram with their heavy guns, they slipped into position and hammered away with powerful broadsides. The noise inside the ram was deafening. Surgeon Conrad referred to the impact of broadsides as "fast and furious, so that the noise was one continuous roar. You could hear voices when spoken close to the ear, and the reverberation was so great that bleeding at the nose was not infrequent."[24]

During the entire engagement, Commander Nicholson of the monitor *Manhattan* claimed that he had been able to fire only six shots. After each shot smoke from his guns filled the turret and interfered with the gun crew's vision. Farragut observed that Nicholson had failed to close with the ram on several occasions and erroneously attributed the problem to difficulty with the steerage. Nonetheless the few shots fired by the monitor's 15-inch gun caused much of the damage done to the *Tennessee*. Lieutenant Wharton of the ram wrote:

The *Monongahela* was hardly clear of us when a hideous-looking monster came creeping up on our port side, whose slowly revolving turret revealed the cavernous depth of a mammoth gun. "Stand clear of the port side!" I shouted. A moment after, a thundering report shook us all, while a blast of dense, sulphurous smoke covered our portholes, and 440 pounds of iron, impelled by 60 pounds of powder, admitted daylight through our side where, before it struck us, there had been over two feet of solid wood, covered with five inches of solid iron. This was the only 15-inch shot which hit us fairly. It did not come through; the inside netting caught the splinters, and there were no casualties from it. I was glad to find myself alive after that shot.[25]

Both the *Winnebago* and the *Chickasaw* had taken position around the *Tennessee*, firing whenever they had a clear shot. Lieutenant Commander Perkins maneuvered the *Chickasaw* close under the stern of the ram and refused to give it up, following Buchanan through every evasive effort to

escape. Perkins concentrated his 11-inch guns in the forward turret on the *Tennessee's* stern casemate, and his gunners banged away as fast as they could load, index the turret, and fire. At distances varying between ten and 50 yards, Perkins delivered 52 accurate shots.[26]

Direct hits shattered the oak and pine supporting the armor and scattered splinters among the men. The concussion stripped nuts and washers off the bolts that held the plates, and pieces of metal ricocheted inside the casemate. The continuous pounding jammed the after-port shutter, leaving Buchanan without a stern gun to return the *Chickasaw's* fire. Surgeon Conrad wrote:

> The admiral ... sent for some of the firemen from below to drive the bolt outward. Four men came up, and two of them holding the bolt back, the others struck it with sledge-hammers. While they were thus standing there, suddenly there was a dull sounding impact, and at the same instant the men whose backs were against the shield were split in pieces.[27]

The shot described by Conrad probably came from one of the monitors, and because of the great concussion, may have been fired by one of the *Manhattan's* 15-inch guns. As Surgeon Conrad examined the two firemen "split in pieces," he recalled that at the same time:

> An aide came down the ladder in great haste and said, "Doctor, the admiral is wounded!" "Well, bring him below," I replied. "I can't do it," he answered, "I haven't time. I am carrying orders for Captain Johnston." So up I went; asked some officer whom I saw, "Where is the admiral?" "Don't know," he replied. "We are all at work loading and firing. Got too much to do to think of anything else." Then I looked for the gallant commander myself, and, lying curled up under the sharp angle of the roof, I discovered the old white-haired man. He was grim, silent, and uttered no sound in his great pain. I went up to him and asked, "Admiral, are you badly hurt?" "Don't know," he replied; but I saw one of his legs crushed up under his body, and, as I could get no help, raised him up with great caution and, clasping his arms around my neck, carried him on my back down the ladder to the cock-pit, his broken leg slapping against me as I moved slowly along. After I had applied a temporary bandage he sat up on the deck and received reports from Captain Johnston regarding the progress of the fight. Captain Johnston soon came down in person, and the admiral greeted him with: "Well, Johnston, they have got me again. You'll have to look out for her now; it is your fight." "All right," answered the captain; "I'll do the best I know how."[28]

By this time Johnston could not do much to alter the course of the battle. He wrote:

Opposite: **Battle of Mobile Bay, August 5, 1864. USS *Hartford* engaging CSS *Tennessee* during the battle (courtesy U.S. Naval Historical Center).**

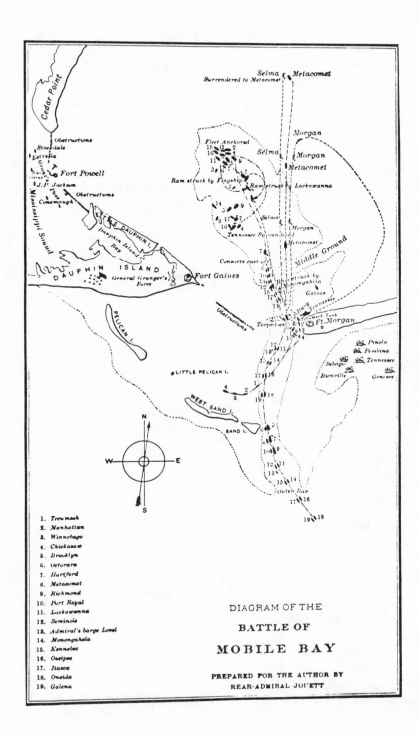

DIAGRAM OF THE

BATTLE OF

MOBILE BAY

PREPARED FOR THE AUTHOR BY
REAR-ADMIRAL JOUETT

1. *Tecumseh*
2. *Manhattan*
3. *Winnebago*
4. *Chickasaw*
5. *Brooklyn*
6. *Octorara*
7. *Hartford*
8. *Metacomet*
9. *Richmond*
10. *Port Royal*
11. *Lackawanna*
12. *Seminole*
13. *Admiral's barge Loyal*
14. *Monongahela*
15. *Kennebec*
16. *Ossipee*
17. *Itasca*
18. *Oneida*
19. *Galena*

While returning to the pilot-house I felt the vessel careen so suddenly as nearly to throw me off my feet. I discovered that the *Hartford* had run into the ram amidships, and that while thus in contact with her the Federal crew were using their small-arms by firing through the open ports. However, only one man was wounded in this way, the cause of all our other wounds being iron splinters from the washers on the inner ends of the bolts that secured the plating.[29]

Johnston observed that the exposed wheel chains had been disabled, and the men were trying to steer the vessel with relieving tackles. When these were shot away, the tiller separated from the rudder head. The enemy soon discovered that the ram could not be steered and converged for the final attack. By this time most of the gunport shutters had become jammed, and for nearly 30 minutes the enemy maintained a continuous fire, but the *Tennessee* did not reply. She lumbered along without steerage and with her perforated smokestack knocked down and lying on its side atop the casemate. The loss of the stack reduced the draft to the furnace, and the vessel could not generate enough steam to stem the tide, which was then running at four miles an hour. The gun crews lingered by their guns, lamenting the loss of many fine opportunities to sink Farragut's wooden ships at close range had their primers not failed. Johnston came down from the pilot house and explained the situation to Buchanan. "Well, Johnston," the admiral replied, "fight to the last! Then to save these brave men, when there is no longer any hope, surrender."[30]

While Buchanan issued a few final instructions to Johnston, Comdr. William E. Le Roy had swung the 1,240-ton *Ossipee* into position to strike the crippled ram. Since being rammed by the *Hartford* and deprived of steerage, the *Tennessee*'s pilot had been unable to maneuver the vessel into position to fire a single gun.[31]

Having the choice of fighting or honorably surrendering, Johnston reported taking the following action:

Upon my return to the gun deck, I observed one of the heaviest vessels of the enemy in the act of running into us on the port quarter, while the shot were fairly raining upon the after end of the shield, which was now so thoroughly shattered that in a few moments it would have fallen and exposed the gun deck to a raking fire of shell and grape. Realizing our helpless condition at a glance, and convinced that the ship was now nothing more than a target for the heavy guns of the enemy, I . . . proceeded to the top of the shield and took down the ensign, which had been seized onto the handle of a gun scraper and stuck up through the grating. While in the act, several shots passed close to me, and when I went below to order the engines

Opposite: **Diagram of the Battle of Mobile Bay (courtesy Edgar S. Maccay's** *History of the Navy,* **D. Appleton, 1901).**

to be stopped the firing of the enemy was continued. I then decided, although with an almost bursting heart, to hoist the white flag, and returning again onto the shield, placed it in the same spot.[32]

Commander Le Roy ordered the *Ossipee*'s engines stopped the moment he saw the white flag, but the momentum carried the vessel into the *Tennessee* and delivered a jarring blow on the starboard quarter that undoubtedly gave Buchanan another shot of pain. As the two vessels came together, side by side, Le Roy leaned over the rail and hailed: "This is the United States steamer *Ossipee*. Hello, Johnston, how are you? Le Roy – don't you know me? I'll send a boat alongside for you." A lifelong friendship had existed between the two men, and when Johnston climbed on board the *Ossipee*, Le Roy met him and said: "I'm glad to see you, Johnston. Here is some ice-water for you – I know you're dry; but I've something better than that for you down below." At a later time Johnston wrote:

> I thanked him cordially, but was in no humor for receiving hospitalities graciously, and quietly followed him to his cabin, where he placed a bottle of "navy sherry" and a pitcher of ice-water before me and urged me to help myself. Calling his steward, he ordered him to attend to my wishes as he would his own. I remained on board six days, during which time I was visited by nearly all the commanding officers of the fleet.[33]

Buchanan, no longer full of fight and immobilized by pain, received a boat sent to the *Tennessee* under the command of Acting Volunteer Lt. Pierre Giraud and surrendered his sword. Giraud commanded the supply ship USS *Tennessee* and had participated in the battle as a volunteer on the *Ossipee*. Giraud explained that Farragut had sent him for the sword without realizing that the admiral had been injured. From his prone position below, Buchanan sent an aide to his cabin who returned with the sword. Shortly afterward the *Winnebago* attached hawsers to the *Tennessee* and towed her to an anchorage near the *Hartford*.[34]

Surgeon Conrad, who observed and recorded much of the fighting on board the *Tennessee*, left an interesting account of the quest for Admiral Buchanan's sword:

> Two creatures dressed in blue shirts, begrimed and black with powder, rushed up to the wounded admiral and demanded his sword. His aide refused peremptorily, whereupon one of them stooped as if to take it anyhow; upon which Aide Forrest [Master's Mate W. S. Forrest] warned him not to touch it, as it would only be given to Admiral Farragut or his authorized representative. Still the man attempted to seize it, whereupon Forrest knocked him

Opposite: **"Monitors Attacking *Tennessee*" from Edgar S. Maccay's *History of the Navy* (D. Appleton, 1901) (courtesy U.S. Naval Photo Center).**

off the shield to the deck below. At this critical moment, when a fight was imminent, I saw a boat nearing flying a captain's pennant, and running down as it came alongside I recognized an old shipmate, Captain Le Roy. I hurriedly explained to him our position, whereupon he mounted the shield and, assuming command, he arrested the obnoxious man and sent him under guard to his boat. The sword was then given to Captain Giraud by Admiral Buchanan, to be carried to Admiral Farragut. Our flag, smoke-stained and torn, was seized by the other man and hastily concealed in his shirt bosom. He was brought before Captain Le Roy, and amidst the laughter and jeers of his companions, was compelled to draw it forth from its hiding place.... These two heroes were said to be the correspondents of some New York and Chicago newspapers.[35]

Farragut did not go on board the *Tennessee* to call upon his old friend Buck. He did invite Johnston to the flagship, where he expressed regret at meeting him under such circumstances. Johnston replied that "he was not half as sorry to see me as I was to see him." Drayton politely interceded and said: "You have one consolation, Johnston, no one can say that you have not nobly defended the honor of the Confederate flag to-day." Johnston thanked him, but declared that all the honor was due Buchanan, "who was the true hero of the battle."[36]

At Buchanan's request Surgeon Conrad went on board the *Hartford* to ask Farragut's permission to remain with the wounded admiral and to see to his care wherever he was taken. When he stepped onto the deck of the flagship, he was astounded by the extent of damage. "The scene was one of carnage and devastation," reported Conrad:

> The spar deck was covered and littered with gun carriages, shattered bolts, disabled guns, and a long line of grim corpses dressed in blue lying side by side. The officer accompanying me told me that these men – two whole guns' crew – were all killed by splinters, and, pointing with his hand to a piece of weather-boarding ten feet long and four inches wide, I received my first vivid idea of what "a splinter" was, or what was meant by "a splinter." Descending, we threaded our way, and ascending the poop, where all the officers were standing, I was taken up and introduced to Admiral Farragut, whom I found a very quiet, unassuming man, and not in the least flurried by his great victory. In the kindest manner he inquired regarding the severity of the Admiral's wound, and then gave the necessary orders to carry out Admiral Buchanan's request.[37]

Fleet Surgeon Palmer had been steaming through the squadron in the *Loyall* when Farragut hailed and directed him to "go aboard the captured ram and look after Admiral Buchanan." Palmer recorded the meeting in his diary:

> It was difficult even from a boat to get on board the *Tennessee*, and I had to make a long leap, assisted by a strong man's hand. I scrambled literally

through the iron port, and threaded my way along the piles of confusion to a ladder, by which I mounted to where Admiral Buchanan was lying in a place like the top of a truncated pyramid. Somebody announced me, and he answered (tone polite, but savage), "I know Dr. Palmer"; but he gave me his hand. I told him was sorry to see him so badly hurt, but that I should be glad to know his wishes. He answered, "I only wish to be treated kindly as a prisoner of war." My reply was, "Admiral Buchanan, you know perfectly well you will be treated kindly." Then he said, "I am a Southern man, and an enemy, and a rebel." I felt a little offended at his tone, but rejoined carefully that he was at his moment a wounded person and disabled and that I would engage to have his wishes fulfilled.... Admiral Farragut would take him aboard the *Hartford*, or send him to any other ship he might prefer. He said he didn't pretend to be Admiral Farragut's friend, and had no right to ask favors of him, but that he would be satisfied with any decision that might be come to.[38]

Buchanan felt severe pain and was in no mood to exchange cordialities with Palmer. He knew his wound was serious and probably anticipated the horrors of amputation. Palmer reported the conversation to Farragut who appeared hurt by the admiral's apparent hostility, claiming that Buchanan had formerly "professed friendship" for him. Knowing Farragut's kind and generous nature, Palmer decided to avoid embarrassment by bringing them together and instead sent Buchanan to Pensacola. In the end Palmer's personal attention to Buchanan's injury probably saved his leg, if not his life. On examination, and over the objections of other doctors, Palmer decided not to perform an operation, and for his skillful management of the case, received Buchanan's gratitude for the remainder of his life.[39]

Farragut sent a flag of truce to Brigadier General Page at Fort Morgan describing Buchanan's injury and asking permission to send a vessel to Pensacola with the wounded, both Confederate and Union. Page asked Farragut to send Buchanan under parole to Mobile, where the admiral could receive "prompt attention." Farragut replied that the request was "out of the question." Page agreed to allow a ship to pass and shortly after midnight the *Metacomet* steamed by the fort without incident. Page also agreed to allow a burial party to bring the dead to Fort Morgan where he designated space for graves.[40]

The following morning Buchanan appeared in better spirits. On the trip to Pensacola he and Lieutenant Murphey, who had been wounded on the *Selma*, received kind and personal attention from Lieutenant Commander Jouett. At breakfast Buchanan commented: "Well, if Jouett had only let me know what he was going to give me for breakfast, I would have surrendered two hours earlier."[41]

Confederate losses were distinctly out of proportion when compared to the odds against which they fought. Although Buchanan lost all his vessels but the *Morgan*, only 12 men were killed and 20 wounded. Another 280 men

were captured when the *Tennessee* and the *Selma* surrendered. Surgeon Conrad reported eight men killed and seven wounded on the *Selma*, but on the *Tennessee*, which had been heavily engaged with the entire Union fleet for about an hour, only two men were killed and nine wounded, attesting to the durability of the ironclad ram. In Fort Morgan, during the heavy exchange of gunfire with Farragut's fleet, only one man was killed and three wounded.[42] Lieutenant Bennett, commanding the *Gaines*, reported two killed and three wounded, and the night following the battle conveyed 129 officers and men safely to Mobile in six small boats.[43] The *Morgan*, which had skedaddled early in the fight and reported only one man wounded, slipped by the Union fleet that night and reached the Mobile defenses, hotly pursued by Farragut's gunboats and shelled most of the way.[44]

By comparison Farragut lost heavily. In addition to 93 men who went down with the *Tecumseh*, the admiral reported 52 killed, 170 wounded and four captured. [45] The *Hartford*, which Farragut kept in the thick of the fight, listed 25 killed and 28 wounded; the *Brooklyn*, 11 killed and 43 wounded. Only the *Port Royal, Seminole, Itasca,* and the three monitors survived the fight without casualties and with practically no damage.[46]

The *Hartford*'s carpenter, George E. Burcham, counted 20 hits; five penetrated the hull, smashing up decks and beams and causing much of the wreckage and most of the injuries. Some of the most serious damage to the hull occurred when the *Lackawanna* collided with the flagship, crushing planks and springing a large section of the quarterdeck. Had it not been for chain armor, three other shots would have hulled the flagship, and the one hitting at the waterline could have sunk her.[47] Thirteen of 30 hits penetrated the hull of the *Brooklyn,* causing considerable damage below deck and contributing heavily to the number of wounded. Two shots entered and passed through just above the waterline.[48]

Of the other vessels, five shots went through the *Lackawanna*'s hull, two barely above the waterline. Five shells ripped through the *Monongahela,* exploding between decks and splintering her insides, but causing only a few casualties. The *Ossipee* reported five shots through her hull; the *Galena* two gaping holes from ten-inch guns. The *Kennebec* was severely damaged by one shell from the *Tennessee*; the *Oneida* was put out of action passing Fort Morgan; and the *Octorara* collected 19 hits, the *Metacomet* 11, and the *Richmond* numerous hits to the hull and the rigging but no serious damage. The *Tecumseh* was sunk by a torpedo and the supply ship *Philippi* abandoned and burned when it grounded on the shoals west of Fort Morgan.[49]

After the battle Captain Jenkins and several other officers examined the *Tennessee* and reported between "forty and fifty indentations and marks

Opposite: **Surrender of CSS *Tennessee* at Battle of Mobile Bay, August 5, 1864 (courtesy Naval History).**

of shot on the hull, deck, and casemate, varying from very severe to slight."
A large number of other marks and smaller indentations were noted but
not counted. Jenkins believed that nine of the deepest indentations on the
afterpart of the casemate were caused by 11-inch shot, probably fired at close
range by the *Chickasaw*. There were no external signs of visible damage
to the *Tennessee's* hull when rammed by the *Monongahela, Lackawanna*,
and *Hartford*, although her rate of leakage had increased. Jenkins sum-
marized his report by writing:

> The *Tennessee* is in a state to do good service now. To restore her to the state
> of efficiency in which she was when she went into the action with this fleet
> on the 5th instant it will be necessary to overhaul much of her iron plating
> on the port and after sides of the casemate and replace some of it. The iron
> gun-port slides . . . must be either removed or repaired. A new smokestack
> is required, and additional ventilators should be added.[50]

Commodore Palmer and a different group of officers appraised the value
of the *Tennessee* at $883,880.29. The Confederates had placed the original
cost of the ram at $595,000.00. There is no record to explain the vessel's
sudden appreciation in value after she had been dented, damaged, demobi-
lized, and surrendered.[51]

For his personal heroism in battle, Buchanan received high praise even
from his enemies. While Brigadier General Granger prepared his forces to
assault Fort Gaines, he had watched the naval battle with interest and
wrote: "After the fleet got into the bay the *Tennessee* gallantly attacked it
all and for more than an hour she withstood the combined pounding of two
hundred guns before surrendering."[52] Commodore Foxhall A. Parker, USN,
after praising the Union fleet, wrote:

> We shall contemplate with hardly less pride, and with similar admiration
> . . . the heroic daring of our brothers-in-arms on board the *Tennessee*, who,
> when the forts were passed, and the Confederate gunboats dispersed, re-
> solved unaided to attempt the "forlorn hope" of wresting victory from three
> ironclads and fourteen wooden vessels.[53]

In the *Photographic History of the Civil War*, author James Barnes made
an interesting comparison when he wrote:

> Among all the daring deeds of the day stands out superlatively the gallant
> manner in which Admiral Franklin Buchanan, C.S.N. fought his vessel. . . .
> The Federal fleet carried more power for destruction than the combined
> English, French and Spanish fleets at Trafalgar, and yet Buchanan made
> good his boast that he would fight. . . . [S]uch boldness was scarce believable.[54]

Perhaps the greatest compliment paid Buchanan was penned in Farragut's notebook when he wrote: "This was the most desperate battle I ever fought since the days of the old *Essex*."[55]

Buchanan's critics claim that the admiral should not have attacked the Union fleet, thereby sparing the *Tennessee* for the defense of Fort Morgan. Had he not made the attempt, he would have been criticized more severely. If he had remained in the shadow of the guns of Fort Morgan, he would have been attacked by Farragut, who had already declared his intention to use his three monitors for that purpose after the first phase of the battle had ended.[56]

Buchanan, while under the care of Surgeon Conrad, explained his reasons for initiating the unequal second phase of the battle:

> I did not expect to do the passing vessels any serious injury; the guns of Fort Morgan were thought capable of doing that. I expected that the monitors would then and there surround me, and pound the shield in; but when all the Federal vessels had passed up and anchored four miles away, then I saw that a long siege was intended by the army and the navy, which with its numerous transports at anchor under Pelican Island, were debarking nearly 10,000 infantry.[57]

If, after doing all the damage possible to the Union fleet, the *Tennessee* still floated, Buchanan had planned to return to Fort Morgan and continue the fight. More importantly, he did not wish to be stigmatized for blowing up the ram without first fighting her to a finish.

For Farragut, worn out by physical exertion and mental strain, the hero of the Battle of New Orleans had now earned another laurel, equally important but far more difficult to achieve. He penned a brief message to his wife: "The Almighty has smiled upon me once more. I am in Mobile Bay. The *Tennessee* and Buchanan are my prisoners.... It was a hard fight but Buck met his fate manfully."[58] The following day, he published General Orders No. 12, thanking the fleet "for their gallant conduct."[59]

Captain Alden of the *Brooklyn* took exception to Farragut's expression of gratitude, claiming that the admiral took credit for "leading" the attack upon the forts with the *Hartford*. He boarded the flagship and accosted the admiral, asking, "Is this so?" referring to Farragut's claim. In an effort to conciliate the irate captain, Farragut invited him into his cabin. The admiral failed to mollify Alden, for thereafter he spoke disparagingly of Farragut, and even went to the amazing extent of saying that the admiral had ordered the *Hartford* to pass the *Brooklyn* on her port side, after that ship had stopped, thereby using the *Brooklyn* as a shield of protection from the guns at Fort Morgan. Later Alden became even more incensed when Farragut's official report became public, and at a gathering of officers refused to shake the admiral's offered hand.[60]

News of Farragut's victory reached Washington by way of the Richmond *Sentinel*. General Butler at Bermuda Hundred, Virginia, first spotted the news in a Richmond paper exchanged by troops at the front. Alone in his tent, Butler voiced three cheers for Farragut and telegraphed the clipping to President Lincoln.[61] When Gideon Welles carried the same news to the White House the following day, he was disappointed that the President did not throw his hat in the air as he had after Vicksburg. Welles confided to his diary: "News of Farragut's having passed Forts Morgan and Gaines was received last night and sent a thrill of joy through all true hearts. It is not, however, appreciated as it should be by the military."[62]

On August 15 the secretary wrote Farragut: "Again it is my pleasure and my duty to congratulate you and your brave associates on an achievement unequaled in our service by any other commander.... Great results in war are seldom obtained without great risks, and it was not expected that the possession of the harbor of Mobile would be secured without disaster.... While the nation awards cheerful honors to the living, she will ever hold in grateful remembrance the memory of the gallant and lamented dead, who periled their lives for their country and died in her cause."[63] A few days later President Lincoln tendered "national thanks," proclaimed a day of thanksgiving, and ordered one-hundred-gun salutes "at each arsenal and navy yard in the United States."[64]

In the afterglow of Farragut's victory, the admiral's attempt to sink the *Tennessee* by ramming was certainly heroic but not sensible. The repeated collisions injured the wooden warships without causing any damage to the Confederate ironclad. It was the gunfire from the monitors that forced Johnston to raise the white flag.

But on August 5, 1864, Farragut's work was not yet done. Confederate forces still held Mobile, three forts in the upper bay, and a series of shore batteries guarding the approaches to the city. This meant more work for the navy, but in Farragut's mind his crisis was over. Buchanan's four ships, 22 guns, and 427 men had been either captured, beached, or chased away.

Chapter 9

The Forts Surrender

When the Battle of Mobile Bay ended on the morning of August 5, Maj. Gen. Dabney Maury telegraphed Richmond explaining that with the exception of the *Morgan*, Buchanan's squadron had been destroyed or captured. "The enemy's fleet," he wrote, "has approached the city and a monitor has been engaging Fort Powell all day."[1] Maj. Gen. Jeremy F. Gilmer, Confederate chief of engineers, replied: "Every effort should be made to hold Forts Morgan, Gaines, and Powell, with the hope of forcing the enemy to withdraw for supplies.... It is believed that the outer works are supplied for two or three months."[2] Great reliance had been placed on the forts, especially Morgan. Jefferson Davis expressed hope that the Union fleet had trapped itself inside the bay. He wired Maury words of encouragement, emphasizing that "the forts on the outer line should be held as long as possible. For that purpose, I hope they are adequately supplied. If there be any deficiencies, they should ... be remedied promptly."[3]

Acting under Farragut's orders, on August 3 and 4 Lt. Comdr. James C. P. de Krafft, USN, took the Union gunboats *Conemaugh*, *J. P. Jackson*, *Estrella*, *Narcissus*, and *Stockdale* into Mississippi Sound and supported Major General Granger's landing of about 2,400 Federal troops on Dauphin Island.[4] With the army unopposed and safely ashore, de Krafft got underway about the time Farragut's fleet passed Fort Morgan. His gunboats took a position to the westward of Grant's Pass within easy rifle range of Fort Powell and opened with two one-hundred-pounder Parrotts and four 30-pounder Parrotts. About 8:32 A.M., the fort responded spiritedly with the only four guns facing west and maintained a brisk fire until about 10:00 A.M., the approximate time of the *Tennessee's* surrender.[5]

Early that afternoon Lieutenant Commander Perkins maneuvered the *Chickasaw* to within 350 yards off the eastern face of Fort Powell and fired 25 11-inch shells at almost point-blank range. Assailed by gunboats front and rear, Lieutenant Colonel Williams withdrew most of his men from their guns and sent them into the bombproof. Before seeking shelter the gunners scored three hits with a 7-inch Brooke gun, two rebounding off the monitor and the other striking the smokestack.[6]

121

At the time of attack, Fort Powell had not been finished. The front, or western face, was nearly completed and in defensible condition, mounting one 8-inch Columbiad, one 6.4-inch rifle, and two 7-inch Brooke guns. The face looking south toward Fort Gaines and Little Dauphin Island was half complete, but the rear of the fort facing Mobile Bay had only been started. Two guns had been mounted, a ten-inch Columbiad and a 7-inch Brooke, but they were without parapets and exposed from the platform up. One shell from the *Chickasaw* entered a sally port, passed entirely through the bombproof, embedded itself in the opposite wall, but failed to explode. Williams wrote that "the shells exploding in the face of the work displaced the sand so rapidly that I was convinced unless the ironclad was driven off it would explode my magazine and make the bombproof chambers untenable."[7]

Certain that the monitor could not be driven away by Fort Powell's two guns, Williams telegraphed Colonel Anderson at Fort Gaines for instructions, stating "that unless I could evacuate I would be compelled to surrender within 48 hours." Anderson commanded the 21st Alabama Regiment and had placed two companies of about 140 men at Fort Powell under Williams. He replied: "Save your garrison when your fort is no longer tenable." Williams wasted little time contemplating the matter of tenability and "decided promptly that it would be better to save my command and destroy the fort than to allow both to fall into the hands of the enemy, as they certainly would have done in two days." At nightfall he waited for low tide and marched his command across the shallows to Cedar Point, leaving Lt. E. G. Jeffers behind to spike the guns and Lt. Thomas J. Savage to prepare a train of powder to the magazine. At 10:30 P.M. Savage lit the fuse and blew up the fort.[8]

Two days later Williams' unwelcome report landed on Maury's desk. The general asked a few questions and learned that no serious injury had been done to the fort besides disabling the carriage of a ten-inch gun. Another gun required repairs because of careless loading. Not a single casualty had been reported. Stored safely under the bombproof were two months' provisions and enough water for 30 days. Williams still had hand grenades, revolvers, muskets, and howitzers to defend his fort against launches, and eight heavy guns to use against gunboats. Furious at what he considered a precipitous evacuation, Maury penned a stiff, harsh endorsement:

> This report is unsatisfactory. Colonel Williams should have fought his guns. They were not more exposed than those in every wooden ship, and vigorously served would probably have compelled the monitor to haul off. Fort Powell should not have surrendered. Colonel Williams is relieved from command until full investigation can be had.[9]

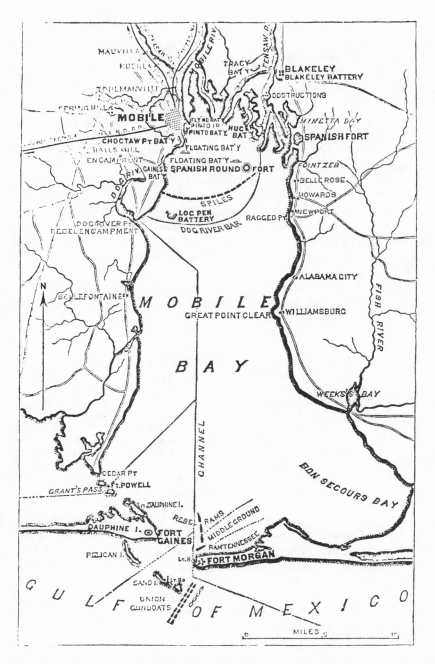

Defenses of Mobile Bay (courtesy U.S. Naval History Collection).

Still distressed over the unexpected loss of Fort Powell, Maury sent urgent orders to Colonel Anderson at Fort Gaines imploring him "to hold his fort to the last extremity."[10] A telegraph wire had been strung between Forts Morgan and Gaines to keep communications open between Brigadier General Page, who was nominally responsible for both forts, and Anderson, about three nautical miles away.

With about 2,400 Federal troops on Dauphin Island poised to attack Anderson's six hundred men at Gaines, Page visited the fort on August 4 to offer words of encouragement, found "good feeling" among the men, and returned to Morgan confident that Gaines would provide "protracted resistance." When the Union fleet entered the bay, captured the *Tennessee*, and forced the evacuation of Powell, Page began to worry about the state of morale at Fort Gaines. Nonetheless Maury remained optimistic and wired Richmond: "Gaines is under attack by land and water. . . . [Forces at] Morgan and Gaines seem resolved. Engineer officer (Victor von Sheliha) just reports damage to Gaines and Morgan slight and thinks their resistance will be stubborn."[11]

Maury's reassuring telegram had barely reached Richmond before more bad news drifted into his Mobile headquarters. On the morning of August 8 Page wrote:

> Yesterday morning at daylight Colonel Anderson communicated with enemy by flag of truce without my sanction. I immediately asked him by signal purpose of it. He made no acknowledgment, though I fired signal guns to gain his attention and telegraphed repeatedly in case he was on lookout, but unable to make signal "Hold on to your fort!" I went there last night [August 7] and was greatly surprised to find Colonel Anderson absent in the fleet, making terms of surrender. I gave peremptory orders, on his return, if the enemy did not return with him, all terms were annulled and he was relieved from command. This morning fired signal guns and telegraphed same effect. No reply. At 9:30 o'clock enemy's flag hoisted on Fort Gaines. Colonel Anderson's conduct inexplicable and disgraceful.[12]

On the heels of a telegram to Richmond, sent hours earlier, stating that "the people of Mobile are all ready for the fray," and "great confidence prevails," Maury suffered more than a little embarrassment when he wired, "It is painfully humiliating to announce the shameful surrender of Fort Gaines at 9:30 this morning by Colonel Charles D. Anderson, of the 21st Alabama. This powerful work was provisioned for six months and with a garrison of six hundred men."

Maury's messages to Richmond had been far too optimistic, and after losing two forts, he somewhat feebly asked Secretary of War Seddon: "Can you spare any good infantry?"[13]

A reporter from the Charleston *Mercury* attempted to minimize the losses on August 6 by informing his publisher that the enemy had merely captured the "outposts," a connotation which the reader might associate with a remote picket line. By the time the report appeared in print, the only "outpost" not occupied by Federal forces was Fort Morgan.[14]

By abandoning Fort Powell on the evening of August 5, Williams simplified Farragut's problems of supply. The admiral's first priority on August 6 had been to force an opening through Grant's Pass so supply vessels could pass from Mississippi Sound into the bay. He had not planned on using the Main Channel, as it was still covered by the guns of Fort Morgan and filled with torpedoes. The evacuation of Fort Powell also came as a pleasant surprise to the men of the *Hartford*. When they spotted the Stars and Stripes floating over the earthwork, sailors climbed the rigging and sent cheers resounding throughout the fleet.[15]

In the early hours of August 6, de Krafft sent the commander of the gunboat *Estrella*, Acting Master Gaius P. Pomeroy, to take possession of Fort Powell. At 7:00 A.M. Pomeroy raised the flag and spent the next few hours assessing the damage. He reported that the fort

> had been blown up, turning the center directly out over the parapet. It is nothing but a heap of rubbish and ruins, with a deep tunnel-shaped hole in the center, which was filled with water.... It had the appearance of being evacuated in great haste, as some of the clothing of men and officers are still remaining in their quarters.

Despite Williams' claims of indefensibility, Pomeroy found many of the big guns serviceable and a substantial supply of shot and shell available. The navy retained possession of Powell until Granger finished his assault on Gaines.[16]

On the evening of August 3, Granger disembarked his command on the western end of Dauphin Island, marched his men across the sand at night, and invested Fort Gaines the following morning. By midnight on August 5 he had moved the light artillery to within 1,200 yards of the fort. The moment Farragut's fleet headed into the bay, Granger's gunners opened on the rear of Gaines and lofted shot and shell over the fort, "taking their water batteries in reverse and silencing them."[17]

That night Granger landed his heavy guns on the south side of Dauphin Island near Pelican Island Spit, but not without some difficulties. He wrote:

> We are getting the 30-pounders into position slowly; the labor is severe, owing to the deep sand and the great distance; everything has to be hauled and packed on the men's backs. All the landings on this island are difficult and uncertain, owing to the wind and surf and shallow water, and nearly the whole of it is a quagmire of deep heavy sand, hot enough during the day to roast potatoes.[18]

On August 6 Granger started moving his troops forward, and as quickly as heavy guns could be placed, the gunners pounded away at Fort Gaines. During late afternoon the *Chickasaw* opened at 2,000 yards and fired 31 11-inch shells, most landing inside the fort and exploding. Gaines returned desultory fire, but after failing to find the range stopped altogether. Through the day and into the night, Granger kept up the pressure, probably not fully appreciating the demoralizing effect his attack was having upon Gaines' young defenders.[19]

On the morning of August 7, Colonel Anderson sent a message to Farragut under a flag of truce offering to surrender to the fleet and asking for the best terms. Maj. W. R. Browne, a reluctant and irritated messenger, carried the proposal to Farragut,[20] which stated:

> Feeling my inability to maintain my present position longer than you may see fit to open upon me with your fleet, and feeling also the uselessness of entailing upon ourselves further destruction of life, I have the honor to propose the surrender of Fort Gaines, its garrison, stores, etc. I trust to your magnanimity for obtaining honorable terms, which I respectfully request that you will transmit to me and allow me time to consider them and return an answer.[21]

The admiral sent for Granger, and together they drafted an agreement calling for the unconditional surrender of Fort Gaines and promised conventional treatment of prisoners of war. Prisoners were permitted to retain their private property but not their arms. [22] Early that evening, Captain Drayton and Col. Albert J. Myer took the *Metacomet* under a flag of truce to Gaines and presented the terms to Anderson. The colonel, accompanied by Major Browne, returned with Drayton to the *Hartford* to argue for more lenient terms. Farragut, in a kindly but convincing tone, expatiated on the hopelessness of attempting to hold the fort. "Gentlemen," he said, "if hard fighting could save that fort, I would advise you to fight to the death; but by all the laws of war, surrounded on three sides by my vessels and on the fourth by the army, you have not even a chance of saving it." Anderson accepted this reasoning without stopping to consider whether his situation was as desperate as Farragut described. Major Browne answered that he, for one, was willing to fight as long as there was a man or a gun left. His courage was not shared by Anderson, and realizing that the colonel had already decided to capitulate, Browne sullenly considered further conversation on the matter useless. Anderson and Browne returned to Gaines about midnight, and on the morning of August 8, surrendered the fort to Captain Drayton of the navy and to Maj. James E. Montgomery, Granger's assistant adjutant general.[23]

In essence, Farragut and Granger made no concessions. Throughout the negotiations Anderson ignored Page's attempts to communicate with him. He had made up his mind to surrender and did. At 8:00 A.M. Federal troops marched into Gaines and at 9:45 A.M. raised the Stars and Stripes to cheers from the fleet. Granger reported:

> By this surrender we have captured 818 prisoners of war, including 46 commissioned officers, 26 guns, a large amount of ordnance stores and ammunition, and subsistence stores for a garrison of 800 men for twelve months.... I shall move my troops without delay to Mobile Point, near Pilot Town, so as to invest Fort Morgan, leaving as small a force as possible to garrison and hold Fort Gaines.[24]

When the 77th Illinois took possession of the fort, they observed that most of the 21st Alabama consisted of "boys" about 17 years old. Only three guns had been dismounted. The fort was in good order and could have withstood a prolonged attack.[25]

At army headquarters in Mobile, Maury understood the consequences of losing both forts Gaines and Powell. Union forces could now freely supply themselves through Mississippi Sound and concentrate on the reduction or capture of Fort Morgan. Suddenly, even the city of Mobile had become vulnerable. Having lost nearly 1,000 men since August 5, Maury wrote the War Office and requested reinforcements:

> The important consequence of these misfortunes is that Mobile is henceforth liable to attack without warning, and must always be ready for siege. I have heretofore ... sent from here troops and supplies to other points which seemed more important or more imminently pressed. Henceforth I must collect and hold here everything necessary for a beleaguered city. The heavy armament calls for a great deal of ammunition. The outer line, Morgan, Gaines, and Powell, was supplied with 300 rounds per gun. The guns near the city have not more than 200. The total number of men now under arms is about 6,000, about 1,000 of whom have been under fire, and a large portion are citizens of this place. The city probably has more women and children in it than at any time since the war began.[26]

Maury had no way of knowing that Farragut did not consider Mobile strategically important and did not intend to attack it. The admiral had confided to Major General Canby: "If I did not think Mobile would be an elephant to hold, I would send up the light-draft ironclads and try that city, but I fear we are not in a condition to hold it."[27] Farragut wanted Fort Morgan, which had now become isolated, permanently out of the way, and he devoted all his attention and most of his naval force to its capture. Maury, on the other hand, feared that General Canby would bring a large force from New Orleans and attack Mobile through Mississippi, thereby squeezing him from both sides.[28]

With several gunboats and two monitors, Farragut stepped aboard the

Metacomet and on August 15 steamed to within 3½ miles of Mobile. Although the mission was a routine reconnaissance, it probably added to Maury's nervousness. Farragut returned, convinced that his decision to concentrate on Fort Morgan had been correct. He discovered a large vessel which he erroneously identified as the unfinished ironclad *Nashville* filled with stone and brick and sunk across the Main Channel. Several soundings verified that the water was too shallow for his gunboats to get within two miles of the fortifications protecting the southern side of the city. More guns had been placed in batteries along the shore, and fields of torpedoes had been scattered in the channels. Farragut wrote Canby that "until these obstructions can be removed there will be no possibility of reaching Mobile with any of our light-draft vessels."[29]

Unlike the commanders of Powell and Gaines, General Page prepared for a protracted fight and expected his men to resolutely defend Fort Morgan. On August 9 the *Lackawanna, Itasca,* and *Monongahela* covered Granger's forces as they landed in the rear of the fort. The *Port Royal* towed the *Tennessee* into position where her guns could assist the attack. Farragut steamed back and forth in the USS *Cowslip,* superintending the movement of vessels and the disembarkment of troops. Later in the morning the *Manhattan, Winnebago* and *Chickasaw* moved into position and lobbed more shells into the fort. Hoping to obtain another easy victory, Farragut sent Lieutenant Watson under a flag of truce to Fort Morgan with a summons to Page demanding unconditional surrender. [30] Not willing to lose a fight by intimidation, Page replied: "I am prepared to sacrifice life and will only surrender when I have no means of defense. I do not understand that while being communicated with under flag of truce the *Tennessee* should be towed within range of my guns." Farragut, sensitive to protocol, had the *Tennessee* towed back to the truce point before bringing her forward again.[31]

In preparation for battle Page destroyed Battery Bragg, a redoubt 2,700 yards from the fort, from which the guns had already been removed. Several outbuildings, including the hospital, quarters, and stables, were burned to remove obstructions and clear the way for firing. The Confederates torched the gunboat *Gaines,* abandoned earlier on the beach near the fort. From all outward appearances, Page had settled in for a fight to the finish.[32]

On August 10 a heavy rainsquall suspended operations in the morning, but in the afternoon Granger landed more troops and began to build siege works, mounting shell guns and mortars. Farragut sent ashore four nine-inch naval guns and placed them under the command of Lt. Herbert B. Tyson, USN, with gun crews from the *Hartford, Brooklyn, Lackawanna,* and *Richmond.* All during this period the navy pounded away at the fort. "Day and night," Page wrote:

Rear Adm. David Glasgow Farragut and Maj. Gen. Gordon Granger photographed after the Battle of Mobile Bay in 1864 (photo courtesy Naval History).

> we were engaged by the fleet, sometimes in a brisk fight of several hours ... at others in desultory firing without any material damage being done to the fort, save a demonstration of the fact that our brick walls were easily penetrable by the heavy missiles of the enemy, and that a systematic concentrated fire would soon breach them.[33]

With almost unending monotony, Farragut's monitors stood off Mobile Point at 1,000 to 1,400 yards and at intervals of 15 to 20 minutes arced shells into Fort Morgan. When the fort replied the gunners took a particular aim at the *Tennessee*, which they struck one day ten times without penetrating the casemate. Granger's short batteries, 30-pounders at 1,200 yards and mortars at 500 yards, added more metal to the daily barrage. It rained every day, disrupting operations, but Granger pushed forward, advancing his entrenchments. "We get along well together," Farragut wrote. "Granger is more of a man than I took him for, attends to almost all the work so far as keeping others up to their mark."[34] Granger's sharpshooters had advanced their rifle pits so far forward that Page's men had difficulty serving their guns without great risk. Pioneers worked with the infantry and in a few days had dug parallels to within 500 yards of the fort. Three 15-inch shells fired from the *Manhattan* on August 15 breached the wall of Bastion No. 4 and disabled the howitzers.[35]

By mid–August Farragut became restive and manifested signs of impatience. Suffering from "Job's comforters," he had difficulty walking, sitting, or standing without great pain because of an outbreak of boils. He wrote his wife, grumbling about his old friend and Norfolk neighbor, "Page is as surly as a bulldog, and says he will die in the last ditch. He says he can hold out six months, and that we can't knock his fort down." The illness had temporarily caught up with the old campaigner. "I am like Brownell's old cove, 'All I want is to be let alone,' to live in peace (if I survive this war) with my family."[36] He did not have long to wait.

On August 17 Brevet Maj. Gen. Richard Arnold, Canby's artillery chief, brought siege guns into the bay and began unloading them at Pilot Town, about three miles in the rear of Fort Morgan. Arnold loaded most of the guns onto barges and floated them up the beach to within 800 yards of the fort. By August 20 he had 34 guns in position with enough ammunition for a 24-hour bombardment.[37]

Every night, Granger moved his work parties forward, extending the entrenchments. Whenever fire from the fort concentrated on an area where men worked, they moved to another spot and resumed their digging, usually well concealed behind sandhills. They joked with each other every time a shell came close. "Lie down! lie down!" someone would yell as a shell whistled overhead. "Grab a root!" There were no roots to grab, but the boys laughed and joked and made good use of their spades.[38] By August 21 the infantry had advanced to within 200 yards of the fort, and preparations had been completed for a heavy combined attack early the following morning.[39]

At 5:00 A.M. on August 22 eight of Farragut's wooden gunboats moved into position with the monitors and opened fire on the fort. Joined by Granger's shore batteries, the bombardment lasted throughout the day. "A more magnificent fire," Farragut wrote, "has rarely been kept up for 24 hours."[40] Shot and shell disabled all the heavy guns bearing on Granger's forces and left only two pieces in service against the Union fleet. A shower of 15-inch shells, combined with accurate mortar fire, breached the walls in several places and reduced the interior of the fort to a mass of rubble. That evening mortars struck the citadel, setting fire to the woodwork, which burned furiously for several hours. The glare of flames gave Union gunners encouragement, and for a while they intensified the bombardment. A correspondent from the *New York Tribune* remarked: "It seemed as if the earth and heavens had come together with a mighty noise."[41] Fires inside the fort threatened to ignite 80,000 pounds of powder stored in magazines. Page moved it outside and flooded it with water. During the night the general learned that the casemates had been breached, making it possible for a direct hit to bring down company quarters and crush the men taking shelter inside.[42]

Page faced a difficult decision. He could "hold [the fort] for this time, gain the éclat, and sustain the loss of life from the falling walls, or save life and capitulate?" Before deciding, he evaluated the situation:

> The enemy's approach was very near the glacis. My guns and powder had all been destroyed, my means of defense gone, the citadel, nearly the entire quartermaster's stores, and a portion of the commissariat burned by the enemy's shells. It was evident that the fort could not hold out but a few hours longer under a renewed bombardment. Page spiked his guns and waited for morning.[43]

At 6:30 A.M. on August 23 a white flag fluttered over the fort. Farragut sent Drayton ashore with instructions to meet General Granger and jointly draw up an unconditional surrender. After trying unsuccessfully to send his sick and wounded to Mobile under parole, Page accepted the terms, and at 2:15 that afternoon, the 34th Iowa Infantry marched into the fort and hoisted the Stars and Stripes. Farragut's gunboats celebrated by booming a one-hundred-gun salute that echoed up the bay. Maury's cavalry sentinels hurried the bad news to Mobile.[44]

The garrison surrendered about four hundred prisoners and 45 guns, 15 of which had been spiked. Most of the guns had been disabled by the bombardment. Over a period of 18 days, 3,000 projectiles had been thrown into the fort, but only one man had been killed and three wounded. Lt. Col. Charles Stewart had been killed when a 32-pounder, rifled from an old pattern, was loaded with a slightly increased charge of powder and blew up. A fragment decapitated the colonel and stunned another soldier standing by the carriage. He died a few days later. Granger's force, consisting of about 4,000 men, reported one man killed and seven wounded. Page had reported firing 491 projectiles during the passage of the fleet on August 5 but provided no report after that date. The casualties had been unusually light on both sides, but most surprisingly so in the fort.[45]

Farragut expressed deep irritation over the conduct of the surrender. Conventional military protocol called for defeated officers to deliver their swords to the victors. Page claimed he had none and surrendered his pistol instead. Other Confederate officers also presented no swords, though broken remnants were later found among the debris. Since the surrender occurred outside, no Union officer had seen beforehand the conditions inside the fort, and when they finally entered to raise the flag, they were astounded by the wreckage. Farragut blamed much of it on Page:

> It was discovered on an examination of the interior that most of the guns were spiked, many of the gun carriages wantonly injured, and arms, ammunition, and provisions, etc., destroyed, and that there was every reason to believe that this had been done after the white flag had been raised.... General Page and his officers, with a childish spitefulness, destroyed the guns which they said they would defend, but which they never defended at all.[46]

The following day, he wrote General Canby, castigating Page without mercy.[47] Farragut, still smitten by boils, probably vented some emotional frustration at his physical torment, as he had more reason to celebrate than complain. On September 1 General Canby appointed a commission of three army officers and one naval officer to investigate charges against Page. Farragut, feeling much better and remembering his past friendship with Page, wrote, "I hope they will prove him truthful and honorable, as I do not wish to change an opinion of a man's moral honesty."[48] Farragut received his wish. The commission exonerated Page, ruling that no public property had been destroyed within the fort after the white flag had been raised at about six o'clock.[49]

Two days after President Lincoln thanked Farragut and Granger for delivering Mobile Bay, Secretary Welles on September 5 sent a formal letter of congratulation to Farragut, which the admiral shared with both branches of the service:

> In the success which has attended your operations you have illustrated the efficiency and irresistible power of a naval force led by a bold and vigorous mind, and the insufficiency of any batteries to prevent the passage of a fleet thus led and commanded. You have, first on the Mississippi and recently in the bay of Mobile, demonstrated what had been previously doubted, the ability of naval vessels, properly manned and commanded, to set at defiance the best constructed and most heavily armed fortifications. In these successive victories you have encountered great risks, but the results have vindicated the wisdom of your policy and the daring valor of our officers and seamen.
>
> I desire that the congratulations which are hereby tendered to yourself, your officers, and men may be extended to the Army, who have so cordially cooperated with you.[50]

Fort Morgan's damaged lighthouse after the battle (photo courtesy Massachusetts Commandery Military Order of the Loyal Legion and the U.S. Army Military History Institute).

Welles' reference to Farragut's "bold and vigorous" mind did not apply to his body. Late in August young Lieutenant Perkins wrote his mother that the admiral "talks a great deal to me when I go to see him – when, all at once, he fainted away. He is not very well, and is all tired out. It gave me a shock, for it shows how exhausted he is."[51]

Farragut admitted physical and emotional strain, but he found himself in the paradoxical situation of occupying Mobile Bay without possessing the city of Mobile. He wrote Welles:

> I am now a little embarrassed by my position. We have taken the forts at the entrance to Mobile Bay, which is all I ever contemplated doing.... I consider an army of twenty or thirty thousand men necessary to take the city of Mobile and almost as many to hold it.... I dislike to make a show of attack unless I can do something more than make a menace.

With only about 4,000 infantry, and another 1,500 now in reserve, he felt he could do more than create a diversion, but he expressed a willingness to carry out the orders of the War Department to the best of his ability. "I fear, however, my health is giving way," he added. "I have now been down in this Gulf and the Caribbean Sea nearly five years out of six ... and the

last six months have been a severe drag upon me, and I must rest, if it is to be had."[52] A few days later he informed General Canby that since occupying the bay, Confederate forces had been confined to the limits of Mobile. "I never was in favor of taking Mobile, except for the moral effect, as I believe it would be used by our own people to flood rebeldom with all their supplies. As my work appers to be at an end for the time," he added, "I shall ask a respite from duty, as I have not felt well lately."[53]

About the same time, the admiral's thoughts turned to his old friend Buchanan, who was recovering splendidly in the hospital at Pensacola. "Though a rebel and a traitor to the Government that had raised and educated him," Farragut wrote to Welles: "[Buchanan] had always been considered one of its ablest officers, and no one knew him better or appreciated his capacity more highly than myself, and, I may add, felt more proud of overcoming him in such a contest," and to refrain from sounding too sentimental, he added, "if for no other reason than to prove to the world that ramming and sinking a helpless frigate at her anchor is a very different affair from ramming steamers when handled by officers of good capacity."[54]

Farragut seemed to be in a mood to let the enemy down easily, show a little forgiveness, and perhaps hope for reconciliation. Assistant Naval Secretary Fox began badgering Welles to recall the admiral and replace him with Acting Rear Adm. Samuel P. Lee, then in command of the North Atlantic Squadron. Welles, always politically sensitive, balked at the suggestion because he thought the public expected an early capture of the city of Mobile, and if he recalled Farragut, failure to take the city would be blamed upon the Naval Office. He also worried that if Farragut took command of the North Atlantic Squadron, the Confederates would interpret the transfer as aggressive, anticipate an attack on Wilmington, North Carolina, and strengthen their fortifications.[55] Nonetheless he believed that Farragut was the best man for the job and ordered him to be at Port Royal by the end of September.[56]

As Welles cut new orders for Farragut, the admiral replied to Fox's letter of congratulation on the capture of Fort Morgan. He reiterated his reasons for opposing an attack on Mobile, complained that all his ships were breaking down, and provided Fox with additional facts on his deteriorating health. "As to myself," he added:

> I have been on board ship so long that the want of exercise has had a bad effect on me, and a few days after we came in I had an attack of vertigo that I fear to have repeated. It kept me down for two weeks, but I am now begin-

Opposite: **Fort Morgan after the surrender (photo courtesy Massachusetts Commandery Military Order of the Loyal Legion and the U.S. Army Military History Institute).**

ning to feel more like myself, but I must have rest and exercise; both my mind and body require them. My mind has been too constantly on the stretch for four or five months. After that I will be ready for any services the Government requires of me.

To Fox's question regarding an attack on Wilmington, the admiral believed the season was too far advanced for such an operation.[57]

Fox laid the matter on Welles' desk. Rather than recall Farragut for a well-deserved rest, Welles left him at Mobile for another two months and gave command of the North Atlantic Squadron to Rear Adm. David Porter.[58] Farragut's health began to improve, but in his heart, he wanted to be at home.

An attack on Mobile continued to be delayed. In late October Canby tapped his fingers on his desk waiting for word from General Sherman.[59] A week later instructions came asking Canby to move 15,000 troops against Selma, Alabama, thereby drawing off Confederate troops from Georgia and opening the way for Sherman's march to the sea.[60]

Deprived of any military support to capture Mobile, Farragut remained at his post, waiting for orders to go home. Finally a dispatch arrived from Welles, advising him "that it is the wish of the Department that you should feel at liberty to turn over the command of the West Gulf Squadron to the next officer in rank to yourself at any time you may see fit and return to New York on the *Hartford*." The admiral transferred his command to Commodore Palmer, and on November 30, he sailed for New York.[61]

The Battle of Mobile Bay resulted in the loss of one of the South's few remaining ports, leaving only Charleston and Wilmington on the Atlantic Coast as major outlets for Southern cotton and heavily blockaded inlets for deliveries of foreign arms, ammunition, medical supplies, and other necessities. West of the Mississippi blockade-runners still ran into small ports along the Texas coast and into Matamoras, Mexico, but because of the great distance to eastern battlefields, few of these supplies ever crossed the Mississippi River.

Farragut's attack on Mobile Bay, supported by General Granger, netted 1,700 prisoners and exposed Mobile to siege by encirclement. The city had never been part of the admiral's objectives. Except as a port Mobile contributed little to the South's defense, and it was a port no longer. After the fall of Mobile Bay, General Canby did not feel that he had sufficient forces to attack the city. Even if it fell, he could not spare the troops to garrison it afterwards, so urgent were the calls for reinforcements to replace casualties in Georgia and Virginia.

Had Canby known the condition of Mobile's forces on August 5, he could probably have captured the city cheaply. There were few troops in or immediately about the city – they had been sent to the forts or moved to other battlefields. Maury had been forced to transfer most of his men north, including much of the artillery, to oppose Major General Smith's attack on Tupelo. When that battle ended on July 15, Maury's Mobile defenders were ordered east to West Point, Georgia, to support Lt. Gen. John Bell Hood's defense of Atlanta. Maury admitted later that if Union shallow-draft transports had come through Grant's Pass after Fort Powell had been evacuated and landed troops up Dog River, Granger's infantry could have marched into the city with hardly any resistance. His force consisted mostly of boys and men too old to join the army.[62] A few months later, this condition would improve, but at the close of 1864, the occupation of Mobile still had little military importance.

In terms of immediate value, the fall of Mobile Bay scored as the first major victory, East or West, in the three months following Gen. Ulysses S. Grant's spring offensive in northern Virginia. Not only did Northerners find cause for celebration, but Lincoln's political supporters needed a victory to solidify the president's chances for reelection in the upcoming campaign, less than three months away.

Strangely enough President Davis and the Confederate War Office never attached proper importance to the defense of Mobile Bay, nor did they fully appreciate the ineffectiveness of forts against 11- and 15-inch guns fired from Union monitors. They seemed to ignore the unexpected fall of New Orleans in 1862, which had provided them with an early example of the effectiveness of improved Union naval ordnance in reducing once impregnable fortifications. Other military priorities dominated their attention, and they continued to draw away men, guns, iron, and other resources from the environs of Mobile to support their dwindling armies. By the time General Canby returned to invest Mobile in March 1865, the war was all but over, but the techniques of fighting had changed. Had the Mobile Campaign occurred at the beginning of the war instead of at its end, the death toll might have been staggering. At that time tactics, both Union and Confederate, had not kept pace with improvements in rifling and artillery.

Back in the spring of 1862, both Welles and Farragut recognized that Mobile Bay controlled the destiny of Mobile, but neither "Beast" Butler nor "Dancing Master" Banks put it on his scrambled agenda. With Farragut's naval support, Granger captured both Gaines and Morgan with about 4,000 troops. He had eight casualties. Farragut could have entered Mobile Bay in the summer of 1862 with light loss, though he could not have held it without control of the forts. Forced to wait two years, he faced a new threat and lost a monitor, a supply ship, and more than three hundred men to the *Tennessee* and a torpedo. The old forts, built of brick and sand, had outlived their usefulness.

Chapter 10
Prelude to the End

With Buchanan injured and taken prisoner, command of the remaining Confederate naval force at Mobile reverted to Commodore Farrand, whose previous performance had been characterized by sluggishness, spells of apathy, and moments of stubbornness. Arriving at Mobile from his station at Selma, Farrand found that his squadron had been reduced to the *Tuscaloosa, Huntsville, Nashville, Morgan,* and *Baltic.* The *Tuscaloosa* and *Huntsville,* although called ironclads and originally intended to be smaller copies of the *Tennessee,* never measured up to expectations. They were partially armored, their undersize engines failed to provide mobility (at times, they could not stem the tide), and neither vessel ever received a full complement of guns. Soon after they arrived at Mobile in March 1863, Buchanan disgustedly downgraded the vessels to floating batteries and thereafter gave them little attention. The huge side-wheeler *Nashville* had never been completed for many of the same reasons. The six-gun wooden gunboat *Morgan* had withdrawn from the Battle of Mobile Bay and retreated to the city, failing to take an active part in the engagement. The *Baltic,* a small converted riverboat, was hardly worth the trouble of manning. Two other gunboats had been started on the wharves of Mobile, but work had never progressed beyond the completion of their hulls.[1]

On August 15, 1864, Farrand observed several Union vessels standing off Mobile and firing at the *Huntsville* and the *Tuscaloosa.* At the time, Farragut was on board the *Metacomet* and had brought several light-draft gunboats with him on a reconnaissance. Farrand returned the fire, probably grateful that the Union vessels came no further. The Richmond *Sentinel* glorified the brief exchange by reporting that "two monitors and five gunboats crossed Dog River Bar, and, coming up to within two miles of the obstructions, opened fire for two hours on our batteries and gunboats, doing no damage. One of our gunboats replied handsomely. Our batteries were silent at sunset. The enemy hauled off." The *Morgan* had steamed into the fray and scattered a few random shots without doing any damage. Nonetheless, to the readers of the *Sentinel,* the mighty Union navy had been driven away.[2] Farragut's reconnaissance represented the last effort on behalf of the Union navy to threaten Mobile for nearly six months, which gave Farrand an opportunity to strengthen his naval squadron.

At the other end of the bay, Lt. George Wiggin, acting under Farragut's instructions, took two steamers into Bon Secours Bay on September 8 and destroyed an important saltworks located on the Fish River. To the people of the Confederacy, salt had become as important as gunpowder. Wiggin burned or blew up two hundred buildings with salt pans producing about 2,000 bushels of the precious preservative a day.[3]

On September 11 the men returned to burn Smith's sawmill and 60,000 feet of lumber. Under a mound of fresh dirt they recovered a large engine that the mill owner had buried to hide it. This time Confederate forces under Col. Harry Maury positioned themselves along a sharp bend in the river and opened fire as the steamers and barges attempted to pass, wounding one officer and two men. During the combined operation, Maj. Augustus H. H. Petibone commanded 250 somewhat disorderly men from the 20th Wisconsin Volunteers. Navy Lieutenant Wiggin registered his disgust at the army's lack of discipline by reporting:

> I hope that I shall not be sent on another expedition with the army. Their main object is to plunder and rob the inhabitants wherever they go, without regard to age, sex or condition. Everyone is on his own hook and does just about as he pleases. The officers have no control of their men whatever, they go on shore when they please and come on board when they get ready.[4]

Aside from chasing an occasional blockade-runner, the Fish River expedition represented Farragut's last naval mission on Mobile Bay and the first military engagement with Confederate forces directly responsible for the defense of the approaches to Mobile. Until March 21, 1865, the Union navy waited for the army to gather a force strong enough to attack Mobile. Gen. Dabney Maury also waited, expecting the campaign to begin at any moment, and spent his waiting days trying to improve Mobile's land fortifications while relentlessly badgering Richmond for reinforcements. With the naval phase of the Battle of Mobile Bay at an end, Union and Confederate armies began marshaling their forces for the inevitable attack and defense of the city.

After the Battle of Mobile Bay, months passed before General Canby could beg, borrow, or recruit troops for an expedition to capture the fortified city. During the summer, General Sherman had drawn off most of Canby's reserves for his Atlanta campaign. At the same time, the Confederate army had taken the initiative and mounted another campaign in the Trans-Mississippi. Maj. Gen. Sterling Price CSA, assumed command of a new expeditionary force at Princeton, Arkansas, to recover Missouri for the South. The campaign lasted until December 2, involved extensive fighting, and prevented Canby from obtaining reserves. All across northern Alabama, northern Georgia and southern Tennessee, Maj. Gen. Nathan Bedford Forrest, CSA, cut up Union communications with his cavalry, dismantling railroads, blowing up bridges, and threatening Union strongholds at Nashville and Chattanooga. When Lieutenant General Hood evacuated Atlanta and started toward Tennessee, Sherman divided his force, sending Maj. Gen. George H. Thomas, USA, on the road back to Nashville. On November 16 the balance of his army started across Georgia on his well-known march to the sea. To support these operations Sherman had drawn troops from the Military Division of West Mississippi. Canby complied by forwarding reserves to Sherman or by threatening other key Confederate positions to prevent the flow of reinforcements to Hood or Price. On December 16 Thomas wrecked Hood's army, and on December 21 Sherman's forces marched unopposed into Savannah. By then it was too late in the season to mount a campaign against Mobile.

Back in early July Maury had received information from a spy at New Orleans that Canby had collected a force of 20,000 men for an attack on Mobile. "I am sadly unprepared at this time," he wrote, "have been drained of everything, especially men."[5] For the defense of the city Maury had about 2,000 effectives, and in desperation he called for 5,000 Negroes.[6] Maury's immediate superior, Lt. Gen. Stephen D. Lee, CSA, had all his forces committed to the defense of Tupelo, Mississippi. He empathized with Maury but did not release any troops. Maj. Gen. Jones M. Withers, nominal commander of all reserve forces in Alabama, received instructions from Richmond to send between 40 and 50 companies to Maury. Withers replied, "I am hunting them up. No authority has ever been given me over enrolling officers, and through them I have not received six companies."[7] Maury already had a morale problem with the few men he commanded; he had not been able to pay them for several months. "There is great distress," he wrote, "among the officers and troops of my command for the want of money."[8]

When Granger landed on Dauphin Island with 2,400 men on the night of August 3, 1864, Maury expected another Federal force to materialize on the doorstep of the city at any time. In far-off Richmond, President Davis considered Canby's alleged campaign a hoax, believed that Maury could repulse Granger's small force, and deliberately shifted his interest back to other fields.[9] As a consequence Maury received no reinforcements. On August 5 he wrote erroneously that "a large force under Canby, estimated at 10,000, are attacking Mobile."[10] This was nonsense and imaginative speculation. Unfortunately, in order to get Richmond's attention focused on Mobile's situation, Maury "cried wolf" so often that his demands became diluted by their frequency. On the other hand, if Canby had been able to raise 10,000 troops, Maury could not have defended the city.

If Maury believed that Richmond had been withholding troops from Mobile without good reason, he soon discovered the causes when Seddon gave him command of the Headquarters Department for Alabama, Mississippi, and East Louisiana. In all, this broadly distributed force consisted of only 9,300 cavalry and about 1,500 Mississippi militia.[11] Maury appealed immediately to Mississippi Gov. Charles Clark for 5,000 more men. About 1,000 reported for duty but were unable to obtain arms. Gov. Thomas H. Watts of Alabama complained that he had organized two companies in Dallas but no one had sent for them.[12] A week passed, and Maury was still trying to locate arms for the few militia who had reported for duty.[13] With his new responsibilities the general now found himself besieged by requests from commanders thoughout his department for the same reinforcements that he had intended to bring to Mobile. Governor Clark estimated that he would raise 8,000 Mississippi militia within a week but he refused to send them to Mobile or elsewhere out of the state. The governor of Alabama did not believe he had the authority to raise additional troops without first convening the legislature and obtaining its approval.[14] To make matters worse, after three months had passed Maury was still trying to obtain enough rifles to arm the few militia who had reported for duty.[15] By then most of the available men had been skimmed out of his department to support General Hood's thrust into Tennessee, and the immediate crisis to reinforce Mobile had temporarily passed.

However, Maury continued to press the govenor of Alabama for laborers and armed militia. Chief Engineer von Sheliha reported unsatisfactory progress on the improvement of Mobile's fortifications because of the "scarcity of hands and of transportation."[16] Heavy November rains washed out traverses on Batteries McIntosh and Gladden and disrupted work on the city's entrenchments. High tides pushed by heavy winds eroded sand supporting shore batteries. Severe freezing weather, mixed with heavy rain, filled trenches with ice and water, suspending work. Men spent the final weeks of 1864 repairing damage caused by the weather. Had von Sheliha's work crew been doubled, their productivity would still have been paced by an unforgivable transportation shortage. Only one small steamer and eight teams supplied about 500 workers with materials needed to complete fortifications stretched across 20 miles of land and water. To make matters worse, even torpedo operations came to a halt for want of powder.[17]

With the bay controlled by the Union navy, the city depended heavily on the Mobile and Ohio Railroad for deliveries of armaments, powder, provisions, pilings, iron, rope, and other essential materials. The M & O stretched south out of Tennessee with connecting points at Corinth and Meridian, Mississippi. At Meridian, the Alabama and Mississippi Railroad, built during the war, ran west from Selma until it connected with the M & O. The Southern Railroad of Mississippi came into Meridian from Jackson, Mississippi.

Maj. Gen. Dabney H. Maury, CSA (photo courtesy Massachusetts Commandery Military Order of the Loyal Legion and the U.S. Army Military History Institute).

These railroads were constantly under attack by Federal cavalry. One other railroad provided service to Mobile—the Alabama and Florida—which came through Montgomery and connected with the Spring Hill short line at Pollard, Alabama, However, the Spring Hill ended at the Tensas River, and from there everything had to be hauled overland or barged to Mobile.

In February 1864 Maj. Gen. James B. McPherson, USA, launched an attack on Meridian and occupied the city for a short period of time. Federal troops tore up 21 miles of track, burning bridges and trestles along 47 miles of road.[18] By April 1 track had been relaid, and trains again ran to Mobile. Beginning in November Federal cavalry again peppered the railroad with raids and disrupted communications all the way down to Mobile. Mississippi militia rushed up and down the line, but always two or three days behind the Federal troopers. Back in Mobile Maury interpreted the raids on the M & O as precursors to an attack upon the city.[19]

The main strike against the railroad came in late 1864. General Canby wanted to close the supply line to Mobile, and on December 19 Brig. Gen. Benjamin H. Grierson, USA, acting under Canby's orders, initiated a cavalry raid out of Memphis, Tennessee, to destroy the M & O. With more than 3,500 troopers, Grierson overpowered resistance at Verona, Mississippi, fought an engagement at Egypt and Franklin, skirmished at Lexington, and clocked about 450 miles after three weeks of riding and raiding. His expedition destroyed about one hundred miles of M & O track, nine locomotives, and a huge supply of Confederate stores, but most of the damage occurred north of Meridian, and other supply lines remained open. Maury had been able to rush enough troops north from Mobile and other points to stop Grierson, thereby forcing the Federal cavalry west, where they turned their attention to wrecking the Mississippi Central.[20]

As Grierson's raiders swept through northern Mississippi, Granger sent a cavalry force from Col. Henry Bertram's 20th Wisconsin Volunteers to strike the Mobile road in the rear of the enemy's camp. At Grand Bay, 22 miles southwest of the city, Bertram ran into stubborn resistance and fell back, reporting 3,000 enemy cavalry in his front. On December 23 Granger sent five companies of the 6th Michigan from East Pascagoula to cover the withdrawal of his cavalry, thereby ending the feint intended to prevent Maury from sending reinforcements to Meridian.[21]

General Canby had sent a third force under Brig. Gen. John W. Davidson, USA, from Baton Rouge on November 27 to break up the M & O in southern Mississippi. Encumbered by a large force with wagons carrying pontoons, artillery, and a supply train, Davidson's expedition had not been designed for speed. Torrential rains flooded streams, carried away bridges, and turned roads into swamps. Heavily laden wagons lingered in mud to their hubs while details chopped trees and corduroyed roads. Losing every element of surprise, Davidson's progress was closely watched by Confederate scouts, and as he neared the Pascagoula River, resistance stiffened.

On December 10 a detachment from Davidson's force crossed the Chickasawhay River but were repulsed by Col. Robert McCulloch's 2nd Missouri before they could damage the railroad. Unable to get his force across the Pascagoula River, Davidson withdrew, having accomplished nothing of strategic value, and turned his road-weary command over to Brig. Gen. Joseph Bailey.[22]

The combined raids distracted Maury but momentarily stimulated the efforts of Chief Engineer Sheliha. Several redans along the trenches, though not yet complete, were hastily put into fighting condition. Batteries Gladden and McIntosh received finishing touches. Improvements progressed at Forts Blakely and Huger and at Spanish Fort. On the eastern shore, men dug rifle pits to the rear and flanks of the forts and placed abatis at points vulnerable to attack from land. Powder finally arrived and Sheliha's engineers anchored 17 Singer and 11 Rains torpedoes in three lines across Bay Minette, about 2,500 yards south of Spanish Fort. Still delayed by the lack of wagons and teams and constantly lacking material, Sheliha's men kept busy, but short days and inclement weather stole precious time. Slowly, each day, the defenses grew stronger.[23]

At Nashville General Hood's Army of Tennessee suffered a crushing defeat, but the devastating loss brought veteran infantry to Mobile. Shattered remnants of Hood's ragged infantry continued to spill into Mississippi as New Year's Day 1865 came and went. Demoralized by defeat and disgusted by the useless shedding of Confederate blood, many of the men threw down their guns and went home. The others, still willing to fight or without any other place to go, followed Hood into Tupelo. On January 23, 1865, and at his own request, Hood relinquished command of the battered Army of Tennessee to Lt. Gen. Richard Taylor. Taylor demonstrated his impatience with red tape by writing the Assistant Adjutant General in Montgomery, "General Hood desiring to leave, I have to-day assumed command of this army without waiting longer for a response from the President. . . . General Hood left this morning for Richmond."[24] Taylor recognized Hood's men for what they had become, a fragmented and tattered collection of veterans but no longer a cohesive fighting force. He disbanded what had once been the Army of Tennessee and dispatched elements to Mississippi, North Carolina, and Mobile.[25]

Prior to the Civil War, Taylor had almost no previous military experience, aside from the distinctive credential of being the son of former president Zachary Taylor. Educated in Europe, and at Harvard and Yale, and a former brother-in-law of Jefferson Davis, Taylor became an influential planter and Louisiana state senator before taking command of the 9th Louisiana Regiment in July 1861. He developed into an outstanding combat commander, and by April 8, 1864, had risen to the rank of lieutenant general, when, with an inferior force, he defeated Major General Banks at Mansfield, Louisiana, and repulsed the Union's disastrous Red River Campaign. Once, when enraged at the perceived lethargy of a superior, he threatened to quit his command, condemning Gen. Kirby Smith as "stupid, pig-headed and obstinate." Despite almost unprecedented vituperation directed toward a superior, he was promoted to lieutenant general and given command of the ailing Department of East Louisiana, Mississippi, and Alabama, which included General Maury and all his problems.[26]

Taylor established headquarters at Meridian, Mississippi, and started funneling forces to Maury. Lt. Col. Calvin H. Moore's 25th Louisiana packed their personal belongings on February 1 and headed for the Mobile trenches. On the same day Taylor ordered Maj. Gen. Samuel G. French's division of Stewart's corps to report to Maury and suggested when they arrived they be given picks and shovels and directed to finish the work that the Negroes had started. Major General Forrest's cavalry had been encumbered with about eight hundred displaced slaves from Tennessee. Taylor sent them to Mobile to work on the forts or to perform other duties. He warned Maury that "any force at Mobile over and above that required to hold the lines and furnish the necessary relief would be a weight and incumbrance." Taylor, a man of action, disliked politics and seldom minced words. He wrote Jefferson Davis: "The navy at Mobile is a farce. Its vessels are continually tied up at the wharf; never in co-operation with the army."[27]

Taylor had confidence in Maury's ability and considered him a competent general, but if Mobile was to be saved, preparations for its defense had to be speeded up.[28] Both generals expected Canby's force to attack along the eastern shore of the bay, converging first on Spanish Fort and then overpowering the smaller batteries as they moved across the head of the bay to Mobile. This created a problem because the fortifications around the city had been designed to resist attack from the western shore. Maury had reported a large buildup of enemy troops at Pensacola and Fort Morgan, with estimates running as high as 50,000 men. Taylor had known Canby for many years, respected him as an opponent, and knew he meant business. As both sides braced for the inevitable fight, Maury put the finishing touches on Spanish Fort and probably felt that he could do no more.

Chapter 11
Blue Tide Rising

In January 1865 Lieutenant General Grant authorized the transfer of Major Gen. Andrew Smith's 18,000 infantry and 5,000 cavalry to Canby's command for an attack on Mobile. Once Mobile fell Grant expected Canby to move into the interior of Alabama and strike either Selma or Montgomery. At the same time he sent Maj. Gen. James H. Wilson's Cavalry Corps of 10,000 troopers on a southward sweep into central Alabama to attack Selma and at some point join Canby's forces as they pushed northward. The city of Mobile, which had been allowed four years to prepare for the attack, was about to have its fortifications tested by an overwhelming assault of veteran infantry dressed in blue.[1]

As men began to arrive in New Orleans, Canby reorganized his force into several units. He assigned Major General Granger command of the XIII Army Corps, consisting of three divisions under Brig. Gens. James C. Veatch, 1st Division; Christopher C. Andrews, 2nd Division; and William P. Benton, 3rd Division. Granger had participated in the Battle of Mobile Bay and had become familiar with the topography, the soil conditions along the approaches to the outer forts, and the Confederate defenses themselves. Major General Smith's XVI Army Corps also contained three divisions under Brig. Gens. John McArthur, 1st Division; Kenner Garrard, 2nd Division; and Eugene A. Carr, 3rd Division. These men, veterans of the Army of the Cumberland, had fought at Nashville and routed Hood's infantry. Major General Steele commanded the "Column from Pensacola Bay" (as it was called by Canby), which consisted of Brig. Gen. John P. Hawkins's 1st Division, containing nine regiments of U.S. Colored Troops; Brig. Gen. Thomas J. Lucas's two cavalry divisions; and three other brigades under Brigadier General Andrews, whom he had borrowed from Granger's corps. Brig. Gen. T. Kilby Smith commanded the District of South Alabama, which consisted of nine artillery and six cavalry companies posted at Mobile Point and Dauphin Island as occupation forces. About 10,000 of Canby's veterans had fought with the XIII Corps at Vicksburg, and had come from various posts scattered along the Mississippi River from Memphis to New Orleans. In all Canby collected 45,200 effectives for his assault on Mobile.[2]

In contrast Maury reported on March 10 that he had about 12,000 men spread throughout the Mobile area with about 9,000 directly assigned to the city's defenses. About 3,000 of the men thinly occupied several miles of fortifications protecting the city on the western shore. Another 6,000 infantry and artillery, along with 1,000 Negroes subject to the orders of the engineer, reported to Brig. Gen. St. John R. Liddell, commanding the Eastern Division of Mobile. Brig. Gen. Francis M. Cockrell commanded French's Division, consisting of four brigades under Cols. James McCown, David Coleman, and Thomas N. Adair and Brig. Gen. James H. Clanton. These units, along with Brig. Gen. James T. Holtzclaw's Alabama brigade, Brig. Gen. Bryan M. Thomas's Alabama Reserves, and Brig. Gen. Randall L. Gibson's Louisiana regiments comprised the bulk of Maury's forces east of Mobile and occupying Spanish Fort, Fort Blakely, and several island batteries.[3] Most of these troops, except the reserves and the cavalry, had fought under Hood and were seasoned veterans.

After the surrender of Fort Morgan, Maury looked for a capable leader to replace Page and take command of the forts along the eastern shore. On September 19, 1864, he assigned the post to Brigadier General Liddell, a 49-year-old, five-foot, nine-inch veteran from Catahoula Parish, Louisiana. Liddell had dropped out of West Point after his first year and spent the next 28 years operating a plantation purchased for him by his father. At the age of 46, he entered the Confederate army as a volunteer aide to Maj. Gen. William J. Hardee, distinguished himself at the Battle of Corinth, and on July 17, 1862, earned promotion to brigadier general. At Perryville and Stone's River, Liddell's reputation as a reliable, hard-hitting infantry commander continued to grow. In 1863 he requested a transfer to the Trans-Mississippi Department and from then until the end of the war he fought in various capacities under Lieutenant General Taylor, whom he personally disliked. When Maury asked the War Department for a tough, competent general, Seddon sent him Liddell.[4]

On January 24 regiments from Canby's Reserve Corps of the Military Division of West Mississippi under General Andrews began to arrive at New Orleans. The 24th Indiana marched on board the steamer *Corinthian* and landed the following day at East Pascagoula. The 34th Iowa and the 114th Ohio clambered off a river transport at New Orleans, scurried over to the train station, and rode the rails to Lake Pontchartrain. Arriving there in the middle of a dark and windy night, they hustled their stores and teams over a long wharf, in many places so rotten that some of the animals broke through. Dismantling their wagons, the men loaded the pieces and their equipment on steamers, making the fourth time their luggage had been handled in 24 hours. On the morning of January 26, they disembarked and reported to General Granger at East Pascagoula, who put them back on the transport and sent them on to Barrancas, Florida, where they finally

Left: Brig. Gen. Eugene A. Carr, USA (courtesy *Photographic History of the Civil War—Review of Reviews*; U.S. Military History Institute). *Right:* Maj. Gen. Frederick Steele, USA (courtesy *Photographic History of the Civil War—Review of Reviews*; U.S. Military History Institute).

went into camp. For the next six weeks troops continued to land at Barrancas, a narrow and sandy peninsula opposite Fort Pickens, where, two centuries before, Spaniards had built a fort to help guard the entrance to Pensacola Bay. Clumps of pine trees, with scattered clusters of live oaks, covered about a third of the peninsula. The men located their camp on the higher ground, not far from a small, clear stream, and as more regiments arrived, many of the men found themselves consolidated with other regiments and reassigned to different brigades.[5]

Major General Smith's XVI Corps left Eastport, Mississippi, on February 5 and 6 by squeezing 18,000 infantry and 5,000 of Wilson's cavalry, horses and all, into 43 river steamers and seven towboats pulling barges. At this time Smith did not know where he and his army were headed and asked Union War Secretary Edwin M. Stanton for his destination. Chief of Staff Henry W. Halleck wrote back: "Continue on your exodus as the Wandering Tribe of Israel. On reaching the land of Canby you will have a number and name."[6] Smith's enormous flotilla moved down the Tennessee River, swung into the current of the Ohio, and continued down the Mississippi to Vicksburg. Not knowing otherwise, Smith disembarked and the entire force went into bivouac around the town. The following day Smith learned that only Wilson's cavalry had been ordered to Vicksburg, so he reembarked his force, continued down the river, and deposited the XVI Corps in the suburbs of New Orleans on February 21, completing 1,335 miles of travel in 11 days.[7]

Left: Brig. Gen. Bryan M. Thomas, CSA (courtesy *Photographic History of the Civil War—Review of Reviews*; U.S. Military History Institute). *Right:* Brig. Gen. St. John Richardson Liddell, CSA (courtesy *Photographic History of the Civil War—Review of Reviews*; U.S. Military History Institute).

For about two weeks the men occupied Gen. Andrew Jackson's old 1812 battlefield east of New Orleans, before steaming over to the main army camp on Dauphin Island. Pvt. Elisha Stockwell of the 14th Wisconsin described the land as "dead-level" truck-farming ground, with ditches every few yards for the water to settle. Several of the men went scouting for fresh vegetables and found a small house with a "fine-looking" garden. Stockwell wrote of his first engagement with rebel truck farmers on Jackson's former battlefield:

> I saw five or six soldiers coming toward it [the garden] from the other side. A very large young woman came out of the house with her sleeves rolled up above her elbows. She swore like a man and called those soldiers nigger thieves, and said if they touched those vegetables she would come over there. They laughed ... and told her they didn't want her truck. But she kept on with the slang, and told them to come up there two at a time and she would lick the whole bunch. I thought I had seen enough and turned back toward camp. I heard later that she was a French Creole.[8]

During the first week of March, the balance of General Steele's command landed at Barrancas. Brigadier General Hawkins' 5,500 U.S. Colored Troops pitched tents on the peninsula and formed a small lively community on a patch of white sand. A few days later General Lucas's cavalry division trotted onto the sandy strip with 2,500 troopers and as many horses.

At Fort Gaines Brig. Gen. James Totten organized seven companies of the 1st Indiana Heavy Artillery, Col. Benjamin F. Hays, and Capt. Albert G. Mack's 18th New York Light Artillery Battery into a 1,200-man siege train. For a while, their destiny was to wait, polish their big guns, and organize their ammunition chests.

The fortifications around Mobile were strong enoughto resist an attack from the western shore and cause a protracted siege. Maury's engineers had built three rows of fortifications south and west of the city. Instead of the direct approach, Canby had decided to move the main army up the eastern shore with support from the navy. After capturing Spanish Fort, Blakeley, and the island shore batteries, he planned to approach Mobile by crossing the Tensas and Mobile rivers and attack the city from the north.

Two huge earthworks stood in Canby's path, Spanish Fort and Fort Blakeley, which had been built along the eastern shore and heavily fortified to protect Mobile from invasion by land or water. A number of shore batteries, redoubts, and small forts containing from two to eight guns surrounded the main works and were positioned in such a way as to provide support for each other. Any attacking force foolish enough to charge across open ground risked being cut up by enfilading naval and ground fire.[9]

For his principal base of operations on the eastern shore Canby used the Fish River, which emptied into Mobile Bay about 20 miles south of Spanish Fort. Shallow-draft vessels could navigate upriver several miles and unload infantry, guns, and supplies from Dauphin Island without a great deal of difficulty or exposure to enemy attack.

As a secondary base Canby chose the town of Pensacola, situated about 40 miles east of Mobile Bay, to which supplies could be hauled overland or brought by water. At this time Pensacola had become remarkable for its ruined and lonely condition. The town once contained about 5,000 inhabitants, and remnants of elegant mansions surrounded by stately shrubbery and delicate flowers recalled a period of past affluence. Continuously raided by troops from both sides, most of the town had been swept away by fire and its population reduced to about a hundred. On March 11 two brigades under Brigadier General Andrews began repairs on a long wharf where two three-hundred-foot sections of the landing had been destroyed. In a few days his men worked 270 piles into the soft bottom by placing a fresh-cut pole, trimmed and sharpened at one end, upright in the mud, and by swaying the pole backward and forward with ropes, inched it into the mud until it stuck tight. With the wharf capped over and planked, Capt. William R. McComas took a detail from the 83rd Ohio, men with railroad experience, and tore up the Montgomery Railroad spur and reset the track and ties on the rebuilt wharf. On March 16 Union supply ships steamed up to the wharf and began unloading ammunition and supplies.[10]

To eliminate the flow of reinforcements from Montgomery into Mobile, Lt. Col. Andrew B. Spurling landed on the east side of Blackwater River with 847 veteran troopers from the 2nd Maine, 2nd Illinois, and 1st Florida, and trotted unopposed into Milton, Florida. Spurling then rode into Andalusia, Alabama, and dallied long enough to destroy government property and plant the impression that his force was headed for Montgomery. Instead, however, he turned west, toward Evergreen. A few miles from town, the column came to a halt, but Spurling rode forward to check his front. He heard talking ahead, cautioned his men to be alert, and stepped forward a few paces. In the dim evening shadows he observed three men approaching and crouched down beside a fence until they passed. As they walked by Spurling sprang to his feet and commanded them to surrender. They demanded to know to whom, and Spurling replied, "I am a live Yankee." The Confederates raised their rifles, but Spurling fired his revolver first, wounding two and capturing the other. The wounded officer, Lieutenant Watts, was the son of Alabama's govenor; the other two men were scouts. By capturing the trio Spurling preserved the secrecy of his mission and was able to begin the work of destruction. At 3:00 A.M. on March 24, at a point five miles north of Evergreen, his men cut the telegraph wires running between Mobile and Montgomery. Detachments spread out and wrecked track and trestles along the Alabama and Florida Railroad. After two locomotives derailed, troopers destroyed both trains, one carrying infantry to Mobile and the other hauling supplies to Montgomery. By the time Spurling returned from his raid, Canby's attack had started along the eastern shore.[11]

At the same time, Major General Steele's Pensacola Column, carrying ten days' rations and consisting of 12,000 infantry, artillery, and cavalry, moved toward Pollard, Alabama, creating the impression that a major force was on the road to Montgomery. Although the expedition was intended as a feint, Canby had the option of ordering Steele on to Montgomery if the Mobile defenses collapsed early in the campaign. If not, he intended to turn Steele around to form a junction with the main army. Burdened by 270 wagons, the column moved slowly over muddy roads and swollen creeks and through dense thickets of pine. Pioneers unsheathed their axes and corduroyed miles of flooded roads and wetlands. Caught by the same rainstorm that delayed the XIII Corps' advance up the eastern shore, Steele's column at times made no more than two or three miles a day. Even solid ground, covered only by a thin grass, yielded to the downpour, plunging parked wagons up to their axles in the quagmire.

The 6th Alabama Cavalry, led by Lt. Col. Washington T. Lary, watched Steele's slow advance, peppering the column with musket fire from behind breastworks, checking its progress from favorable crests, destroying bridges, and nipping at the flanks of the wagon train. Maury received a report, probably through Lary's scouts, that Steele's force contained 25,000 men, twice its actual size. He sent Brigadier General Clanton with Col. Charles G. Armistead's cavalry brigade to meet the attack and develop Steele's intentions. Fighting daily skirmishes, the Union column lumbered across Florida's

Maj. Gen. Christopher C. Andrews, USA (courtesy *Photographic History of the Civil War—Review of Reviews*; U.S. Military History Institute).

panhandle, pushing aside Armistead's weak force. Confederate cavalry destroyed a bridge over the Pine Barren Creek, forcing Steele to halt until engineers could replace it. Every delay depleted Steele's rations, and supply vessels expected from Barrancas failed to arrive at the landing at William's Station. In two days Capt. Eugene H. Newton, in pooor health and working much of the time in water, assembled a large detail of both black and white pioneers and threw a three-hundred-foot bridge across the Escambia River. The cavalry crossed, followed by the artillery and wagons. Coming out of the Pine Barren, the ground suddenly gave way under the wheels of the 2nd Division's wagons, bringing the train to another stop. That night the men camped beside a dismal marsh, slapped mosquitoes, and ate half rations to the rattle of distant picket fire.[12]

Aware that the Confederates were bringing up reinforcements, Steele sent Brigadier General Lucas's Cavalry Division ahead to take possession of the bridge over the Big Escambia River and prevent the Confederates from destroying the only bridge between his army and a line of supply. Steele saw his provisions dwindling at an alarming rate, with no ready means for sustaining 12,000 hungry soldiers. Lucas ran into resistance at Mitchell Creek, where Col. Charles P. Ball's 8th Alabama Cavalry had partially destroyed the bridge and then entrenched along the opposite bank. Clanton's brigade, some distance in the rear, waited in reserve.

Lucas sent a detachment from the 2nd New York Veteran Cavalry, led by Col. Morgan H. Chrysler, a mile upriver to find a crossing, and if possible, ride in on Ball's right flank. He then ordered three companies of the 1st Louisiana (U.S.) Cavalry, under Col. Algernon S. Badger, downriver to dismount, cross to the opposite bank, and attack Ball's left. After a few minutes of spirited firing, the Louisianans drove Ball back to Clanton's line, and Chrysler returned, unable to ford the river. Lucas organized details to repair the bridge and with the remainder of his force, moved on, encountering more resistance from Ball at Cotton Creek and again at Canoe Creek as the Confederate cavalry fought as they retreated.

At Pringle's Creek, about a mile above Bluff Springs, Florida, both Ball and Armistead retreated to William's Station, leaving Clanton's brigade under Lieutenant Colonel Lary alone and in the immediate front of Lucas. Because Pringle's Creek offered a poor defensive position, Ball believed that Lary would have enough sense to move on, but Lary remained, dismounted his men, and threw up a breastwork of fence rails on a rise north of the creek and formed his men. Clanton had not yet arrived from Pollard, but as soon as Lucas advanced, Lary opened with his dismounted cavalry. A brief, sharp fight ensued. Within ten minutes the 6th and 8th Alabama had fallen back two hundred yards. General Clanton galloped onto the field and ordered a halt. Lary argued that he was rapidly being flanked, but Clanton demanded that "we must fall back in order." The general ordered the men: "Dress up on the colors." While Clanton paused for a drill exercise, Badger ordered his troopers to charge. The 1st Louisiana rode forward with a cheer, wounded General Clanton, and captured 17 officers and more than one hundred enlisted men. From a rather impetuous charge, the 1st Louisiana lost a first lieutenant, one bugler, and eight wounded. During the fight, Pvt. Thomas Riley of the 1st Louisiana wrenched the Confederate battle flag from the hands of the enemy and later received the Congressional Medal of Honor for his part in the skirmish. Steele reported: "Of those who escaped capture, some sought refuge in the swamps and the rest were so hotly pursued to Big Escambia bridge that some of them, not knowing that a span had been swept away by the flood, jumped into the river and were drowned with their horses."[13]

From Bluff Springs, Steele's column plodded on to Pollard, where an advance detachment under General Andrews secured a large quantity of government property and some badly needed supplies, but most of the corn and subsistence stores had been carried off by local troops when they learned of Clanton's defeat. Despite disappointingly slow progress, Steele's force captured or destroyed tons of material and supplies needed at Mobile and tore up all the track in the vicinity of Pollard. Returning from Evergreen, Spurling rejoined Steele at Pollard on the evening of March 26 with 120 prisoners, 200 Negroes, 250 mules and horses, but few provisions.

Steele's column headed west and reached Canoe Station before the townspeople had hauled all their corn to safety. The cavalry entered the town ahead of the main force and found several ox teams laden with corn and about to depart for the country. Details slaughtered the oxen and divided fresh meat among the brigades.

Two hundred picked cavalrymen under Maj. Raymond H. Perry started for Montgomery Landing in search of corn, beef, information, or even a steamboat if one could be captured to haul provisions. Perry returned on March 30 with enough cattle and sheep to feed the army another day. By then Steele had communicated with Canby, who wanted the column back with the main army, but his force could not move far without provisions. On the afternoon of March 31 a detachment of cavalry trotted into Stockton, Alabama, and located enough corn and beef to stretch one more day. Steele, reprovisioned at Stockton, put his column back on the road, and headed for Holyoke, a few miles east of Fort Blakely.[14]

On March 17 Colonel Bertram's 1st Brigade, 2nd Division of the XIII Corps, left Fort Morgan at 5:30 A.M., marched along the peninsula, and headed for the Fish River, building bridges and corduroying roads for the 3rd Division, trailing behind. Brigadier General Veatch's 1st Division crossed from Fort Gaines to Navy Cove, disembarked, but found the ground impassable from recent rains and spent several days trying to move over saturated roads. Wagon trains could barely get under way. Every team seeking an untried path got mired, and wagons sank to their hubs. The animals, struggling to haul the teams, half buried themselves and fell exhausted. Corduroyed roads washed away or sank out of sight under the weight of artillery. Men tried to muscle forward through waist-deep mud and water. Foot soldiers fastened long ropes to heavy field guns and pulled with the animals just to gain a few yards. For more than a week, Granger's regiments were scattered all over the lower eastern shore, watched by Confederate scouts, and vulnerable to hit-and-run attacks.[15]

Pvt. Carl Bernhardt, 35th Wisconsin, described from personal experience the toilsome overland march and the exhausting efforts made by the men to move the wagons:

> Then we pull the donkeys, mud up to our knees, but those long-ears weren't dumb. When things didn't move, they layed down. The drivers, standing in the mud, waited for relief to come. That arrived soon because we 2-legged ones with the back pack and the three day ration on our backs had to pull the carts out of the mud and, again, the long rope came out. . . . We had 28 wagons and pulled these, one at a time, through 24 miles of mud . . . 125 men per team, up to their knees or body in water and mud, the wagons up to their axles, but it worked.[16]

The 33rd Iowa, wading through marshes with their trousers rolled up, ascended to a pine wood, where an old black woman, apparently overjoyed at the sight of the Union army, stood near the road, crying and laughing almost hysterically as the men trudged by. "Glory, Hallelujah!" she shouted. "Glory, Hallelujah! The Lord's done heard us. There's eight hundred of us praying for you at Mobile! Go on! Go on! Glory, Hallelujah!"[17]

Avoiding the rigors suffered by Granger's Corps, Smith's XVI Corps scrambled onto transports at Fort Gaines, steamed across scenic Mobile Bay on March 19, and after a pleasant voyage, disembarked about six miles up Fish River at Dannelly's Mills.

Within five days, about 16,000 fully equipped infantry with light artillery batteries, supply wagons, reserve ammunition, horses, and fodder completed the trip from Dauphin Island to Fish River. Conversely Benton's brigade, which had left Fort Morgan on March 17 and suffered a miserable, rain-drenched march over muddy terrain, crossed the north fork of the Fish River on March 23 and went wearily into camp on the right of the XVI Corps, the bands playing: "Oh, ain't you glad you're out of the wilderness." Three more days passed before Benton had all of his division over the river and safely in camp.[18]

On the morning of March 24 Lt. Origen Sibley, Jr., with eight men of the 15th Confederate Cavalry, spotted Veatch's Division loosely stretched out along the road about two miles above Magnolia. The small scouting party halted and watched for stragglers. They located five men resting by themselves, spurred their horses to a brisk gallop, and captured all five without firing a shot. Brig. Gen. James R. Slack, the brigade commander, was not far off. After disarming the prisoners, Sibley left three guards and half an hour later charged a wagon train but was driven off by the 99th Illinois. He returned to Greenwood and, after questioning the prisoners, sent a hurried message to General Liddell at Blakely that he had learned from the prisoners that

General Smith had placed a large command on the *western* shore to operate against Mobile – an error that, whether or not fabricated by the prisoners, might have compensated for their capture.[19] Federal troops engaged in a feint up the western shore had already withdrawn, but General Maury had been receiving conflicting reports from all fronts and had not been able to determine Canby's intentions.

At this time Liddell and Maury had probably not expected an attack on the western shore because the only major movement by the enemy had been on the eastern shore. A week earlier, on March 18, Col. Jonathan B. Moore had taken his 1st Brigade, 1st Division, XVI Corps, with 1,700 infantry and two Rodman guns of the 1st Indiana by steamer from Dauphin Island to Cedar Point on the western shore. The 72nd Illinois, under Lt. Col. Joseph Stockton, drove away a small Confederate force, paving the way for the brigade to advance to Alabama Point, about two miles farther up the bay. Late in the afternoon, the 95th Illinois, under Col. Leander Blanden, brushed off about two hundred Confederate cavalry before camping for the night. The following morning, the brigade advanced to Fowle River, met light resistance at a bridge set afire by retreating cavalry, and threw skirmishers across the river. Without orders to advance farther, Moore halted, but he was gratified to learn from local citizens that the strength of his force had been reported as 6,000 in Mobile. On March 22, Moore withdrew and rejoined his division at Dannelly's Mill on the Fish River.[20]

By March 25 Canby had enough of his force in position to initiate an attack. At that time he had not heard from Steele, who he presumed was handling his own affairs in the vicinity of Pollard. A few regiments of the XIII Corps had not reached Fish River but were still on their way overland. Most of the XVI Corps had crossed the bay and had pitched tents around Dannelly's Mill. Totten's Siege Train had not been brought over because Canby did not know where or when he would need them. Divisions of both Smith's XVI Corps and Granger's XIII Corps moved out that morning and started toward Spanish Fort, about 20 miles away. Confederate skirmishes pecked away at the moving columns but were easily brushed aside.[21]

On March 23 the 16th Confederate Cavalry, led by Col. Philip B. Spence, scouted toward the Fish River while the 32nd and 58th Alabama infantry, under Col. Bushrod Jones, waited in support near Hollywood. The following morning, Brigadier General Gibson's Brigade of Louisianans, along with a column of artillery, moved eight miles below Spanish Fort and formed a defensive position. Two days later Colonel Bertram's blue brigade reached Montrose, about three miles south of the Confederate position. Gibson observed activity in his front, faced about, and threw up breastworks on a hill just north of D'Olieve's Creek. Cockrell had posted his Confederate division about four miles northeast of Gibson at Alexis Spring, and about three miles south of Sibley's Mill. Liddell ordered Capt. J. V. Tutt, who had been watching Union activities at Pensacola, to move his command at Greenwood back to Sibley's Mill and to scout the road to Durant's.[22]

Spence's cavalry made contact with Bertram's brigade, strung out skirmishers to develop the size of the force, and mistook the brigade for a full Federal division. At this time, Liddell believed that the only force in his front was Granger's divided XIII Corps. Although Liddell had not left Spanish Fort to personally assess the scope of the attack, he believed that Gibson could cover the Village Road from D'Olieve's Creek, and Cockrell could meet an attack along Durant's. Because of bad roads he believed that the attack would come first at D'Olieve's, and that the force on Durant's road would continue to remain separated from Bertram's brigade. Gibson's two Confederate brigades, about 3,000 men, entrenched on the high and hilly ground on the north bank of D'Olieve's Creek and prepared to meet Bertram's attack on the right. Cockrell moved his three brigades a few miles south to cover the left of the Confederate line and to intercept any advance along the Sibley Road. Spence fell back to cooperate with both Gibson and Cockrell and to keep his cavalry active on the flanks and the open center. Liddell held Holtzclaw's brigade in the rear, intending for it to move around and strike the Federals on their right flank soon after the engagement opened.[23]

On March 25 Liddell had been active throughout the day gathering intelligence and attempting to make the best possible use of his troops. Late that night he was startled to learn that the XVI Corps was advancing so rapidly on his left that he did not have time to properly concentrate Cockrell's force. His worst fears were realized the next morning when scouts reported that his left had been flanked by Smith's XVI Corps. Liddell issued orders pulling all of his brigades back to the fortifications — Cockrell to Blakely and Gibson to Spanish Fort — but he asked each commander to offer resistance long enough to develop the size of the attacking force.[24]

By March 26 an overpowering tide of blue had amassed a huge force on a still-distant doorstep from Mobile. The bulk of Canby's two army corps, about 30,000 men, were stomping up the eastern shore, determined to capture or eliminate the string of fortifications guarding the city. Steele's column of 12,000, still struggling in the forests and swamps to the east, soon turned westward to add their force to the power of the tide. Farragut's old naval squadron, now commanded by Acting Rear Admiral Thatcher, waited off Hollywood and Montrose, ready to support the movement of the army and add the weight of their guns to the reduction of the forts. Another 10,000 blue-clad cavalry under General Wilson were swooping down from the north, interim destination Selma, but ready to trot on down to Mobile if Canby needed help.

Maury and Liddell were both game fighters, but probably questioned whether their 9,000 veterans could stand long against such odds. For four years they had prepared for this moment, but with the Confederacy collapsing on all sides, they must have asked themselves – was the further loss of life worth it? Hood's veterans, battered at Atlanta and decimated at Nashville, proud but beaten men, accustomed to battle but demoralized by poor generalship, garrisoned the forts and snuggled behind protective breastworks. If attacked they would defend as long as life lasted, but they no longer believed they could win. Fighting had become a way of life, and, they must have asked themselves, When would it end?

Chapter 12
Spanish Fort

Spanish Fort was a line of field fortifications built at the mouth of the Apalachee River where it emptied into Mobile Bay. The city of Mobile lay due west across the bay, about 13 miles distant. The outer fortifications stretched some one and one-half miles above the shore in a clearing surrounded by woods on a high, red bluff. At its deepest point, one-half mile inland, earthworks had been dug and faced by breastworks and abatis that overlooked several hundred yards of open terrain cleared for gunners. The northern rim of the fort terminated at a swamp covered with fallen timber on the southern shore of Bay Minette. The southern flank ended on the edge of a hilly rise that sloped into another swamp formed by the mouth of D'Olieve's Creek. Both flanks were open and unfortified at the edges of the swamp. The fort itself was a network of batteries facing both into the bay and across the clearing into the woods in the rear. Inside, a bastion known as Old Spanish Fort had been built above the shore and facing the bay. On the southeastern corner of the earthworks, Fort McDermott, slightly smaller and shaped differently, faced both ways. Another string of batteries behind redoubts faced inland, guarding the outer perimeter of the main line.[1]

Old Spanish Fort was a strong work, nearly enclosed, and built on a bluff that projected into the water. The parapet on the bay side was partially natural, but additional earth had been excavated to increase its thickness to 30 feet. The fort was armed with 8-inch Columbiads and 30-pounder Parrotts. Originally Old Spanish Fort had been built to protect Forts Huger and Tracy, two earthwork island batteries located upriver on marshes. Fort Huger was on the opposite side of the river about one mile above Spanish Fort; Tracy was located about three hundred yards upriver from Huger. Inside the main works Fort McDermott, about four hundred yards to the right of Old Spanish Fort and one hundred feet above the water, covered the high ground with a battery of ten heavy guns and held the most commanding position on the field. To the north and left of McDermott, the ground descended gradually. A long line of rifle pits stretched to a ravine filled with brush and a small stream, and then extended up a slope to

159

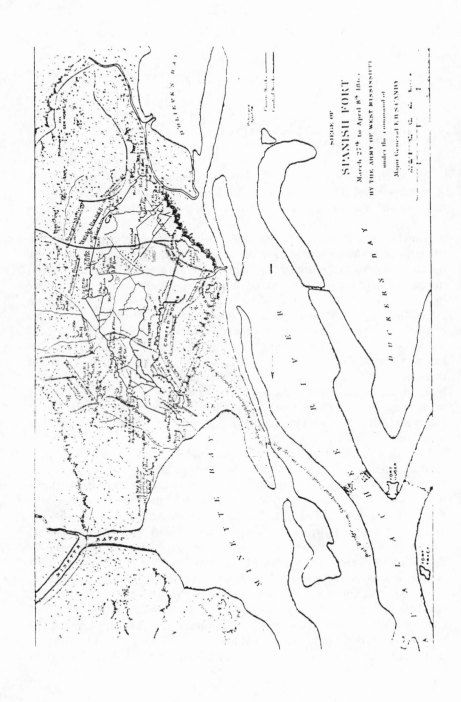

SIEGE OF
SPANISH FORT
March 27th to April 8th 186.,
BY THE ARMY OF WEST MISSISSIPPI
under the command of
Major General E. R. S. CANBY

another strong battery designated as No. 3, where Lt. J. Adolph Chalaron had placed Slocomb's battery. From there a line of works called Red Fort continued north another six hundred yards, with four redans manned by Capt. J. W. Phillips' batteries, before turning toward the bay and striking the marsh on Bay Minette. Lt. A. C. Hargrove had placed his battery (Lumsden's) along the northern approaches to guard the open far-left flank, thereby completing the fort's primary defenses.[2]

Opposite the outer line of works, crews of Negroes had cut back a dense growth of trees, leaving an almost impassable obstruction of slashed timber, underbrush, and vines for about 1,400 yards in front of Spanish Fort. If the enemy fought its way through the entaglements, it faced a ditch five feet deep and eight feet wide in front of well-constructed breastworks. The Confederates had also dug detached rifle pits for sharpshooters in front of every battery and constructed a line of abatis 15 to 20 feet wide. The abatis had been formed from tree branches, cut back to limbs two inches in diameter, sharpened with a drawing knife, and stripped of bark to make them difficult to set on fire. It was laid about 50 feet from the breastworks at almost point-blank range for the defenders. A road had been cleared through the entanglements for the convenience of the fort, but guns covered the opening. Outside the abatis long logs had been placed, called "sheep racks," with pointed stakes fitted through bored holes in such a way that if the log was rolled over, the other point of the stake came up. On March 27, almost as an afterthought, the Confederates, worried that their extreme left flank had never been completed, hurriedly requested picks, shovels, and carts to close it.[3]

At daylight on March 27 four hundred of Gibson's Confederate cavalry under Col. Richard Lindsay fired a volley into General Veatch's pickets and, with a yell, charged between the flanks of the 47th Indiana and 161st New York, driving both units back in some confusion. Gibson had considered launching an attack, but Lindsay's cavalry got near enough to the main force to see, for the first time, the strength of Granger's XIII Corps. After a short gallop Lindsay returned with several bloodied troopers. "After a closer examination," Gibson advised Liddell, "I concluded not to attack."[4]

On the previous evening, a few miles east of Veatch's division, Brigadier General Carr had learned his division would take the lead when the XVI Corps attacked Spanish Fort. Up to that moment the division had expected to bypass the fortifications and strike for the Alabama River, cross it, and attack the city from the north. With dawn came the prospect of heavy rain. Veteran soldiers who had grown accustomed to interpreting a downpour as a precursor to battle steadied themselves for a fight. They buckled on

Opposite: **Map of the seige of Spanish Fort (courtesy *History of the Campaign of Mobile*).**

their cartridge boxes with the customary 40 rounds, rolled up their blankets and slung them over their shoulders, picked up their entrenching tools, grabbed their muskets, and fell into line. Carr's 3rd Brigade, under Col. James L. Geddes, stepped out with the 81st Illinois in front, and in the dim light of daybreak, led the division into the woods to the right of Spanish Fort.

Carr had entered West Point in 1846, graduated 19th in his class in 1850, and received a commission in the Regiment of Mounted Riflemen. For the next decade he fought hostile Indians on the Western frontier. He loved the cavalry and eventually became "perhaps the most famous and experienced Indian fighter." When the Civil War started, he joined Brig. Gen. Nathaniel Lyon's forces in Missouri, participated in the Battle of Wilson's Creek on August 10, 1861, and six days later became colonel of the 3rd Illinois Cavalry. At the Battle of Pea Ridge, he sustained a severe wound, but for his gallantry there he received the Medal of Honor and promotion to brigadier general of volunteers. Carr commanded a division at Vicksburg but saw limited action after the city surrendered. Early in 1865 Canby recalled him from Arkansas to lead a division in the Mobile campaign.[5]

Carr had marched about four miles when the 21st Alabama, under Lieutenant Colonel Williams, opened from ambush on the 81st Illinois, scattered several companies, and narrowly missed an opportunity to shoot General Smith. The 81st Illinois held their position while the 124th Illinois, under Col. John H. Howe, took the advance and brushed back the Confederates. Carr resumed the march and, when within a mile of the fort, deployed in line of battle from a concealed position. With two brigades formed to the front, Smith rode along the lines before ordering the assault, but the men, unaware of the general's intentions, rent the stillness with a cheer easily heard behind Confederate lines. Seconds later, a shell from the fort screeched through the trees and dropped close to the 49th Missouri, causing the entire regiment to flinch. Smith, angered by having his position disclosed, snarled: "Stand up to it! You had no business cheering."[6]

The 1st Division, under Brigadier General McArthur, took position between Carr's left and the right flank of the XIII Corps, completing the investment of Spanish Fort. The long blue line stretched across a three-mile semicircle as the troops advanced through open woods with banners unfurled and the air filled with the clamor and stir of a moving army. Confederate sharpshooters, hidden in pits or crouched behind felled logs, peppered away at the approaching enemy, and here and there, blue-shirted infantry stumbled to the ground, leaving tiny openings in a solid line, but only for moments as others closed up. Carr ordered Geddes to send out more skirmishers, and the colonel detached the 8th Iowa and 108th and 124th Illinois. The men rushed forward and drove the sharpshooters back to the safety of their pits. As he led his company forward, Capt. W. M. Bullock of the 108th Illinois fell, his thigh shattered by a musket ball, but he ordered his men on, and when all had passed, dragged himself to the rear. In the 124th Illinois, Lt. W. E. Smith had taken his color sergeant and rushed ahead, leaving the brigade a half mile behind; they made conspicuous targets and fell together with mortal wounds. Shortly after noon Carr's 14th Indiana Light battery, under Capt. Francis W. Morse, came up and opened from a ridge at eight hundred yards, joined later by the 1st Indiana Light, under Captain Lawrence Jacoby, who positioned his artillery to the left and front of the 14th. Spanish Fort responded, and as rain started pouring from the skies, the crash of exploding shells mingled momentarily with the torrent.[7]

Carr, expecting an order to assault the fortifications, struggled to keep his lines compact, but the order never came. Geddes's men charged forward and occupied about three hundred yards of the enemy's outer works, and by flanking entrenchments on either side, drove many of the Confederates back to the main fort. Col. Jonathan B. Moore's 1st Brigade came up behind Geddes, fanned out to the flank, and began entrenching about six hundred yards from Spanish Fort. Skirmishers of the 14th Wisconsin, under Maj. Eddy F. Ferris, climbed through the slashings until they reached the abatis. "We worked our way up until we drove all the Rebel skirmishers into the fort and then we had things all our own way," wrote Sgt. James K. Newton. "We fired so lively that they dare not show their heads above the works. We were so close that they could not depress their cannon enough to touch us and some of the boys in front of one of the portholes completely silenced the Gun it contained."[8] Carr complained that "we might have gone at once over the whole interior, but I did not feel justified in risking too much on my own responsibility."[9]

McArthur's 1st Division, on Carr's left, moved to with in four hundred yards of Red Fort, named for the huge pile of red earth excavated in its front. Slocomb's battery, commanded by Lieutenant Chalaron, occupied two redoubts along Red Fort and kept up a galling fire. The Confederate skirmish line collapsed from McArthur's pressure, but as Union skirmishers scurried forward, their lines became tangled and men became separated. A corporal in the 12th Ohio had gotten so far forward that he received a severe wound in the foot from someone in the rear. Shortly after noon, the 3rd Indiana Light Artillery, under the command of Capt. Thomas J. Ginn, opened with a battery of Rodman guns on Red Fort, and the 2nd Iowa Light Artillery, led by Capt. Joseph R. Reed, brought four 12-pounder Napoleons up, sighted on the works, but did little damage. Lt. Henry F. Folsom of the 7th Minnesota suffered a thigh wound from fragments of an exploding Union shell. Several companies that had advanced to within 200 yards of Red Fort began looking for shelter, as minié balls and shells whizzed past their heads from both directions. Later that evening, the men crawled out of their hiding places and returned to the main line, which had been established about four hundred yards from Red Fort.[10]

General Smith asked permission to attack with two divisions. Canby doubted Smith's ability to carry the works and asked McArthur's opinion. After a close inspection of the works, McArthur replied: "My division will go in there if ordered, but if the rebels stay by their guns it will cost the lives of half my men." Canby answered: "It won't pay."[11]

Veatch's 1st Division of the XIII Corps deployed on the right. The men had been up most of the night entrenching, and those who had been able to find time for a few hours rest were awake at 3:00 A.M. and warming their coffee. Though somewhat jaded, they formed in line of battle and moved out at 7:00 A.M., ready for a fight and believing they would take Spanish Fort by direct assault. Brigadier General Slack's 1st Brigade held the right, Lt. Col. William B. Kinsey's 3rd Brigade took the left, and Brig. Gen. Elias S. Dennis's 2nd Brigade followed in reserve.

Benton's 3rd Division moved at 9:00 A.M. and in three columns of regiments filed into the gap between Veatch's right and the XIII Corps left. The 91st Illinois, under Lt. Col. George A. Day, attacked Confederate skirmishers and picked them off as they attempted to fall back over the slashings. Lt. Col. Albert H. Brown's 96th Ohio passed through the right of Veatch's division and at a point opposite Fort McDermott drove Confederate skirmishers into the main work, opening the way for the 7th Massachusetts Light Battery, led by Capt. Newman W. Storer, to place its guns on a rise of ground about 750 yards from McDermott. All along the line regimental colors popped up, making targets for Confederate gunners.[12]

Early in the afternoon General Granger came on the field and ordered a further advance. The 20th Wisconsin and the 19th Iowa scrambled forward through the slashings but could not move fast. Confederates hidden in rifle pits and gunners in the fort waited until the Federals had advanced about two hundred yards before opening with a devastating fire. Blue-shirted infantry slipped behind fallen logs and returned the fire, but not before some fell, dead or wounded. Capt. Joseph Foust hurried Battery F, 1st Missouri Light Artillery, into position about 1,300 yards in the rear of the fort, got the range, and distracted the enemy by plunging well-timed shells into their midst with unerring accuracy. The forward regiments set to work entrenching, digging late into the night throwing up breastworks.[13]

By dusk Granger's XIII Corps had established its main line about eight hundred to one thousand yards from Spanish Fort. After dark, large details set to work entrenching, and the thud of axes and the scraping of digging tools could be heard by Confederate pickets. Granger's casualties had been light, considering the amount of firing throughout the day, 77 men killed or wounded, including Granger's orderly, who was carrying the corps colors as the general rode casually along the line of skirmishers. Smith's XVI Corps, entrenching on Granger's right, had sustained 91 casualties when Carr's regiments forced the action early in the day.[14]

Brigadier General Gibson, commanding Spanish Fort, had been expecting an assault and had saved most of his available firepower for the contest. His own brigade, under Col. Francis L. Campbell, counted only five hundred rifles. Brigadier General Thomas's brigade of Alabama Reserves and Col. Isaac W. Patton's artillery added another 950 muskets and 360 gunners, giving him a force of about 1,810 effectives. About two miles upriver, Batteries Huger and Tracy constituted a part of Gibson's command and provided a source for obtaining additional reserves. All in all, Gibson reported his strength at 3,400 men. From information gleaned from prisoners and maps taken from a captured XVI Corps engineer, he estimated Canby's force at about 20,000 effectives and prepared his men for an unequal contest. His greatest dismay was the imperfect condition of the fort to repulse an attack by land, and he hurriedly added additional field pieces from wherever they could be obtained.[15]

When Gibson entered the Confederate service, he had no military experience. Born near Versailles, Kentucky, on September 10, 1832, he received both a private and public education on his parents' plantation in Louisiana. After graduating from Yale University in 1853, he studied law at New Orleans, traveled in Europe, and served briefly as U.S. embassy attaché in Madrid. When Louisiana seceded from the Union, Gibson joined the 1st Louisiana Artillery as captain. Later commissioned colonel of the 13th Louisiana Infantry, he led the regiment at Shiloh and there commanded the 1st Brigade of Brig. Gen. Daniel Ruggles's division in early assaults on the enemy's "Hornets' Nest." He fought with the Army of Tennessee's 1862 Kentucky Campaign and at the Battle of Chickamauga. Promoted to brigadier general, he joined Hood's army and led brigades at Atlanta, Franklin, and Nashville. When that army was dispersed, he was ordered to Mobile and placed in command of Spanish Fort. Gibson inspired men, but on March 27, 1865, he probably wondered if inspiration alone would be enough to hold off Canby's host of blue veterans.[16]

On the day of the first assault, Gibson's thin gray line huddled behind its fortifications and stopped the Federal attack a few hundred yards from the main works. When his men were not fighting off an attack, those that had picks and spades dug, and the work went on day and night. On the first day, Gibson lost five killed and 44 wounded, a small number compared with Federal casualties but hardly affordable nonetheless. He complained to Liddell that the Confederate navy stood silent off the Federal right during the attack, failed to commence firing until sunset, and then retired after lobbing a few token shells. Most of his men could not protect themselves outside the fort because they had no entrenching tools. To compound Gibson's problems, Selma was preparing for General Wilson's cavalry attack and calling for reserves needed at Spanish Fort and for the defense of Mobile. In a final attempt to retain his reserve regiment, mostly youths under Brigadier General Thomas, Gibson asked Liddell to come down from Blakely and "take a look at things."[17]

On the evening of March 27 Gibson did not know that Canby had no intention of blindly assaulting Spanish Fort without first developing its strength. The Federal army had outrun its supplies, forcing Canby to wait a few days for his wagons to arrive. He had not heard from Steele's Column, mired somewhere to the east along the Alabama-Florida border. Canby established his headquarters on the main road, near Wilson, two miles from Spanish Fort, and waited.

Gibson expected the Federal assault to resume in force the following morning and had sent details outside the main fort to dig advance rifle pits. Men lit hundreds of campfires to give the impression of exaggerated strength, stringing them out in a manner that concealed the actual location of Confederate positions. The Alabama Reserves worked together with Negro crews to strengthen the left, felling trees and extending abatis into the muck of the swamp. Inside the fort exhausted men got little sleep, cleaned their muskets, counted their ammunition, and waited for dawn.[18]

In the morning Gibson looked out across the field of fire and saw the landscape dotted with fresh mounds of red earth, hastily dug throughout the night to protect the enemy from Confederate sharpshooters. In the distance gabions and fascines had been started. Even some of the slashings, felled by his men to impede Canby's advancing regiments, had been chopped up and used as supports for bombproofs and revetments for batteries. At the sight of so much spadework, Gibson probably suspected that with Spanish Fort invested on three sides, he would be faced with a siege by a superior force and slowly squeezed into submission, but for the moment he braced for an attack.

There had been occasional shooting during the night, but as daylight broke on March 28, musketry rattled from both sides, grew in intensity, and then the artillery opened spiritedly on both sides. Overnight Gibson's men had hacked an opening in the timber to the shore of Bay Minette so Fort Huger, situated on a marsh 1,800 yards to the north, could bring its heavy guns to bear on the XVI Corps' right flank. After some excellent shooting a stray shot landed inside the garrison, and Gibson ordered the battery silenced.[19]

The erratic firing from Fort Huger also wrought havoc on the rear of the Federal position. The 14th Wisconsin, camped about three-quarters of a mile from the front, complained about "125-pound shells" enfilading their lines. "We could see it coming," wrote Private Stockwell, who continued:

> [B]ut [we] couldn't tell where the darned thing was going to light. Some would go clear over, and some would light before they got to us. We could run several rods while it was coming. But it always looked like it was coming

Brig. Gen. Randall Lee Gibson, CSA (courtesy *Photographic History of the Civil War Review of Reviews***; U.S. Military History Institute).**

right where you were, so those that were down at the foot of a hill ran up, and those up the hill ran down. Everyone moved and all were excited until it had hit, when we would quiet down until the next one was on the way.[20]

During the night the XVI Corps brought up its guns. The 14th Indiana Light Battery, under Captain Morse, had advanced to a prominent exposed position about 550 yards from Red Fort. They had worked all night throwing up works, but the earth was so hard that by morning only a few logs had been rolled over and covered with dirt. Morse opened at daybreak, but batteries from Lumsden's Alabama and Phillips's Tennessee concentrated their fire on him, and by 10:00 A.M. the guns fell silent. Morse called in the pioneers to strengthen the works while a mortar battery of the 1st Indiana came up and joined the 14th. Gunners hauled another battery, a Whitworth and a steel rifle, to a crest where it could engage Fort Huger and draw fire away from the corps' right flank.[21]

Geddes's brigade of Carr's division had spent the night digging and finished a parallel that started at a crest two hundred yards from the Confederate works, bent inward, and terminated only 120 yards away from the main line. The 8th Iowa and 124th Illinois finished their parallel about one hundred yards farther back. Moore's brigade was back another one hundred yards with Col. Lyman M. Ward's 2nd Brigade posted far in the rear. With four parallels opened, the XVI Corps was in good position to beat off a surprise Confederate attack.[22]

Much of the Confederate artillery fire fell randomly in the Federal rear. During a lull in the firing, General Carr stopped to refresh himself near several boxes of reserve ammunition. "I had an ammunition chest exploded by an enemy's shell within five steps of me," he declared, "which injured two poor fellows, forcibly tearing off their clothes and blackening their faces. . . . [I]t would have been comical if it had not been that they were burned so badly." Carr escaped the explosion unscathed and unblackened.[23]

Granger's XIII Corps spent the night in similar discomfort; short water, short rations, without sleep, but with interminable digging. At daybreak, four companies from different regiments of Benton's division were placed under Capt. James Gunn, 27th Wisconsin, and ordered to advance across a ravine filled with a labyrinth of slashings and relieve skirmishers who had been under fire throughout the day. They progressed slowly, being directly under the guns of Fort McDermott and in the sights of Confederate sharpshooters. The men reached the pits with only one killed and 18 wounded, but many of the relieved troops preferred to remain where they were until dark rather than face a gauntlet of fire by racing back to the rear. Capt. George E. Croft, 7th Vermont, made it back to safety with valuable information about the Confederate works. During the night he had crept closely enough to see some of the activity in and around the fort and observed many of its weaknesses.[24]

When no attack came on March 28, Gibson bided his time and looked for an opportunity to take the initiative. At dusk he spotted a large detail of Federals moving to the front to work on a battery. This group had been placed under the command of Capt. J. L. Noble, 21st Iowa, and consisted of one hundred men with arms and three hundred men from other regiments without arms – an unusual oversight. Lieutenant Colonel Lindsay mustered 550 Louisianans for the attack, led his men over the fortifications, and silently crept up to Noble's outlying pickets. About midnight, in the middle of a heavy rainstorm, Linsday's men charged, driving in the skirmishers and sending part of Noble's command running to the rear. For a few minutes the combat was hand to hand. Noble maintained a stiff resistance and kept the Louisianans out of the battery until reinforcements arrived from General Slack. Skirmishers all along Granger's left got rolled back during the attack, but the Federals gave no ground. Lindsay returned with about seven killed and 14 wounded, bringing with him a few prisoners and a handful of captured arms and equipment. He reported that the enemy had a large force in "heavy and extended line of battle." Gibson prepared for a siege, knowing that the investment would be temporary and eventually followed by an overwhelming attack.[25]

Fortunately for Gibson the Union fleet had been unable to invest Spanish Fort from the river. Canby had counted on this help but did not get it. Shallow water on the Blakely bar combined with elaborate obstructions and strings of torpedoes had prevented Thatcher from risking his vessels. Nonetheless, on March 28 the gunboats *Octorara* and *Genesee*, with the river monitors *Kickapoo*, *Milwaukee*, *Winnebago*, and *Chickasaw* left Howard's Wharf and steamed for the Blakely River. The monitors passed over the bar, but the *Octorara* grounded in eight feet of water. With the tide falling, Lt. Comdr. William W. Low burst a tube in the starboard boiler trying to get the vessel off the bar, and for the remainder of the day the vessel remained stuck and out of action. The *Winnebago* and the *Chickasaw* advanced up the river and opened on the fort. The Eads turrets had been designed to allow the guns a maximum elevation of 20 degrees, and after a few trial shots fell short the gunners looked for other targets. Before returning to the bar, the *Winnebago* fired a few shells at a transport bringing supplies to the garrison and chased it back upstream, but not a single shot reached Spanish Fort.[26]

When the monitors returned downstream, the *Milwaukee* followed, dropping with the current, her bow headed upstream, and drifted to within two hundred yards of the anchored *Kickapoo*. The area had just been swept and supposedly cleared of torpedoes, but a violent explosion shook the vessel's port side, abaft the after turret and 40 feet from the stern. Lt. Comdr. James H. Gillis saved his entire crew and sent them to the *Kickapoo*. The stern of the vessel sank in three minutes, but the bow stayed on the surface for nearly an hour, allowing the men to rescue most of their personal belongings.[27] The officers of Spanish Fort peered downriver, their eyes fastened on the gunboats, wondering whether one had gone down.[28]

By March 29 Low had repaired the *Octorara*'s boiler, shifted sandbags and shot, placed four heavy guns each weighing 9,600 pounds on tugs, and at noon passed over the Blakely bar and anchored inside. By evening, a 100-pounder Parrott had been returned to the gunboat. Low remained at anchor throughout the following day, waiting for a detail to cleanse the channel of any stray torpedoes.[29]

That afternoon the ironclad *Osage*, under Lt. Comdr. William M. Gamble, lay at anchor with four other vessels inside the Blakeley bar. A strong easterly wind had dragged the *Winnebago* alongside the *Osage*, and to avoid a collision, Gamble weighed anchor and moved to a safe distance off her starboard bow. As the men prepared to let go the anchor, a torpedo exploded under the bow, killing four men and wounding eight. The *Osage* filled and sank in minutes. Her position had just been thoroughly dragged by boats, and Gamble believed that the torpedo that struck her had been submerged and drifting.[30]

On March 30 the *Octorara* steamed upriver and at 5,700 yards opened on Spanish Fort, adding to the misery of the garrison. From that distance Low could not tell whether his firing did any damage, and he worried that some of the shells would overshoot the fort and explode over Canby's lines.

On April 1, the six-gun tinclad stern-wheeler *Rodolph* received orders from the flagship to bring a barge alongside carrying apparatus to raise the *Milwaukee*. Acting Master N. Mayo Dyer weighed anchor, crossed the bar, and was standing toward the wreck of the *Milwaukee* when he struck a torpedo under the starboard bow and sank in 12 feet of water. The explosion ripped a hole in her hull about ten feet in diameter, killed four of the crew, and wounded 11.[31]

Although Canby continued to press both Thatcher and Palmer to get the fleet up the river and seal off the rear of the fort, a dread of torpedoes had stirred fears among ranking naval officers. Thatcher had disrupted the flow of supplies to the fort, but after losing three gunboats, he hesitated to expose the squadron to further losses without first taking every precaution. He suspected that Confederates were laying torpedoes at night and sent picket boats upriver to capture them. Every morning boats redragged the channel, and every day more torpedoes popped to the surface or exploded below. On April 2 Thatcher asked that boarding nets be collected from each vessel, spliced together, and stretched across the channel above the fleet. Later a second net was anchored about a mile and one-half farther upriver. Torpedoes had temporarily prevented the navy from taking an active role in the campaign.[32]

On March 29 the siege at Spanish Fort continued as Federal troops slowly dug their way closer to the main work. Artillery boomed throughout the day, but most of the action occurred along the skirmish lines, where little land disputes came with every nightfall. Details deepened parallels throughout the day, but the lines were only advanced at night and many mixups occurred.

One evening Col. Henry M. Day detailed Capt. L. K. Myers, 29th Iowa, brigade officer of the day in the forward trenches. Myers took four companies and advanced at night with instructions to dig new rifle pits within one hundred yards of the fort. Across the way men from Gibson's Louisiana brigade, under Colonel Campbell, quietly listened and watched. After dark, Myers took eight men and crept forward to gauge his distance from the fort. A sentinel, five or six steps away, fired high, sending Myers and his detail to the ground. He backed away, finished his scout, and began digging pits about 50 yards from the enemy. After midnight he started to the rear to report progress when he met eight men from Company C of his own regiment, without arms, bringing out ammunition. The men were lost, and Myers agreed to lead them to the pits.

In coming to the rear, Myers had guided on a large tree, but on returning to the pits he became confused and followed a different tree farther to the right. After retracing his steps the approximate distance, he spoke softly: "Boys, I am coming back again." A voice answered: "Come on." A few steps later Myers found himself facing a Confederate officer and 12 armed men. At first neither man recognized the other, but the Confederate officer asked: "Do you know where you are – do you belong to us?" Myers answered: "Of course we belong to you, ain't you Confederate soldiers?"

Myers tried to convince the enemy officer that his men were bringing ammunition to the Confederate fort and asked for guidance in getting there safely. With some hesitation the officer agreed, and both parties started through the pits to Red Fort. Myers later wrote:

> I had feared that some of my boys would run and the rest of us would be fired on, but they all stood quiet, trusting me to manage affairs. I knew the reb. knew what we were, and was afraid to order us to surrender; perhaps wanted to double his force at the next post. I wanted to get on the move, and gave the word to my men to run. We had only gone a few steps when one of the rebs. next [to] the officer said, "Hold on, these are not our men!" I said, "You are certainly mistaken"; and while trying to satisfy him, the officer became too much alarmed to stand it any longer. He sang out, "Retreat," turned and ran; most of them discharging their guns at me before running. The balls passed close on both sides of me. I called out, "Fire on them, boys, fire on them!" I also drew my revolver and fired four shots. By this time my men had got started back. I turned to follow them, and was about to run on to their [Confederate] advance sentinel, who was squatting down behind the brush and [who] raised and fired, when I was within two or three feet of the muzzle of his gun.... [He] hit me in the right hip, the ball hitting the bone, glancing round, and coming out about five inches from where it went in. I fell beside him, and as he turned to run, I gave him the two remaining shots from my revolver; he fell within a few steps of me and lay quiet. I lay there a few minutes, and the rebs., from their breastworks some fifty yards distant, poured a heavy fire into the brush. I could see day breaking fast, and knew they could soon see me. So I began to crawl off. Could not stand on

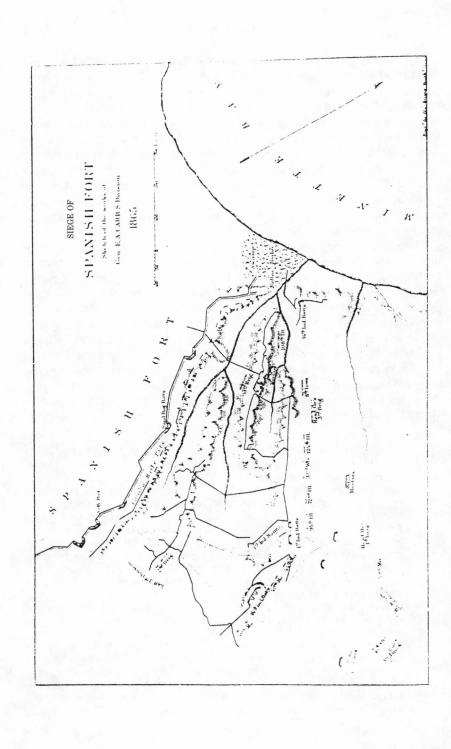

my wounded leg. Soon came to one of my boys, who had been with me and was lost in the brush. While he and I were cautiously making ourselves known to each other, two of our Company C boys, in their rifle-pits, raised their guns to fire at me, but their lieutenant knew my voice, and told them not to fire. They then called me by name, "Capt. Myers," and the rebs. following up behind me, called, "Come this way, Capt. Myers, come right this way." Lieut. Stocker ordered a few shots fired at them, which stopped their hallooing, and I came into the rifle-pits . . . and was assisted back to my regiment.

The man of my squad who carried the box of one thousand cartridges, threw it down before retreating, and the rebs., next day, were afraid to touch it, and would call out to our men . . . to come and get that infernalmachine. When the fort was taken, my colonel sent and got the box. The rebs. would also call out, "How is Capt. Myers?" Our men would reply, "He is not dangerous," and then inquire about the officer who ran from unarmed men.[33]

Gibson complained that the Confederate navy gave superficial support to the fort. On a few occasions when Farrand's gunboats shelled Union positions, the enfilading fire caused many injuries and suspended work on trenches. One shell struck down 18 men of the 32nd Wisconsin and another shell killed two men of the 8th Iowa. A shell fragment struck Pvt. William H. Wilson, "cut off both his hands, and cut him so nearly in two that . . . a part of him fell one side up, and a part the other. . . . But the rebels did not know what they were doing, and only one more shell was fired."[34]

Another Federal sortie on March 31 ran into unexpected difficulty. The day before Capt. Riley B. Stearns, 7th Vermont, had relieved a company on the skirmish line in front of Slocomb's battery. At night Stearns advanced his line about 25 yards and began to dig new pits some 150 yards from the battery. The following day musket fire from his men killed Confederate artillery chief Col. William E. Burnet and narrowly missed General Gibson.[35] Slocomb's battery and Fort McDermott opened on Stearns' company and drove it into a ravine for protection, but as soon as the artillery let up, Stearns' marksmen popped back up and harried the gunners with miniés. At dark Stearns expected to be attacked and sent a corporal back to regimental headquarters to request artillery support when he fell back. The Confederates then set fire to the slashings and brush to his right. Stearns anticipated being smoked out of his position and ordered a retreat, but as soon as one man exposed himself, hundreds of bullets whizzed over him. Stearns countermanded his orders, and the men hunkered down in the pits as the smoke rolled over them.

Just before sunset the guns of the garrison opened furiously, driving the men deeper into the pits. "In less than ten minutes," Stearns wrote, "fifteen shells were exploded inside and directly over the pit in which

Opposite: **Map of the Union investment of Spanish Fort (courtesy *History of the Campaign of Mobile*).**

myself and ten men stationed. I had my men cover themselves as best they could, and ordered bayonets to be fixed in anticipation of a charge being made." Suddenly the cannonading ceased. Capt. Clement S. Watson, Gibson's inspector general, led a detachment of 31 men over the earthworks and, screened by the smoke, descended on Stearns' pits, capturing the captain and 21 men. "The charge was so sudden and vigorous," said Stearns, "that we could offer but little resistance." Over supper General Gibson complimented Stearns for his courage, but on the following day shipped him to the Meridian stockade for the balance of the war.[36]

On March 30 General Maury visited Spanish Fort, examined the lines, and decided to replace Thomas's youthful Alabama Reserves with Brigadier Holtzclaw's veteran brigade. Holtzclaw marched into Spanish Fort to relieve Thomas, but Gibson asked to retain the youngsters, claiming that garrison duty "is a school of instruction for the Reserves." Though he failed in his appeal, he managed to retain one of the regiments a few days longer.[37]

When the Union navy threatened to choke off Confederate communications from the river, Gibson organized work parties to build a treadway across the swamp in the left rear of Spanish Fort. About 1,200 yards long, the 18-inch-wide footpath stretched across two marshes, bridged an outlet from Minette Bay, and terminated opposite Fort Huger. Each day men lengthened the walk, concealing it with high grass and covering it with moss, while gunners of the XIII Corps splattered shells around the workers. Although Gibson built the treadway to bring in a few supplies and take off the wounded, he probably considered its potential as the only means of escape when Canby's superior force finally hurled itself on the fort. In the meanwhile, he bided his time, counted his casualties, clamored for reenforcements, asked for more guns, and waited for the end.[38]

Every trench had diggers and sharpshooters, and while the diggers dug, the sharpshooters huddled behind portholes and fired at anything that moved. The typical porthole had an opening slightly larger than the barrel of the musket, and as long as the musket filled the hole, an enemy bullet could not get through. A true sharpshooter was deadly accurate. One day when Private Stockwell was deepening a trench, he noticed that a sharpshooter from the 48th Missouri stood in front of his porthole while reloading. "I told him he ought to stand to one side as the Rebs were good at shooting," Stockwell warned:

> But he laughed at me, and to show he wasn't afraid, he jumped on top of the breastworks and took a shot at the Rebs' rifle pits. This was what we called foolhardy, so I saw there was no use talking to him. He was about eighteen years old and a nice-looking young man. That afternoon he was killed by a bullet coming through the porthole.[39]

**Brig. Gen. James T. Holtzclaw, CSA (courtesy *Photographic History of the
Civil War — Review of Reviews*; U.S. Military History Institute).**

After the 12th Iowa had dug its way to the abatis, it developed a new
method for harassing the enemy from the trenches. The men cut a section
from the trunk of a gum tree, about three feet long, and bored out one end
to receive a charge of powder and a shell on top. Two men carried the
wooden mortar into the trenches, and by adding a small amount of powder,
they could discharge a shell with a very short fuse into the Confederate
works.[40]

Union forces continued to converge on Spanish Fort. Brigadier General Totten's Siege Train came up from Dauphin Island and established batteries of the 1st Indiana Heavy Artillery at different points around the fort. Batteries H and K placed eight 30-pounder Parrotts in a sunken position on the shore of Minette Bay and banged away at Confederate transports and supply ships. Battery B, with eight 8-inch mortars, landed at Stark's Wharf on the night of March 28 and split their force, sending four guns and 40 men to extreme left and the other four guns and 50 men to a knoll in the rear of the left of Geddes's brigade. In Granger's front on March 31, Battery C set up on the brow of a hill eight hundred yards from McDermott, got the range, and drove Confederate gunners into bombproofs. The 18th New York Light Artillery, with six 20-pounder Parrotts, took position on Granger's left center seven hundred yards from the fort. Four ten-inch mortars and four 8-inch howitzers of the 6th Michigan Heavy Artillery were hauled into position just behind the center of Colonel Bertram's forward rifle pits. Until April 8, the day of the final attack, Canby continued to push artillery further to the front.[41]

By the beginning of April, Spanish Fort had been reduced to about 1,700 infantry and 500 artillery. Gibson wrote: "I have not ammunition for the day." At the same time General Maury anticipated pressure on Fort Blakely from General Steele's column, which had been moving in from the east. Maury withdrew Ector's brigade from Spanish Fort and moved it to Blakely. Gibson could not believe the order and pleaded to keep the brigade "a day or two longer." Maury snapped back: "I decided this matter when at Blakely. Ector's brigade must come up." Gibson felt he could not hold Spanish Fort with a reduced force.

Liddell tried to encourage Gibson by writing that "greater credit will be due General Holtzclaw and yourself by holding out gallantly with your small force, and no one will more readily accord this credit to you, General Holtzclaw, and your garrison than myself." Gibson accepted his orders and prepared for the final blow, probably wondering what kind of insanity inspired his superior's decisions.[42]

Maury faced an enormous dilemma when Steele's column reached Stockton with his force of 12,000. He had moved most of his Mobile defenders to the eastern shore. Steele had the option of uniting with Canby, attacking Blakely, or crossing to the north and assaulting Mobile at its weakest point. Maury did not know which of Steele's options to anticipate, but he knew he could not retrieve the force from Spanish Fort if Gibson's back door got shut off by the Union navy or a sudden attack by Canby. Transports could still move troops back and forth by using the Blakely wharf, and for this reason, Maury wanted to save as many men as possible. He did not expect Spanish Fort to hold out for long against the huge Union force in its front; he could not afford further losses; and he hoped that if

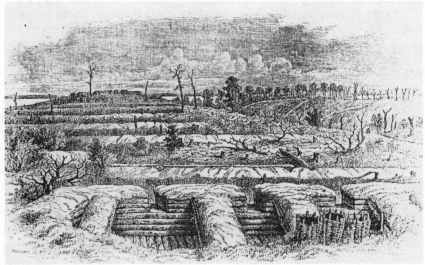

Two views of Spanish Fort bombproofs (courtesy C. C. Andrews' *History of the Campaign of Mobile*).

Blakely also fell, he could rescue those troops for the final defense of Mobile. While Gibson worried about the defense of Spanish Fort, Maury worried about the defense of Mobile, but Steele's column turned south and headed for Blakely.

Chapter 13
Investment of Fort Blakely

The small town of Blakely was located on the east bank of the Apalachee River, directly opposite its confluence with the Tensas River and about ten miles northeast of Mobile. Spanish Fort, separated from Blakely by Minette Bay, lay what would today be some five air miles to the south. At the time of the war, Blakely, although a county seat, had a population not greater than one hundred. The town had been built on a slight bluff of high and dry ground that followed the river upstream for one and one-half miles, but on each side of this rise were low marshes, densely covered with timber and a rank growth of weeds and vines. About a mile from the town landing, on a plateau of equal elevation, stood an incomplete bastion of red earth.[1]

From Blakely Landing two principal roads diverged, both gravelly but much worn and washed, one bearing northeast to Stockton and the other veering southeast to Pensacola. Both roads passed through the Confederate fortifications, and together with Blakely's deep water landing, provided a nearby line of supply for Confederate operations on the eastern shore.

A mile back from the landing the ground gradually rose to a height of 60 feet, and all along this height Confederate engineers had established a semicircle of breastworks. The surface beyond the breastworks was uneven, thickly wooded, congested with brush, abounding with springs, and on the extreme open flanks of the fortifications, wet with swamps. The Confederate fortifications, three miles in length, surrounded the town and included nine strong redoubts, or lunettes, armed with about 40 pieces of artillery, but the ditches in front of the line were shallow, only four to five feet deep. Much like Spanish Fort, the area out from the lines for a distance of six- to eight hundred yards had been cut down and covered with slashings. A line of abatis had been erected 50 yards from the main line, and in front of some of the redoubts, a second line had been built. Three hundred yards to the front and running parallel to the main works ran another line of abatis, behind which detached rifle pits had been dug. Along many of the external approaches to the fort, details had buried hundreds of land mines. With the exception of shallow ditches along the main line and open flanks adjacent to swamps, Fort Blakely was a well-designed line of defense, although somewhat long and narrow.[2]

Blakely's garrison consisted of French's Division, under Brigadier General Cockrell, and Thomas's brigade of youthful, inexperienced Alabama Reserves, who had been transferred by Maury from Spanish Fort. Cockrell occupied the left wing with three brigades of veterans, mostly from Missouri and Mississippi. Several artillery companies manned the guns, bringing the garrison to about 3,500 effectives, all under the overall command of Brigadier General Liddell.

Born October 1, 1834, at Johnson City, Missouri, Cockrell grew up on a farm, attended log-cabin schools, and at age 20 graduated with honors from Missouri's Chapel Hill College. Admitted to the bar in 1855, he practiced law, developed strong secessionist views, and in 1861 entered the pro–Confederate Missouri State Guard, led by Gen. Sterling Price. Rising quickly to captain, he served in the 3rd Missouri at Carthage, Wilson's Creek, and Pea Ridge. Captured during the Vicksburg Campaign and later paroled, he rose in grade to brigadier general on July 18, 1863. Under his tutelage the 1st Missouri Brigade became one of the best-drilled and most effective commands in the Army of Tennessee. During the Atlanta Campaign the brigade served under Major General French, often with distinction. Cockrell accompanied General Hood's army into Tennessee and was wounded seriously during the fight at Franklin. After recovering he received command of French's Division and brought his veteran brigades to Mobile.[3]

At the end of March, Liddell received scouting reports that a large Federal force under Major General Steele had reached Stockton, 15 miles to the north, and was headed for Blakely. He recalled Col. James McCown's infantry detachment at Sibley's, three miles east of Blakely, and instructed them to plant torpedoes in and along the road before leaving. The bridge at Sibley's was to have been burned, but a company of the 2nd Illinois Cavalry, under Maj. Franklin Moore, arrived in time to save it. Liddell also considered sending Cockrell's brigade out of the fortifications to make a surprise night attack on Steele's position, but he could not find enough men to occupy the advanced rifle pits and still protect the fort.[4]

On the morning of April 1, Steele's U.S. Colored Troops started toward Blakely. Earlier, at 5:00 A.M., Lieutenant Colonel Spurling's 2nd Cavalry Brigade, Lucas's Division, left Stockton to ride ahead and open communications with General Canby at Spanish Fort. Five miles from Blakely, Spurling found the 46th Mississippi, led by Capt. J. A. Barwick, posted behind a barricade of fence rails three tiers deep. He dismounted the 2nd Maine Cavalry, deployed them on each side of the road, and kept the 2nd Illinois saddled with sabers drawn in the rear. When the 2nd Maine's repeating carbines splattered the rail fence with a flurry of bullets, the 46th Mississippi hastily withdrew and scattered to the rear. When Spurling saw

Brig. Gen. Francis M. Cockrell, CSA (photo courtesy *Photographic History of the Civil War—Review of Reviews*; U.S. Military History Institute).

the enemy about to run, he ordered two companies of the 2nd Illinois forward and pursued the fugitives to within a half mile of Fort Blakely, capturing three officers, 41 men, and the regimental colors. By the time Spurling got back on the road, Steele's main column had marched into sight.[5]

On March 31 Canby started a supply train of 75 wagons to Steele, along with a small force from Veatch's division and a detachment from the 4th Tennessee Cavalry. Canby knew that Steele was somewhere on the road to Blakely, but he did not expect to find his bedraggled and hungry column already there.

After crossing the Escambia River and overcoming miles of mud, Steele had moved rapidly eastward, then down the Stockton Road to Blakely. On the evening of April 1, his column bivouacked just east of the fort, and detachments of U.S. Colored Troops filed into skirmishing positions on the right.[6] The rumble of guns could be heard from Spanish Fort, but to the Negro troops the sound of artillery was no longer new. In a somber mood, the men slept by their guns, and with empty stomachs, but before they moved out the following morning, Veatch's wagons arrived with corn and provisions, and cheers rippled down the lines as rations were distributed.

From the extreme right of Steele's force, Col. Charles W. Drew's 3rd Brigade led the advance with a detachment of pickets from the 68th U.S. Colored under Lt. Albert H. Taisey in the van. When morning broke Taisey found no enemy in his front, and taking an officer from a cavalry detachment, made a reconnaissance toward Blakely. After they had proceeded some distance and begun to suspect that the Blakely force might have evacuated, a heavy volley spat from a clump of trees near the edge of the slashings, followed by brisk fire from Confederate artillery. As Taisey fell back, Drew sent two companies of skirmishers forward from each regiment and ordered an advance in line of battle, the 68th U.S. Colored on the right, the 76th in the center, and the 48th on the left. The brigade brushed Confederate skirmishers away and advanced to within one-half mile of the fort when Drew received an order to halt. At that point a ravine filled with slashings was in his front, his right rested on a swamp, and his left could find little shelter. Confederate artillery opened on his exposed lines and wounded 15 men before Drew obtained permission to move into the ravine and find cover.[7]

The 1st Brigade, under Brig. Gen. William A. Pile, advanced in echelon behind Drew, halted about nine hundred yards from the Blakely works, and closed on the 3rd Brigade's left.[8] Col. Hiram Scofield's 2nd Brigade followed but remained in reserve, thereby completing the deployment of Brigadier General Hawkins' 1st Division on the first day of Blakely's investment. By being in the rear, Scofield was continuously harassed by Confederate artillery, which overshot more advanced positions.[9]

On the evening of April 1, two brigades under Brigadier General Andrews, commanding the 2nd Division, bivouacked at Hall's, about halfway between Stockton and Blakely. Before sunrise Andrews had his force on the road. They had not gone far before they heard the distant thud of artillery fire. Andrews hastened the pace, joined the main force at about 10:00 A.M., and located Steele with several other officers sitting on logs and holding a conference by the Stockton road, about a mile from Blakely. Steele's first intention had been to strike the small Confederate force at

Holyoke, but the scarcity of provisions had taken him down the Stockton road to Blakely, where he hoped to intercept Veatch's supply train. Learning that Steele had already partially invested the fort, Canby instructed him to keep applying pressure.[10]

Born in 1829, Andrews graduated from Harvard Law School, practicing in New England, Kansas, and eventually Minnesota, where he became a state senator. Early in the war, he enlisted as a private in the 3rd Minnesota, and a short time later the regiment elected him captain. Captured near Murfreesboro by General Forrest's cavalry in July 1862, he was later paroled and promoted to lieutenant colonel, and after fighting at Vicksburg, rose in grade to colonel. Andrews continued to serve in the West, receiving his star January 5, 1864, along with his first brigade command. Just prior to the Mobile Campaign, Canby assigned him to command of the 2nd Division, XIII Corps, where he was breveted major general, United States Volunteers.[11]

When Andrews reported his arrival, Steele ordered him to deploy his two brigades on Hawkins' left. Col. Frederick W. Moore's 3rd Brigade advanced in line of battle, filling the gap between Hawkins' left flank and the Pensacola Road. At first Col. William T. Spicely's 2nd Brigade remained in the rear, but when Andrews discovered a huge gap off his left flank, which extended all the way to Minette Bay, he brought most of Spicely's brigade forward and extended his lines to a length of two miles. After a careful reconnaissance of the enemy's advance rifle pits, Andrews sent the 114th Ohio, under Col. John H. Kelly, and the 20th Iowa, led by Lt. Col. Joseph B. Leake, forward as skirmishers. Two hundred yards out, they met resistance, took shelter, and kept up a steady fire. One wayward minié ball struck Pvt. Josiah Robinson, 34th Iowa, in the face, shattering both his upper and lower jaws and tearing out nearly all his teeth.[12]

At Blakely, Liddell did not know that Canby had instructed Steele to invest but not attack the fort. When Hawkins' skirmishers engaged his left, Liddell braced for an attack. He asked Farrand for naval support, some heavy guns to "rake the right of the enemy's lines." A little later in the day he observed more skirmishers in his front and asked Maury to send additional light artillery. By the end of the day, he observed a force of undetermined strength on his right, Andrew's skirmishers, but still the expected attack did not come. At nightfall, he ordered the artillery to pound away at Federal positions, thereby preventing the enemy from advancing his lines. Joined by the *Huntsville, Nashville,* and *Morgan,* shells of large caliber plunged randomly all along the line, exploding like flashes of lightning but doing little damage. Small groups of skirmishers from both sides advanced slowly in the darkness, often overlapping each other's lines in the rough terrain and dense shrubbery, firing on anything that moved. By the morning of April 3, Liddell was still uncertain of the enemy's intentions.[13]

The ground between Steele's force and Liddell's defenders appeared from a distance to be level, but it contained many ravines and numerous undulating depressions filled with brush and vines. Springs trickled through most of the ravines, creating marshy bottoms and slippery banks, as the water seemed to ooze from the soil. High ground around the fort rose to about 80 feet, but men plunging into a ravine for cover could slide 60 feet to the bottom if not stopped by the dense vegetation. A Federal assault, launched from Steele's present position, would encounter great difficulty just navigating through the topography. Positioned about 1,000 yards from the fortifications, Andrews' division occupied slightly higher ground that gradually declined for about three hundred yards to the front. Hawkins' Negro regiments held a rise about level with the Confederate left. Both divisions occupied positions protected by woods with an abundance of good running water. Steele had no heavy artillery to support an assault, just Capt. Walter S. Hotchkiss' 2nd Connecticut Light battery, which did not get into position until April 5.

On April 3 Veatch's division, XIII Corps, and Garrard's division, XVI Corps, reinforced Steele's extended lines. At first Veatch remained in reserve near Sibley's, but Garrard went into position to the left of the Pensacola road, allowing Andrews to tighten his lines on the far left. Confederate gunboats continued to harass Hawkins' far right, making it hard for the men to complete their approaches to the fort. Without artillery Steele could not reply, and Canby was unwilling to ease the bombardment of Spanish Fort by sending batteries to Blakely. Instead Canby sent pontoniers from the 114th Illinois, under Maj. John M. Johnson, to lay a bridge across Minette Bay to enable reinforcements to be rushed to Steele if needed.[14]

Steele's force received entrenching tools on April 4 and began to advance its lines. Confederate skirmishers banged away and attempted to slow the enemy's progress. Toward evening a tremendous bombardment at Spanish Fort could plainly be heard all along the Blakely lines. Steele's skirmishers started cheering, followed by the shouts of thousands of voices in the rear. The Confederates in forward positions pulled back, anticipating an assault, and Federal skirmishers all along the line moved forward and occupied new positions at little cost. Moore's brigade gained about three hundred yards, and Spicely's about 150, but on the far right, gunboat fire kept most of Hawkins' division pinned down.[15]

During the day Steele's chief of staff, Lt. Col. Luther H. Whittlesey, went to the front line to make observations. About 50 yards in front of the 52nd Indiana skirmish line he spotted an old log building, once used as a barracks, and ran through picket fire to get inside. After Whittlesey perched himself on the rafters where he could get a good view, Cockrell's pickets reported his position back to the artillery and soon enemy shells were crashing all around him, one passing clear through the building. With no

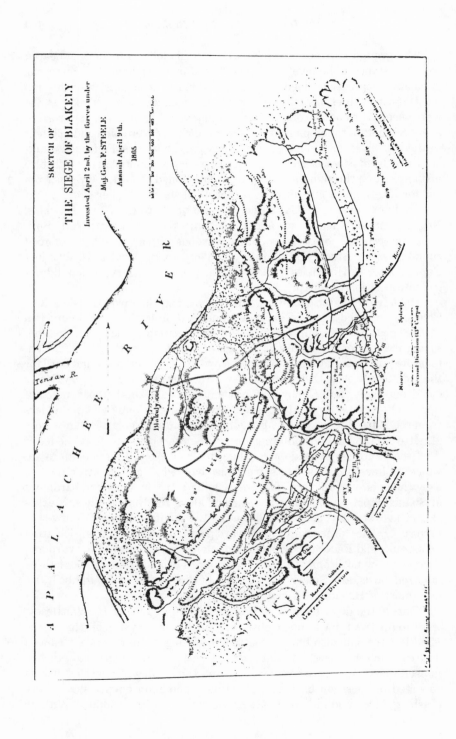

SKETCH OF

THE SIEGE OF BLAKELY

Invested April 2nd, by the forces under

Maj. Gen. F. STEELE

Assault April 9th.

1865

sign of concern Whittlesey continued writing in his notebook, finished his observations, descended to the floor, and returned with his report to the rear.[16]

On April 5 Steele had only one ten-pounder in place and after firing a few rounds, Confederate artillery got the range and made life miserable for the solitary gun crew. Steele emplaced two more guns that night, still barely enough to support a regiment of men. Canby had batteries placed on a rise along the south side of Minette Bay to harass Batteries Huger and Tracy and to chase gunboats away from his right flank at Spanish Fort. Every once in a while the gun crew pitched a shell into Fort Blakely, which was barely in range. The Minette Bay battery became bothersome to Liddell's defenders, but Steele could not depend upon it for coordinated support.

When Liddell realized that the enemy gained as much as two or three hundred yards of ground every night, he asked Maj. Henry Myers, chief ordnance officer, to make up some fireballs for the 24-pounder Cohorn mortars. After nightfall, Liddell's batteries had been depleting dwindling supplies of ammunition to keep the enemy from advancing, but gun crews had literally fired into the dark. With fireballs, Liddell hoped to illuminate the field and "allow the artillery to be used with effect."[17] Fireballs increased the risk of starting fires, and there is no record to confirm that Liddell used them.

Without fireballs Liddell depended on sorties to probe the night and slow the advance of the enemy, but his small force was repulsed at every point. At 3:00 A.M. on April 6, his men crept out of the fort and charged detachments of the 89th Indiana, 119th Illinois, and 11th Wisconsin, which had just advanced about two hundred yards and occupied freshly excavated rifle pits. Lt. Angus McDonald of the 11th Wisconsin took advantage of a lull in the musket fire to shout: "First and Second brigade supports, forward!" The Confederates skedaddled, not knowing that the Federals had no supports in the rear and were down to about four rounds of ammunition per man.[18]

Every night Federal lines advanced and Confederate outposts fell back. In Garrard's division, men fell into line with spades at midnight, and at the given signal, advanced about three hundred yards under constant gunfire. Because of the darkness casualties were remarkably light. In one regiment Maj. Jonathan Hutchison advanced companies of the 32nd Iowa by forming a line, placing himself on the right, and ordering the men to dress on him as they moved forward. He counted the paces until gaining the required distance and then ordered the men to start digging. Neither artillery nor skirmishers in advance rifle pits slowed the 32nd Iowa, and there was no report of casualties, attesting to the ineffectiveness of night firing.[19]

Opposite: **Sketch of the siege of Fort Blakely (courtesy *History of the Campaign of Mobile*).**

By April 7 Steele's engineers had several batteries underway in positions to enfilade the fort. At the edge of a bluff on the far right, Capt. Eugene H. Newton installed four 30-pounders that could cover the river and shell the entire length of the Blakely works. When the battery was completed on April 8, Capt. William P. Wimmer, 1st Indiana Heavy Artillery, turned his Parrotts on Farrand's gunboats and drove them away after sending seven shots into the *Morgan*. He then swung the guns around, shelled the redoubts, and chased away a steamboat landing supplies at the Blakely wharf.[20] Lt. Albert Rowse, 15th Massachusetts Light Artillery, opened from the left center with four 12-pounder Napoleons, hurling shells into the fort from the opposite flank. Three ten-pounders of the 2nd Connecticut kept up a fire from their position near the Pensacola road.

Annoyed by Federal artillery, Liddell obtained three seven-inch siege guns and worked through the night to have them in position on the morning of April 8. At 8:00 A.M., he opened with every gun, concentrating his fire on Steele's scattered artillery. After an hour of intensive bombardment, Liddell noticed that the Federal batteries were still responding with spirit and abandoned the effort. Many of the shells had passed over artillery positions and exploded in the Federal rear, landing among infantry reserves and wounding several men, but the men on the front lines escaped with little injury.[21]

At Spanish Fort, General Gibson's force was being worn down by attrition and overpowered by Canby's heavy guns. Liddell could not send reserves to Gibson when he could not get them for himself. On April 2 Maj. Gen. James H. Wilson's cavalry force had captured Selma, and Maury worried that Wilson's next stop would be Mobile. By April 8 Maury, Liddell, and Gibson probably recognized that the end was near, but they all still held their positions and waited for the final attack. With Federal forces in overwhelming strength, Liddell probably wondered why Canby needed to make such elaborate preparations to force the surrender of his thinly manned earthworks. On the other hand, Canby had witnessed the fall of Forts Powell and Gaines with little resistance from the garrisons. Fort Morgan stood longer and surrendered to a much smaller force, but the difference had been the heavy guns of the navy. What Canby had not considered was the resolve of General Gibson to hold out at all costs, fight his guns beyond the point of hope, maintain a high level of morale under constant bombardment, and breathe life into the harried Confederate forces defending Mobile by holding onto the fort with exemplary courage.

Gibson had become the pivot upon which final Confederate resistance rested, and that pivot was about to fall.

Chapter 14
All Fall Down

Since the beginning of April, Canby's forces had been inching toward Spanish Fort through a labyrinth of trenches, parallels, and saps. Each night the men spaded further forward, as shells from both sides of the line whooshed over their heads. During the day sharpshooters squinted from under embrasures made of thick, heavy planks and discharged their weapons at the slightest movement along enemy lines. A Federal artillery officer wrote: "The siege progresses splendidly. How different from [*Vicksburg*]. There it was charge! charge! charge! Here a little more good sense is shown, and a regard had for human life; and the end approaches much more rapidly."[1]

As the sun rose on April 7, Gibson looked at the fresh dirt piled up just outside his line of last defense and wrote Maury: "I can't get along without subterra shells, hand-grenades, more negroes, a company of sappers and miners, a cutter or launch from the navy, [and] two howitzers. The enemy made great progress yesterday.... He will soon dig up my main line at the rate he is advancing." At midnight, he added, "We cannot ... arrest his progress. Will send off all surplus articles."[2]

On the morning of April 8, Generals Gibson and Holtzclaw agreed the time had come to evacuate. Lieutenant Colonel Williams, 21st Alabama, had been working on a battery of four 12-pounders on Holtzclaw's left and expected to have them in position to enfilade the enemy's left by nightfall. Gibson decided to hold on another day and give Williams an opportunity to try his guns. At 4:00 P.M. he opened with a full artillery barrage, but concentrated and accurate Federal fire disabled Confederate guns and drove their crews into bombproofs.[3]

Along the Federal lines Granger's XIII Corps had dug 10,500 yards of parallels and sap. Bertram's brigade had excavated to within one hundred yards of Fort McDermott. McArthur's division, XVI Corps, had constructed 3,975 yards of parallels and 2,035 yards of sap. The sap of Col. Lucius F. Hubbard's brigade extended to within 60 yards of Red Fort. Carr's division, XVI Corps, had constructed batteries for about 50 guns, including mortars. Col. Jonathan B. Moore's brigade had dug to within one hundred yards of the garrison's main works. In addition to six heavy guns positioned on Minette Bay, Canby's force had 53 siege guns, including mortars, and 37 field guns bearing on Spanish Fort; 13 of those mounted in enfilading positions. At 5:30 P.M. Federal guns opened on Spanish Fort and continued the bombardment for two hours. A newspaper correspondent declared: "The earth actually trembled from this mighty fire." Canby had decided to wait no longer and issued instructions to assault the fort at 8:00 A.M. on April 9.[4]

Carr's division had pushed its line far forward on the extreme right of the Federal line. During the heavy artillery fire the evening of April 8, Geddes attacked the skirmishers on the Confederate left, and drove them off a strategic crest and into the fort. Colonel Geddes advanced two companies of the 8th Iowa Infantry, under Lt. Col. William B. Bell, to the crest and discovered that the new position overlooked the rear of the Confederate garrison scattered along Red Fort. During the movement forward, the left of Carr's division cheered loudly to give the impression that an assault was being mounted along a different position of the line, thereby distracting the attention of Ector's Brigade from the real point of attack. Several companies of Texans remained on the left, temporarily stalling Geddes' attack. Bell sent another company forward but became troubled when he saw his forward line pinned down on ground with little cover. He feared if his men were forced back, they would be shot up badly. Bell sent Lt. Alexander M. Clark to the rear to apprise Geddes of the difficulties and return with instructions. Before Clark returned Bell took matters into his own hands and brought up the entire regiment. The 8th Iowa advanced to the crest, but finding the skirmishers hotly engaged by the Texans, moved by the right flank around the crest and attacked Confederate rifle pits on the extreme left, just outside the main works. The flank attack carried about five hundred yards of Confederate fortifications before Geddes came up and ordered the men to take position along the outer side of the works, using them as breastworks when firing into the fort. A Federal mortar battery, seeing the commotion along the Confederate works, burst several shells over Bell's infantry. Bell placed the regimental colors over a captured parapet and waved his hat at the gunners, motioning them to direct their fire farther up the line.[5]

During the assault, a minié ball struck 1st Lt. Henry Vineyard, 8th Iowa Company G, in the left arm, but he continued to wave his company forward. Near the crest of the vital hill, another ball fractured his left thigh, mortally wounding him. Some of the men gathered around to give him comfort, but he said: "Pay no attention to me, boys – move on."[6]

The 8th Iowa scrambled over the parapet and into the main works on the left and began driving Ector's Brigade back, collecting prisoners as the enemy retreated. Texans in detached rifle pits had heard the musket fire but did not know the fort had been breached until they looked up and into the points of enemy bayonets. Some fought to the last, firing into the 8th Iowa at point-blank range, and, after discharging their muskets, glumly surrendering. A few men fought to the end and died in a fearless manner.[7]

Near nightfall reinforcements from the 81st Illinois, under Lt. Col. Andrew W. Rogers, filed into the fort and took supporting positions along the line established by Bell. A little later the 108th Illinois, under Col. Charles Turner, and the 124th Illinois, under Brevet Colonel Howe, entered the works and formed a line to repel an expected counterattack. The 8th Iowa climbed back out the works, advanced along the outer line, and placed themselves in a position to pour flanking fire into the attacking force.[8]

What started as a strong counterattack fizzled in confusion. Capt. Frederick P. Kettenring, 8th Iowa, reported that a strong column of the enemy was advancing in force. Bell steadied his men for the shock, but at a distance of "thirty or forty yards," the Confederates called out "we surrender," hurriedly fired their rifles, and then broke and ran. Sergeant Newton of the 14th Wisconsin lamented: "If they had only been driven a little further we would have captured the whole garrison: but the Gen'l [Carr] seemed to think he had done well enough for one day, so he stopped to fortify & get ready to 'give it to them' in the morning."[9] A little later Geddes returned to the field and found no resistance in his front. He formed the brigade and marched it through the fort to the bay, picking up a few prisoners, but Gibson's main force had skedaddled.[10]

Once inside the fort, some of Carr's brigade mounted the breastworks, and with a cheer, moved down the line toward Red Fort. Skirmishers of the XVI Corps "thought the Rebs. were going to make a charge," wrote Sergeant Newton, "and they began to fire at a great rate into our own men. They felt rather sheepish when they found out who they were shooting at."[11]

Near the center of the line, pickets from the 96th Ohio had crept within speaking distance of the enemy. Cheered by a rumor circulating among the trenches, one of the pickets shouted: "Johnnie, listen a minute: Lee's surrendered to Grant; you're gone up. Don't I often told you so!" After a moment of silence, Johnnie replied: "Yank, if that's so, we don't need this old fort; come and take it!"[12]

On the opposite side of the fort, intensive Federal firing had silenced Fort McDermott. The 19th Iowa, under Lt. John Bruce, had established advance rifle pits so close to McDermott that gun crews risked their lives every time they became exposed. Because of his advanced position, Bruce expected a strong Confederate sortie would be organized to drive his men away. The 23rd Iowa, under Col. Samuel L. Glasgow, came to the front double-quick to help Bruce beat off the expected attack—but no attack came, only silence and the distant rattle of muskets far to the right.[13]

As soon as Gibson learned the line on his left had been broken, he directed Holtzclaw to restore it. The general looked at the line, found the

Texans and North Carolinians doubled up and in confusion, and reported the Federal attacking force too strong to be driven back. Gibson pulled reinforcements off the main line to hold the left long enough to evacuate the garrison. Colonel Coleman gathered his North Carolina regiment together and, with help from Gibson's provost guards, collected a force of about three hundred men, deployed them in a line perpendicular to the main works and told them to check the enemy's advance. Knowing that the safety of the garrison depended upon their valor, they charged the 8th Iowa. After a stinging repulse, Col. Francis C. Zacharie brought up about 60 men from the 25th Louisiana to help restore the line. By then Gibson had called most of his force to the rear and sent the first detachments over the treadway to safety. Zacharie's small force formed with its left covering the treadway and his right thrown forward. Scouts returned claiming that they could find no enemy in their front. Zacharie did not believe them and ordered a captain, one sergeant, and two men from the 22nd Louisiana to go forward until they found the Federal line. They went out but were captured. By then the evacuation was well under way.[14]

The moss-covered treadway, about 1,200 yards long, was commanded throughout the day by Federal batteries, making evacuation by day a difficult maneuver. Gibson wanted all his troops over the bridge and into Battery Huger before daylight. The night was dark, making progress slow, and men pulled off their shoes to make the movement as noiseless as possible. From the opposite end of the treadway, they crossed the river in boats, marched by the earthwork, and boarded steamers for Blakely.[15]

As the rear guard stepped on the footbridge to cross the swamp, they heard cheering at McDermott, probably from the 94th Illinois when it discovered the fort evacuated. A few shells passed over their heads from batteries on the right of the XVI Corps. Without enough transports to move his men out of sight before daylight, Gibson sent about 1,000 of the men to Blakely, a distance of five miles, by marching them over the Minette Bay swamps. The route lay through mud and water, across marsh grass and canebrakes, around thick underbrush, and over narrow but deep bayous. Men sank in the swamp and had to be pulled out by their comrades. Slack's brigade of Veatch's division had been sent down to the shore of the bay and were talking and laughing as Gibson's muddied men made their escape. The garrison passed within a few yards of idle Federals and could hear their conversations. They reached Blakely at daylight, thoroughly exhausted but safe.[16] Most of the balance of Gibson's force, including the general himself, continued by transports to Mobile and received assignments for the defense of the city.

In the early stages of the siege, Maury had asked Gibson to hold Spanish Fort as long as possible, but when the capture of the garrison seemed imminent, to make every effort to evacuate the force for the defense of Mobile.

With never many more than 3,000 men, Gibson resisted nearly 30,000 infantry and artillery for 13 days with Canby in his front and Thatcher's gunboats harassing his rear. On the night he evacuated Spanish Fort, details removed all the sick and wounded, dispersed most of the remaining provisions, spiked the guns, and withdrew the garrison in good order. Despite Gibson's insistence that everyone be withdrawn, a few officers failed to recall all their skirmishers. "I deeply deplore the capture of even a part of these brave men," Gibson wrote, implying that their officers had better have a satisfactory explanation for leaving them there.[17]

About midnight Colonel Blanden's 95th Illinois, Moore's brigade, wheeled left and charged along the garrison works in reverse and flank, collecting a few stray prisoners. On reaching Old Spanish Fort, Blanden discovered the garrison gone and hastened down to the footbridge, but Gibson and his men had vanished. Geddes came up with the rest of the brigade and, finding no enemy, allowed the men to stack arms and enjoy the few hams and cornmeal left behind. As weary, exhausted men sat on the ground relishing their unexpected midnight meal, the USS *Octorara* fired a one-hundred-pounder shell at Old Spanish Fort that screeched overhead and exploded just outside the works. The men shuffled to a safer position and finished eating. Geddes collected his prisoners and, after leaving a detachment posted at the fort, marched the brigade back to its quarters.[18]

In the morning Canby's troops moved into Spanish Fort to collect the spoils. The ground in front of the main line had been heavily mined with torpedoes. Men from McArthur's division found a number of Confederate dead just outside the fort; one appeared to have been killed while planting a torpedo and a detail buried it with him. In round numbers, Canby's force collected about 500 prisoners, nearly 50 pieces of artillery, 1,300 projectiles, and huge reserves of ammunition, powder, and cartridges. The artillery had been spiked, and the gun carriages and implements smashed or rendered unserviceable.[19]

On Sunday, April 9, Canby began transferring men and artillery to new positions at Blakely. By late afternoon ten batteries, including the heavy artillery of the 1st Indiana and other detachments of Totten's Siege Train had rolled into position and begun to shell the fort in front and along both flanks. Three lines of entrenchments had been completed and skirmishers posted about 140 yards from the main line of the enemy's forward rifle pits. Up to this time Federal casualties had been light – about 20 killed and one hundred wounded.

In the morning General Smith visited Garrard's headquarters and asked the division commander to assault Fort Blakely "at the earliest practicable moment," promising support from McArthur's and Carr's divisions and all the artillery he wanted. Garrard placed two batteries of the 1st Indiana, consisting of four 30-pounders each, on his extreme left and bombarded the enemy line until late afternoon. Captain Mack's Black Horse Battery (18th New York) of six 20-pounders went into position on Garrard's right with orders to withhold fire until the enemy opened and then silence those batteries. The general issued similar orders to the 17th Ohio (four Napoleons), 2nd Illinois (four ten-pounder Parrotts), and the 3rd Indiana (four ten-pounder Parrotts), as he did not want his division harassed by enemy artillery when making the assault.[20]

Shortly before noon observers posted in trees reported that boats had been seen leaving Blakely loaded with troops. Soon afterward, the news traveled through the trenches, and speculation increased that the enemy was evacuating. Unusual silence along the front led to a general desire up and down the line to push forward and "feel" the enemy. Garrard pulled his commanders together and ordered an advance at 5:30 P.M. to be spearheaded by two heavy skirmish lines and followed by the main force.[21]

General Andrews, commanding Steele's 2nd Division near the center, sent his aide-de-camp, Lt. Herman D. Pettibone, to headquarters for permission to advance the division "as far as it could go." Pettibone found both Steele and Canby at Hawkins' headquarters and returned with information that the entire line should prepare to make a general assault at 5:30 P.M. that afternoon.[22]

The silence along the Blakely lines deceived Federal commanders. The supposed evacuation, reported by treetop observers, was nothing more than part of Gibson's jaded swamp crossers leaving for Mobile. Early in the day, Colonel Patton had signaled Liddell from Battery Tracy that "wagon trains and heavy columns of infantry have been crossing Bay Minette bridge all morning." Liddell now considered his open right flank threatened and moved men into position to cover it against attack. With Canby's overpowering force moving into his front, Liddell expected to be attacked and sent instructions to his division and artillery commanders to hold themselves "in readiness for an assault at any moment." The artillery had suffered a severe bombardment during the morning, having two guns dismounted, but since noon Confederate gun crews had saved their ammunition and prepared to repel the assault.[23]

On the far left of the Blakely line, opposite Brig. Gen. William A. Pile's brigade of U.S. Colored Troops, fire from Confederate sharpshooters had quieted. Pile probed the defenses, scattering several shots from the guns of the 4th Massachusetts Light Battery, but received no reply. Shortly after 3:00 P.M. he deployed companies from the 73rd and 86th Colored regiments to the forward skirmish line, and at a given signal, the men charged the Confederate advance rifle pits. They drew a galling fire from sharpshooters and artillery. The garrison held a strong line behind abatis, and the sharpshooters took advantage of the exposed condition of the attackers and shot many down. The 73rd's company commander fell, mortally wounded, but the men continued their advance, jumping over fallen logs, tripping over vines, and scrambling across washed-out terrain. Pile supported the attack with five more companies, instructing them to hold the ground gained and to entrench in the immediate rear of the enemy's abatis.[24]

Liddell, alerted to an attack on his left, sent reinforcements forward to strengthen the skirmish line. As they arrived, skirmishers were already falling back from the abatis to the main breastworks, and the contest grew more obstinate.

About 4:00 P.M., Scofield's 2nd Brigade, on Pile's left, and Drew's 3rd Brigade, each sent four companies forward to support Pile. The men had three hundred yards to cover, and to facilitate the movement through thick brush, they shed their coats and charged in their shirtsleeves. Skirmishers climbed out of their pits and rushed to the front, followed closely by a second line, all moving double-quick and cheering at the top of their voices. Confederate skirmishers picked up their muskets and retreated, firing and running, until they tumbled behind the main line and reformed along the breastworks. Effective artillery fire took its toll, but the Negroes pressed forward until they reached the abatis and formed next to Pile's men.[25]

Colonel Drew, confident that the 68th and 76th could carry the works in his front, or perhaps impelled by the enthusiasm of the moment, ordered both regiments to charge, waving his hat and shouting, "Forward on the enemy's works." Both regiments surged toward enemy lines in disorder and became hopelessly mingled. Grape, canister and shells ripped through the Colored regiments. The 68th's Lt. Charles Manhardt tried to execute an order to close the men to the right but fell, riddled by grape-shot. At the same time, Capt. George Giger received a mortal wound while trying to direct the men to the left. The regimental commander, Col. J. Blackburn Jones, felt something tugging at his trousers, and looking down, saw a man mortally wounded in the first charge asking that his remaining cartridges be "taken to the boys." Soon after, Jones fell, stunned by an exploding shell.[26]

Drew and his two regiments moved along the ground on a point level with Blakely's left redoubt and faced a deadly fire. He found a little protection below the brow of a bluff and worked the men around to the right, intending to assault the extreme left of the Confederate works and force his way inside. When Drew finally reached the last depression offering any protection, he paused to rest and count his men before ordering the assault. With one hundred yards to go, he counted only 19 officers and 65 men, too few to occupy and hold a lodgment inside the garrison. The men did not attack, but they cheered, fired a volley, and cheered again, looking for reserves and wondering where their comrades were. Worried about the welfare of the few men around him, Drew left Lt. Col. Daniel Densmore in command and hurried to the rear to find the reserves.[27]

The men in the garrison suspected that the force behind the bluff was in trouble and organized a sortie. Three companies of Drew's brigade, which had become separated from their regiment in the assault, occupied a brow of the bluff near the main works and to the left of Densmore's position. Neither knew where the other was. When the Confederate sortie came out, they got squeezed in a crossfire and hurried back to the breastworks. Densmore's men resumed firing in the air, cheering, and praying for reinforcements to come up. When Drew failed to return, Densmore sent back a captain to bring up the reserves. When the captain did not return, he sent a lieutenant, charging him to let nothing but death prevent him from bringing back men or orders. While waiting for some word from his two messengers, three Confederate gunboats steamed into sight and moved into position to fire. About the time Densmore thought he would have to send a third messenger, an officer showed himself and, with his hat, waved the remainder of the force back from its exposed position. Too indignant to hurry, the men retreated in order, bringing off their dead and wounded. Densmore and his men returned to the trenches in time to see the reserves move into position for the 5:30 P.M. attack. The three companies isolated behind the brow of a hill remained where they were, and when the main assault force moved up to their position, they fixed bayonets, charged down the line parallel with the fort, and drove the enemy sharpshooters into Fort Blakely.[28]

At 5:30 P.M. Pile heard cheering to his left and learned that the 2nd Division was charging the main works. He ordered his brigade forward. The assault became general along Hawkins' entire front as Scofield's and Drew's brigades picked up the cheer and charged on the right. When the Colored troops got close to the works, some of Cockrell's Missourians, dreading capture by Negroes, ran off to surrender to white troops. In Drew's front another detachment of Cockrell's veterans posted outside the works refused to surrender and maintained a cool and desperate struggle until they fell. In Scofield's line a single torpedo exploded, killing and wounding 13 men of the 51st Regiment. As his men advanced, they heard a Confederate officer behind the works shout, "Lay low and mow the ground – the damned niggers are coming!" Lt. Col. Henry C. Merriam led the 73rd Colored Regiment – all New Orleans troops – in a desperate charge. The Colored troops fixed bayonets, shouted at the top of their lungs, sprinted forward, and became the first of Pile's brigade to plant their colors on the parapet. Merriam, leading the assault at the very front of the brigade, earned the Medal of Honor. A soldier of the 50th ambled into the fort behind the 73rd and found his former young master among the prisoners. They shook hands and refreshed themselves with a drink from the same canteen.[29]

In Andrews' 2nd Division Colonel Spicely's brigade led the assault with the 97th Illinois, under Lt. Col. Victor Vifquain, initiating the charge. Moore's brigade followed in echelon, the 83rd Ohio posted to the front. At the designated time, Vifquain placed his regiment in two forward trenches and carefully walked the line, supervising the deployment of the men. Just prior to the assault a torpedo exploded, injuring several men and tearing off the leg of Capt. James W. Wisner as he spoke to his company. The explosion delayed the assault while a detail carried injured men to the rear.

At 5:45 P.M. Vifquain drew his sword and ordered the charge, "Forward, Ninety-seventh!" The men sprang from the trenches, tripped and fell over obstructions, weaved forward on the run, and stumbled into a shower of enemy bullets. Twenty yards from their trenches, men began to fall. A few steps behind, Lt. Col. William H. Baldwin's 83rd Ohio followed, cheering as they dashed for the enemy redoubt in their front. Garrison artillery opened, firing rapidly with grape and cannister as the two forward regiments closed on Confederate rifle pits. Any notion that the enemy had evacuated was dispelled by stiff resistance all along the line. Vifquain hurried a prisoner to the rear who verified the strength of the enemy.

At first Confederate sharpshooters held their position and returned a bitter musket fire, but as the skirmish gathered in strength, they slowly gave way, overpowered by numbers as the enemy converged on their front and flanks. Swarms of Confederate infantry left their pits, scrambled up a low hill, and retreated into the main fortifications near Redoubt No. 4. A few paces behind, men dressed in blue followed with a cheer, driving skirmishers so hard that the enemy did not have time to take up the footbridges across the ditch as they tumbled over the parapets.[30]

Behind Vifquain's and Baldwin's regiments, the rest of the 2nd Division sprang forward on the run. The 69th Indiana, under the command of Lt. Col. Oran Perry, took the Stockton Road, veered slightly to the left, and entered the Confederate works. The 76th Illinois, under Col. Samuel T. Busey, charged the redoubt directly in their front and to the right of the Stockton Road. The men held their formation until they became entangled in a second row of abatis. There the battle became fierce and bloody. While part of the regiment delivered a spirited fire, others crossed the abatis and formed on the redoubt. Lt. William F. Kenaga was shot through the leg at the abatis, but he limped forward. Nearer the works he received a ball in the ankle joint of his other leg. Unable to walk, Kenaga rose to his knees and crawled toward the enemy, cheering his men forward. The color sergeant fell 20 feet from the works. Corporal Goldwood grabbed the colors and planted them on the parapet. Concussion from a gun knocked him senseless and he fell to the ground, the colors wrapped in his arms. His body was later found with the charges of three muskets in his chest, fired at close range while he lay unconscious.

The 76th Illinois and the Confederates fought for several minutes across the works, at times engaging hand to hand. Running along the front with his revolver blazing at the enemy, Colonel Busey encouraged his men to fix bayonets and hurdle the parapet. He wounded a gunner about to fire a howitzer, which afterwards proved to be double-charged with grape and canister. Collecting about 50 infantry, Busey charged the front and right flank of the redoubt and drove the enemy out of the works. Fifty yards to the rear, the Confederates re-formed behind a row of brush and fired another volley, this time wounding Busey. The 76th charged again and sent the enemy flying into the woods and toward the Blakely landing. Busey sent detachments in pursuit, and when the firing finally ceased on that section of the field, the 76th had collected about four hundred prisoners. Referring to the spirited assault of the 76th Illinois, General Andrews wrote: "No regiment on the field that day suffered so heavily, nor exhibited more intrepid bravery. And higher praise than that cannot be awarded troops."[31]

The 24th Indiana entered the works on the right of the 76th Illinois. During their charge they passed over Confederate skirmishers without stopping to capture them. One skirmisher raised his hands to surrender, but when no one bothered to disarm him, he fired at a passing soldier and nicked his ear. The latter turned and killed him. Before the charge a man in Company C predicted where he would fall. During the assault his comrades looked back and saw him lying on the spot. Colonel Spicely and his staff entered the works with the 24th Indiana.[32]

The 97th Illinois planted their colors on the works between the Stockton Road and the redoubt to the south of it, almost simultaneously with the colors of the 83rd Ohio. Both regiments faced Cockrell's Missouri Brigade, among the most famous fighters in the Confederate army. These troops stood up behind their breastworks and delivered a steady and deliberate fire. Supporting artillery spat round after round of grape and canister, but most of the shots went high. With the 69th Indiana and the 97th Illinois on his right, Lieutenant Colonel Baldwin put the 83rd Ohio to work clearing an opening through the abatis. Both flagstaffs carrying the colors of the regiment were shot in two and the flags riddled with bullets. A staff officer hastened to the rear to bring up the main line of the 3rd Brigade to support the 83rd Ohio, but Baldwin got through the abatis and charged the works before reinforcements arrived. Running near the front of the regiment, Baldwin leaped over the parapet and into the works, shouting, "Surrender!" A Confederate officer asked, "To whom do we surrender?" Baldwin replied: "To the Eighty-third Ohio." The officer then commented: "I believe we did this once before," referring to a similar occasion at Vicksburg.[33]

In leading the assault Lieutenant Colonel Vifquain's 97th Illinois exposed themselves to severe fire in the race to the Blakely works. The regiment hit the outposts of the Confederate skirmishers so hard that they began falling back all along the line. Although several regiments planted their flags on the enemy works at about the same time, Vifquain was credited for spearheading the attack, and his regiment sustained the heaviest casualties. For his personal heroism and leadership in the assault on Fort Blakely, he received the Medal of Honor.[34]

Veatch's division, posted to the left of Andrews, advanced with Brigadier General Dennis's 2nd Brigade in front. Veatch held the 3rd Brigade, under Lieutenant Colonel Kinsey, in reserve, and left Slack's brigade, which had just returned from Spanish Fort, in camp. The 8th Illinois, a veteran regiment under Col. Josiah A. Sheetz, occupied the forward trench and led the advance. The 11th Illinois, under Col. James H. Coates, followed in line of battle to the left, and the 46th Illinois, under Col. Benjamin Dornblaser, followed on the right. Veatch instructed Sheetz to move forward as soon as he saw Andrews' division advancing. By the time Sheetz got his lines moving, Baldwin's 83rd Ohio had covered half the ground to Fort Blakely.

The 8th Illinois rushed forward with a yell, navigated through a ravine, leapt over slashings, and hurdled a cordon of wire obstructions. Barely pausing to empty Confederate rifle pits of their occupants, the boys in blue pushed abatis aside and rushed headlong into rapid fire from four batteries and a volley of musket fire. At one hundred yards from the Confederate line, men started to fall. The 11th and the 46th lagged behind. Garrard's division on the left seemed to falter, and the 11th and 46th were ordered to halt. The orderly carrying the instruction rushed forward to stop the 8th, but by then Sheetz's men were on the parapet and driving the defenders back. Capt. Alexander Coleman fell with a dangerous wound, but after being brought to the ground, he continued to wave his sword, cheering on his men. Seeing no reason to delay the advance, the 11th and the 46th Illinois resumed their attack and joined the 8th in pursuing the Confederates to the Blakely wharf, collecting three hundred prisoners during the chase.[35]

Garrard's division, posted on the left of the Federal line, had been primed for the assault since early in the afternoon. The right of Col. John I. Rinaker's 1st Brigade and the left of Col. Charles I. Harris's 3rd Brigade held positions closest to the Confederate works, and Garrard decided to launch his attack from there. Because extensive obstructions covered most of the six hundred yards on his front, Garrard started two lines of heavy skirmishers in front, followed by the main force, which he directed to charge after the skirmishers reached the main line.

Harris formed two lines, with three regiments in the front and two in the rear. The forward line from right to left consisted of the 58th Illinois, under Capt. John Murphy; the 178th New York, under Lt. Col. John B. Gandolfo; and the 11th Wisconsin, led by Maj. Jesse S. Miller. The 11th Wisconsin advanced three companies of skirmishers at 5:45 P.M., but after they had covered only one hundred yards, they stalled under a withering fire from Confederate rifle pits. Fearing a repulse, Major Miller ordered the entire regiment forward. The men sprang out of the trench, and with ringing cheers, the veterans of the 11th Wisconsin charged the retreating Confederate skirmishers so closely that the guns of the fort could not open without risk of killing their own. As the skirmishers dived over the parapet, musketry, grape, and canister leapt from the fort, thinning Miller's ranks, but the 11th came on in good formation, fixed bayonets, and ascended the parapet. At first the Confederates fought back hand to hand, but the blue tide pouring over the parapet proved too strong. Lt. Angus R. McDonald, backed by several men from the 11th, tumbled over the parapet and demanded surrender. Eight Confederates threw up their hands, but ten yards to their right another officer in charge of 12 men shouted: "No quarter to the damned Yankees!" and continued to pour lead into the right of the regiment. Several men with bayonets charged Lieutenant McDonald and Sgt. Daniel B. Moore. McDonald parried with his sword, killing two and injuring others, but he received two bayonet thrusts in the chest and a musket ball in the thigh which sent him stumbling to the ground. A dead Confederate fell on him and McDonald used the body for a shield as another soldier picked away at him with a bayonet. Moore, also injured by a bayonet, grabbed a loose musket and shot McDonald's assailant "dead."[36]

Behind the 11th Wisconsin Colonel Harris and the rest of the brigade clambered over the parapet, but most of the enemy force had retreated to the landing. Anxious to pocket at least some of the credit, Harris sent a detachment into Blakely to gather prisoners.[37]

Brig. Gen. James I. Gilbert's 2nd Brigade had advanced just behind Harris's right. The general formed his five regiments into three lines and deployed the 10th Kansas, under Lt. Col. Charles S. Hills, and Company B of the 27th Iowa as skirmishers to lead the assault from the forward trench, about six hundred yards from the main works. Directing their attack on the Sixth Redoubt, the 10th Kansas charged out of their trench in good formation, but Confederate artillery drove them into a ravine. An enfilading fire greeted them there. Hills led the men back to high ground, where they pushed their way through two rows of abatis. The men had lost their formation but they gathered in small groups, dashed to the ditch in front of the works, and in columns mounted the parapet. With fixed bayonets, the 10th Kansas swept along the works to their right, overpowering the thin gray line and taking prisoners by the score. Capt. Robert W. Wood, Company A, confronted a Confederate captain and demanded his surrender. The man picked up a musket and fired at Wood but missed. Finding a second and third musket at hand, he fired twice more and missed both times. Corporal Schultz came up before the captain could find a fourth musket and put a ball into his head. About this time many of the Confederate officers came forward, presenting their swords, and asking that the "butchery" be stopped.[38]

Maj. Jonathan Hutchison, 32nd Iowa, with eight men held off a large force of Confederate infantry and kept them in the sights of their own

Confederate gunboats. Farrand withheld his fire for fear of shelling Liddell's defenders. Hutchinson's determined stand spared attacking Federal troops from a devastating enfilading fire and eliminated the Confederate navy from the action.[39]

Garrard's 1st Brigade, under Col. Rinaker, occupied the extreme left of the Union line, its left flank resting on the swamp. The 119th Illinois, under Col. Thomas J. Kinney, deployed as skirmishers about three hundred yards in front of the main fort, but as they formed for the assault, they observed Confederate sharpshooters abandoning their pits and falling back to the works. Kinney got his men in motion, and a race for the fort began. Two redoubts turned their guns on Kinney's men, but most of the projectiles passed over the heads of the 119th Illinois and scattered among the regiments in the rear. General Thomas' Alabama Reserves comprised the force behind the works, and these youngsters had not developed a hardened taste for battle. As Rinaker's men started to scale the parapet, the Reserves headed for Blakely landing, leaving the artillery to fend for themselves. The gunners, armed with rifles, put up a stiff resistance until the 21st Missouri and the 122nd Illinois bounded into the works, turned left, and charged down the rear of the fort to the last redoubt. The 21st Missouri chased a number of Cockrell's Missourians down to the Apalachee River, and about 150 Confederates dived into the river and swam to safety. Other men improvised rafts and poled across the river or hid in the marshes until dark. A few days earlier these same men had occupied opposing picket lines, and each night little social gatherings had taken place under an informal truce. Tobacco, coffee, and newspapers had been traded as the men rested on their muskets and talked about home. Rinaker's brigade captured 520 prisoners and 37 commissioned officers, including General Thomas and General Liddell.[40]

Prisoners from Thomas' Alabama Reserves filed to the rear and seemed amazed at the great number of "so many boys in blue." Some of the youngsters asked: "Where did you Yanks all come from?" Many of the men behind Confederate lines never imagined the odds they faced until after the fight ended.[41]

Unlike Gibson, who built a treadway over a swamp, Liddell had provided no backdoor exit. The force at Blakely surrendered in pieces, overpowered and overwhelmed by 16,000 Federal troops from 35 regiments attacking simultaneously along a line three miles long. As each Federal regiment breached the Blakely defenses, they rounded up prisoners in their front, and by the evening of April 9 Canby's force had collected about 3,700 prisoners, including three generals and 197 commissioned officers. Partial accounts of Confederate losses at Spanish Fort and Blakely list 73 killed and 320 wounded, but these reports do not include Steele's campaign from Pensacola or losses sustained prior to the investment of the forts. During a campaign lasting nearly three weeks, Canby reported 1,508 casualties: 177 killed, 1,295 wounded, and 36 captured or missing.[42]

Considering the tremendous amount of ammunition consumed, combined with Canby's assault over a field covered with obstructions at Blakely, the light casualty list reflects a new concern for the lives of men. At this stage of the war, commanders had learned how to attack strong fortifications without excessive bloodshed. Spades and axes had replaced glorious charges. Four years of fighting had taught the men how to protect themselves, and they no longer took unnecessary risks with their lives. Col. Lucius F. Hubbard, 5th Minnesota, reported that McArthur's 2nd Brigade had excavated 7,000 cubic yards of dirt and expended 169,000 rounds of musket ammunition during the campaign. His brigade lost only five killed and 94 wounded. Dirt had replaced death.[43]

As evening fell on April 9, no musket or artillery fire boomed along the front lines, but as men searched the ground for their fallen comrades, the sharp report of exploding torpedoes echoed through the night, spilling the victors' blood.[44] For several decades after the Civil War, buried mines, or subterra shells, continued to kill and mutilate Southerners as they walked through peaceful woods or flower-filled fields once defended by Confederate infantry.

With the fall of Blakely, the reduction of Batteries Huger and Tracy became a foregone conclusion. Thatcher cleared the river of torpedoes and brought up his gunboats, the *Octorara* opening on Huger at 5,400 yards. At the same time, Federal batteries on Minette Bay and two unspiked one-hundred-pounder Brooke rifles in Old Spanish Fort under Capt. Joseph Foust, 1st Missouri, added more metal to the bombardment. In all, 20 guns from land batteries banged away at Huger and Tracy.[45]

On April 11 Canby organized a night attack on the forts and asked Thatcher for support from his tinclads, cautioning him not to fire on his boats. That evening General Smith led a detachment down to the shore of Minette Bay and prepared to shove off for the forts at about midnight. However, at 9:00 P.M. a cutter from the *Octorara* on picket duty below Huger captured a skiff with eight men who claimed they had just deserted from the fort. When questioned they stated that both Huger and Tracy had been evacuated after dark. The information was communicated back to Thatcher, who ordered cutters out to investigate. Federal batteries continued to pound the forts, and when Thatcher's force landed and found the Confederates gone, signals were passed to the gunners to cease fire, and Smith's party returned to camp.[46]

On April 11 Granger's 1st and 3rd divisions marched to Starke's Landing and with five days' rations embarked for Catfish Point, about five miles south of Mobile. The general made his temporary headquarters on the steamer *General Banks*, and as the vessel approached the western shore, the morning mist lifted, revealing transports and gunboats, in single and double lines, majestically crossing the bay. One gunboat advanced some distance ahead of the fleet and fired a single shell to challenge the shore. No reply came. Acting Rear Admiral Thatcher came alongside the *General Banks* in his flagship and signaled: "I propose to shell the shore." Granger lifted a glass to his eye, scanned the shore, and signaled back: "By _____, you'll shell a flag of truce if you do." Andrew F. Sperry of the 33rd Iowa looked shoreward and observed that "all this tremendous array of fleets, armies and artillery was thus brought to bear against a solitary negro, whose feeble hand waved a white flag tremblingly."[47]

Granger's XIII Army Corps disembarked at Codfish Landing, a rotten and broken old wharf. The general met the city's mayor, Robert H. Slough, trotting down the Bay Road toward them in a carriage bearing a white flag. Granger received the surrender of the city from the mayor "to the land and naval forces of the United States," and at 10:30 A.M. marched unopposed along a beautiful shell road and into Mobile. A little later Union ships moved to the dock at the foot of Government Street, and troops came marching off with bands playing. Showing relief rather than fear, a curious crowd gathered to watch. They were back in the Union again.[48]

After four years of relentless work to build and strengthen three lines of fortifications that protected the wrong side of the city of Mobile, Maury collected the remnants of his dwindling army and skedaddled on the night of April 11 without firing a shot. With half of his force captured at Blakely, he had no hope of holding out against Canby. He knew that Federal forces could move across the delta without opposition and place batteries on Blakely Island to shell the defenseless city. Lieutenant General Taylor approved the withdrawal, and on April 11 Gibson ordered all the remaining infantry and artillery at Mobile moved up the road leading to Meridian.[49] Lt. Col. Philip B. Spence, 16th Confederate Cavalry, guarded the rear of the withdrawal. As Granger's force marched into Mobile, Maury's rear guard moved to Citronelle, about 30 miles north. His riders stopped along the way to burn bridges and trestles, but their hearts were no longer in it, and to most of them the war had come to an end.[50] Some simply turned their mounts around and rode home.

At the conclusion of the Mobile Campaign, Canby reported the capture of 5,000 prisoners, 12 flags, nearly three hundred pieces of artillery, several thousand stands of small arms, and large stores of ammunition and other war materiel. He thanked the officers and men of the army for their "zeal, energy, and gallantry," and the navy for their "zealous and hearty co-operation."[51]

But the war had not quite ended in the Deep South. Regiments fell into marching order and headed north. Wagon trains rumbled over dusty roads to Meridian and to Montgomery, but most of Canby's infantry would fire no more at the Confederates. For everyone the killing was almost over.

Chapter 15
In Retrospect

The capture of Confederate forces at Fort Blakely left General Maury with 4,500 troops, too few to defend Mobile and about half the number he commanded prior to Canby's invasion of the eastern shore. Gen. Pierre G. T. Beauregard considered it a mistake for Maury to have garrisoned any part of the eastern shore. He believed that Huger and Tracy should have been self-sustaining forts, with the main garrison at Mobile. Had Maury not lost half his force defending Blakely and Spanish Fort, his concentrated army could have delivered stiff resistance behind the Mobile fortifications.

Huger and Tracy, along with numerous other shore batteries, had been designed to prevent the Union navy from approaching Mobile and forcing the city's surrender by heavy bombardment. The bay had always been shallow around Mobile, making it difficult for even medium-draft vessels to reach the city without grounding. The opposite shore was deeper, but the distance too great for naval guns to reach the city. Huger and Tracy had been built to keep enemy gunboats away from the deep water. Maury believed that by holding Spanish Fort, Huger and Tracy would be protected, and, in turn, Mobile. So often during the Civil War, military commanders overlooked or ignored the improvements in artillery since the Mexican War, especially technological advances in sighting, rifling, and explosives. Had Canby chosen to circumvent Spanish Fort and concentrate his batteries on Huger and Tracy, guns placed on the shore of Minette Bay would have crushed the forts within two weeks.

On the other hand, Canby did not want his supply lines harassed by well-organized sorties launched from Spanish Fort or Blakely. Had he ignored the forts and swung around to the Alabama River, his extended lines would have been under constant attack. Canby might have found a way to force the evacuation of Spanish Fort by indirect means, but he preferred the direct approach, and his light losses justified his decision, although it took time.

On March 27 Gibson expected Spanish Fort to be overrun by Federal troops, but Canby saw no critical objective to be gained by an immediate assault. He did not know the strength of the fort, but he knew that most of the defenders were veterans. After four years of bloody repulses by Federal infantry assaulting strong Confederate fortifications, Canby did not wish to add another grim chapter to the "butcher's bill" because of personal impatience. Had Canby ordered an assault that day, Gibson's garrison officers agreed it would have been stubbornly resisted but probably successful, although at a high cost in Federal lives.

Prior to March 27 Canby had probably not planned on a tactical siege with heavy artillery. He had left General Totten's Siege Train at Fort Gaines and did not order any part of it to Spanish Fort until March 28. On the other hand, by delaying the call for heavy artillery until he needed it, Canby was able to use Starke's Landing, about four miles from Spanish Fort, thereby avoiding a difficult haul up the Fish River and over rain-drenched roads.[1]

Both Gibson and Liddell failed to construct strong and connected works down to and across swamps on their flanks. Canby launched his assaults on those flanks, forcing the evacuation of Spanish Fort and rolling-up the lines at Blakely. For some reason, Confederate engineers believed that swamps represented impassable natural obstructions. General Andrews of the XIII Army Corps wrote: "The swamp was narrow, and could have been bridged, and there was not good excuse for the investment being incomplete."[2]

Gibson commented that Federal artillery fire from land batteries was heavy but not generally accurate. He credited the navy with better marksmanship. Col. Benjamin F. Hays, 1st Indiana Heavy Artillery, complained that the Hotchkiss pattern of solid shot would "end over" when fired and that shells would burst prematurely, occasionally scattering shrapnel over the pits and trenches of Federal skirmishers. Eventually artillerists replaced the powder with sand and converted the shells into solid shot, but against earthworks, gunners preferred using shells.[3]

The slashings and obstructions strewn across the field of fire from both forts benefitted Federal skirmishers by providing convenient protection from Confederate sharpshooters. Canby's force would have sustained severe losses by charging over a half mile of obstructions, but by gradually advancing their lines with parallels and sap, the infantry dug their way to forward striking positions, thereby saving lives. Had Canby charged Spanish Fort on the first or second day of the investment, his men would have had little or no artillery support.

By eliminating Spanish Fort as a threat, the capture of Blakely probably became less bloody. Although the 3,500 Confederate infantry and artillery at Blakely conducted themselves commendably, once Spanish Fort fell, they faced the demoralizing reality that another 20,000 Federal troops, flushed with victory, would join those already in their front. Canby's simultaneous assault along the entire front of the Blakely works was so sudden and in such strength that, in several instances, retreating Confederate skirmishers were only a few footsteps ahead of the attackers, preventing defenders within the works from firing. Most of the official papers covering the assault on Blakely reported that the enemy works were carried in "five to ten minutes from the advance of the skirmish line." Compared with months of preparation and days of arduous digging, the fight was over in "the blink of an eye."[4]

Maury probably made a tactical mistake by defending Blakely after the fall of Spanish Fort. Every possible effort should have been made to remove the garrison before the morning of April 9. Gibson had enough foresight to build a treadway to Fort Huger, but Liddell had provided for no means of escape and depended on a few transports that could not operate during the daylight without drawing enemy fire. When Gibson evacuated Spanish Fort, Maury transferred the swamp crossers to Mobile. There seemed to be no contingency plan for the Blakely defenders if Spanish Fort fell. Lieutenant General Taylor did not believe that Maury planned to ignore or desert the force at Blakely. Years later he wrote:

> Maury intended to withdraw Liddell during the night of April 9. It would have been more prudent to have done so on the night of the 8th, as the enemy would naturally make an energetic effort after the fall of Spanish Fort; but he was unwilling to yield any ground until the last moment, and felt confident of holding the place another day.[5]

On the other hand, Liddell claimed that he had depended on retaining the troops from Spanish Fort to assist in the defense of Blakely, but Maury ordered them to Mobile.[6]

Had Spanish Fort not fallen for a few more days, General Steele would have advanced his parallels at Blakely another one to two hundred yards. The closer diggers came to the main Blakely works, the more torpedoes they uncovered. After the assault, detachments began to clear the ground and discovered that the advance trench on the right of Andrews' Division had been dug between two rows of "infernal machines." Any additional digging would have increased Federal casualties.[7]

After the surrender of Mobile, Farrand took the *Nashville*, *Morgan* and two transports up the Mobile River and anchored them in the Tombigbee, just above its junction with the Alabama River. For protection small-boat details scattered torpedoes all along the channel below him. Before retiring, Farrand ordered the floating batteries *Huntsville* and *Tuscaloosa* scuttled to obstruct the Spanish River.[8]

The twin batteries had been foolish additions to the Confederate navy and should never have been built. They provide a sad testimony to the Confederate government's inability to produce ships. With limited resources and little shipbuilding skill, Southern aspirations for a combative navy rested almost exclusively in the imagination of Secretary Mallory. He championed the cause and got what he paid for, overweight sloths built with riverboat technology. The money wasted on useless vessels could have been spent to finance better projects. By concentrating resources, instead of one *Tennessee* Mallory could have built two or three. The three ironclads started on the Tombigbee River, the *Nashville* built at Montgomery, and the two floating batteries all took time and material and contributed nothing to the defense of Mobile Bay. Had Buchanan met Farragut with three *Tennessee*s, the Union's wooden gunboats could not have survived.

Torpedoes destroyed more Union warships than all the ironclads in the Confederate navy combined.[9] Had more effort and money been spent to promote the development and deployment of reliable torpedoes, Admiral Farragut might not have forced an entry to Mobile Bay or paid a much higher price in doing it. While clearing the rivers and estuaries of obstructions and torpedoes, Thatcher lost four more vessels, the tugs *Ida* and *Althea*, a launch from the *Cincinnati*, and the gunboat *Scotia*, bringing his total losses between March 12 and May 12 to eight vessels, including two monitors.[10] Torpedoes were inexpensive and the Confederacy's only practical defense against Union monitors; unfortunately too few of them worked.

Submarine technology, which had once been given an opportunity to be developed on Mobile Bay, was whisked away to Charleston by owner Hunley when he was offered a huge bounty for sinking Union blockaders. Submarines of the Hunley design had a much better chance of damaging Farragut's fleet inside the quieter water of the bay compared with ventures into the Atlantic Ocean or the Gulf of Mexico. One can imagine what Buchanan or Farrand might have accomplished with three or four Hunleys creeping through the mist of the bay toward Farragut's snugly anchored squadron. After Hunley's departure John P. Halligan tried to build a submersible torpedo boat at Mobile. His prototype, the *Saint Patrick*, successfully attacked the USS *Octorara*, but struck with a torpedo that misfired. After one excursion the boat returned to Mobile and settled into obscurity.[11] By not vigorously promoting the development of submarine warfare, Secretary Mallory missed an opportunity to move Confederate naval technology – at little cost, compared with enormous expenditures for unfinished ironclads – closer to the twentieth century.

Brevet Major General Wilson's cavalry campaign in central Alabama prevented General Taylor from sending reinforcements to Maury. When Steele's Pensacola column marched across the Florida panhandle and into southern Alabama, Taylor intended to attack it and frustrate Canby's advance by defeating the force in detail.[12] Brig. Gen. Abraham Buford left Selma with a brigade of cavalry and trotted south to intercept Steele. On March 28 Taylor became aware that Wilson's incursion from the north consisted of a large force and recalled Buford. Nonetheless he assured Maury that as soon as he whipped Wilson, he would assist in the defense of Mobile "with all the force of the department."[13] Wilson's 10,000 troopers, armed with repeating carbines, brushed aside Confederate resistance and on April 2 captured Selma. From there he could have ridden south and supported Canby, but instead he struck eastward toward Montgomery, forcing Taylor to follow, thereby depriving Maury of reinforcements.

If the objective of Canby's campaign had been the capture of Mobile, why did he choose the lengthiest approach to the city? Neither Canby nor Farragut considered the capture of Mobile a strategic military objective, although both recognized the political appeal. By attacking along the eastern shore, Canby intended to open the Tensas and Alabama rivers as a supply line to the interior of the state. With the rivers in Union control, he could march into central Alabama and attack Montgomery, thereby establishing a second line of supply from Pensacola. The further he advanced into Alabama, the more troops he would have to shed to garrison captured towns and railroads. For this reason he started the campaign with 45,200 men.

Maury did not have a strong force at Mobile, and Canby knew it. By capturing the forts along the eastern shore, he hoped to draw troops away from the Mobile defenses and gain control of the rivers. Mobile's strongest fortifications faced south and west. Once the forts fell, Canby intended to cross the Mobile River and fall upon the city from the north, but he did not intend to become detained by a long protracted siege. His objective continued to be Central Alabama.[14] Wilson's cavalry got there first, and Maury, unable to defend Mobile, handed it to Canby without a fight.

Compared with other battles of the Civil War, losses during the Mobile Campaign were light. Canby reported an aggregate total of 1,678 casualties, but only 13 officers and 219 men were listed as killed. There is no record of Confederate losses, but a good estimate is probably about five hundred men since most of the action occurred from positions of defense.[15]

The small number of casualties is remarkable considering the number of troops engaged, but after four years of war, men had learned how to protect themselves, and officers no longer insisted on frontal attacks against heavily fortified and strongly held earthworks. Liddell explained the reason differently. Because he had so few men, he had spread them about one yard apart, thereby sparing the enemy from a volume of concentrated fire at any point among his widely scattered men.[16]

At the same time Liddell credited Canby with superb generalship. Having been a witness to many other battles, he wrote: "Canby's assault was one of the most magnificently timed and executed assaults in the Civil War. (35 regiments, 16,000 attackers, three mile front)." The sudden charge of so many men against so few defenders gave Liddell's force little time to reload or offer resistance.[17]

After the Battle of Mobile Bay, Farragut compiled his naval losses and reported 52 killed and 170 wounded, but 93 drowned when the *Tecumseh* sank, increasing the death toll to 145 and the casualty list to 315.[18] Until World War II, the sinking of the *Tecumseh* remained as one of the worst disasters to befall a U.S. warship in action.[19]

Admiral Buchanan and the officers of his squadron reported 12 killed and 18 wounded. Most of the casualties occurred on the *Selma*.[20] Commander Johnston in his report to Buchanan noted that losses in the Union navy "made a number nearly as large as the entire force under your command."[21] Casualty returns for joint operations against Forts Powell, Gaines, and Morgan were negligible. Williams claimed one wounded at Powell, Anderson reported none at Gaines, and Page sustained one killed and three wounded at Fort Morgan. Granger, whose force was spared from mounting an assault on either Gaines or Morgan, reported one killed and seven wounded. The scourge of both armies had been sickness, not bullets, with dysentery and malaria taking the heaviest toll.

Canby captured Fort Blakely on the same day that Gen. Robert E. Lee surrendered the Army of Northern Virginia to General Grant at Appomattox. The distressing news, though disappointing, probably came as an overwhelming shock to no one in Alabama. On April 26 Gen. Joseph E. Johnston surrendered all Confederate troops east of the Mississippi, with the exception of General Taylor's department. Then at Meridian on May 6, Taylor met Canby and surrendered the remaining forces under his command.[22]

On April 26 an emotional shock of universal pain gripped the Union army. Suddenly the joy of victory gave way to silent despair. "President Lincoln has fallen by the assassin's hand," rippled down the ranks. Surgeon Woods of the 96th Ohio described the reaction: "Immediately the most intense and painful sorrow enshrouded us in a pall. Few knew till then how much, how deeply they had loved him whose heart held 'Malice towards none, and charity for all.'"[23] Maury's men, also horrified by the news, stood in silent amazement and asked if it was possible that any Southern man had committed such an insidious act. They seemed relieved when they learned that "the wretched assassin had no connection with the South, but was an actor, whose brains were addled by tragedies and Plutarch's fables."[24]

Maury gathered his small force at Cuba Station and Demopolis and marched to Meridian. On May 8 he dispersed the remnants of Gibson's Louisiana brigade, Ector's Texans, Holtzclaw's Alabamans, and a few men from North Carolina and Georgia. In a final address to his men, he said: "Conscious that we have played our part like men, confident of the righteousness of our cause, without regret for our past action and without despair of the future, let us tomorrow, with the dignity of the veterans who are the last to surrender, perform the duty which has been assigned to us."[25] By then attrition and desertion had thinned Maury's command to the size of a brigade. The Louisiana band—the only band left in the Confederacy—came to the final encampment and played for the last time. After the musicians finished the last bars of "Dixie," they packed their instruments and went home.[26]

Typical of so many displaced Confederate soldiers, Maury returned to civilian life in poverty. He held teaching positions in Virginia and Louisiana, volunteered as a nurse at New Orleans during the yellow fever epidemic of 1868, and settled for a time in Richmond. He died at his son's home in Peoria, Illinois, on January 11, 1900, but spent the intervening years establishing and promoting the Southern Historical Society, whose papers provide a richly detailed record of the War of the Rebellion, and whose pages still ring with the clash of sabers, the beat of drums, and the rattle of musket fire.

The city of Mobile, the Gem of the Gulf of Mexico, survived the war without a scratch—but not the aftermath. On May 25 Marshall's Warehouse, the main ordnance depot for the Union army, blew up, creating enormous loss of life and great destruction of property. Canby wrote: "The cause of the explosion is not yet known, but as it occurred when a train of captured ordnance stores from Meridian was being unloaded, it is probably due to the explosion of a percussion shell."[27] The accident was investigated, but no definite conclusion was reached. Details poked through the rubble looking for clues but found nothing.

Visitors to the depot had commented on the carelessness with which Negroes rolled wheelbarrows full of live shells over cobblestone streets and roughly unloaded them onto platforms, laughing and singing as they worked. Then, on May 25, a great cloud of smoke rose in the morning air, hung for a few moments, then split apart, blown in every direction by flames and bursting shells. Explosion followed explosion as fires spread. Two ships sank in the river. Men and horses died of concussion in the street. Several blocks away a man was blown off the wharf by the force of the blast. Late into the night shells and rockets arced skyward and cast their light over the entire city. People rushed to the country to escape the flying debris. The fires burned until all the ammunition had been set off and everything consumable destroyed. Hundreds of buildings were leveled by the blasts. The northern part of the city lay in ruins. Where the warehouse once stood a great hole had formed, which eventually filled with water and for many years remained a pond. Caldwell Delaney, Mobile's historian, wrote: "No estimate could ever be made of the number of people killed or the exact property loss, but certainly both were greater than the losses suffered by the city in four years of siege."[28] Mobile had escaped the battle but not the war.

Six weeks after Lee's surrender at Appomattox, General Canby accepted the surrender of the last Confederate army in the field, Lt. Gen. Edmund Kirby Smith's Trans-Mississippi command. After the war Canby remained

Admiral David G. Farragut, USN (courtesy Scribner's *Battles & Leaders of the Civil War—1888*).

in the army with the permanent postwar rank of brigadier general and returned to his earlier profession of fighting Indians. He received command of the Department of the Columbia on the Pacific Coast in 1870. Three years later, while leading a peace mission at Siskiyou, California, he was attacked and murdered by Modoc Indians.

Admiral Buchanan recovered from his fractured leg but languished in prison until March 4, 1865. Naval Secretary Mallory sent him back to Mobile to assist in the final defense of the city. Buchanan hobbled into Mobile just in time to join the general surrender. After the war he returned to his Maryland estate, rebuilt his home, cultivated his acres, and in 1868 accepted the post of president of the Maryland Agricultural College. Buchanan reorganized the dilapidated school, increased enrollment from six to 80, raised funds, paid off debts, restored financial credit, elevated the school's standards, and preserved for future generations an institution of higher education that eventually became the University of Maryland.

After accepting in 1870 the position of manager of the Alabama branch of an insurance company in Mobile, the infirmities of age began telling on "Old Buck." He resigned his lucrative post and returned to live out the balance of his years on his Maryland estate. On May 11, 1874, surrounded by his family and physicians, Buchanan died of pneumonia at the age of 73. A eulogist summed up his life by writing: "In him died a man who never feared another, whose whole life was his answer to the call of duty, whose name is a proud heritage to his children, whose record gives honor to his native state, and whose memory will be an enthusiasm to the heroes of the future."[29] By fighting the Union fleet first at Hampton Roads and again at Mobile Bay, he demonstrated the potential strength of ironclads, which ultimately led to the obsolescence of the wooden navies of the world.

In late 1864 Admiral Farragut returned home from Mobile Bay exhausted and ill, but before the war ended, he was back on duty in the James River. Like Buchanan, Farragut belonged to the "wooden age" of warships. He held the opinion that though a hostile shot might go clear through a wooden ship, it would cause less damage than a shot that penetrated the armor of an ironclad. Toward the end of the war, his attitude toward ironclads changed, and at Mobile Bay he lobbied for four monitors before making his attack. To his dying day, however, he refused to serve on one.

After boisterous banquets and celebrations at the close of the war, Farragut became the navy's first full admiral, and during 1867–1868 commanded the European Squadron. Secretary Welles feared for the admiral's health, but Farragut returned from a long cruise in splendid condition. On his way home from a trip to Chicago with his wife, he became violently ill and suffered serious damage to his heart. He never fully recovered, and on August 14, 1870, the honorable admiral died in Portsmouth, New Hampshire, at the age of 69.[30]

With Farragut went the last champion of the wooden navy. Despite his fine record, the admiral went to his grave with one regret. In July 1864, when he heard that the USS *Kearsarge* had sunk the dreaded Confederate cruiser *Alabama*, he threw up his arms in celebration. "The victory of the *Kearsarge* over the *Alabama* raised me up," he wrote. "I would sooner have fought that fight than any other fought on the ocean."[31] From the age of nine he had lived on wood and fought on wood, and no contemporary had done it better or longer. He left a legacy of courage, skill, and determination, but he deeply regretted that all his battles were fought against forts, and he never had that glorious opportunity to fight a victorious battle on the open seas against other ships.[32] The decisive Battle of Mobile Bay marked the last major naval engagement in which wooden gunboats fought an enemy squadron in open combat. The era of wood had ended.

The Battle of Mobile Bay, which ultimately led to the surrender of Mobile, also gave military tacticians an excellent example of the results which could be achieved by well-organized and well-executed combined land and sea operations. In the past armies and navies too often acted independently. During the Civil War the Confederate services failed to cooperate; each had different agendas and strived toward different objectives. Welles had first selected Farragut to lead the Fort Fisher expedition because the admiral understood how to coordinate naval operations with the army. Farragut was ill and declined the post. As a consequence the first attack on Fort Fisher failed because of poor tactics, poor preparation, and poor leadership.

Although the Battle of Mobile Bay and the Mobile Campaign did little to change the ultimate outcome of the war, the strategies and tactics applied were immensely superior to those employed in the early stages of the war. Combined operations, trench warfare, coordinated attacks, submarines, torpedoes, minesweeping, land mines, rifled artillery, hand grenades, and naval combat between armored vessels all scientifically evolved throughout the war, and when Union forces invaded the environs of Mobile Bay, nothing had been omitted.

European military professionals studied the American Civil War with keen interest and began reshaping their attitudes toward tactics and weapons. While a reconstituted Union licked its many wounds, reconstructed the country, and developed its internal resources, Germany, France, Austria, Russia, Great Britain, and even Japan and Italy replaced their wooden navies with armored cruisers and mighty guns. European engineers perfected the submarine, the torpedo, water and land mines, and all the new weaponry tested in the fields and along the shores of the South. Fifty years later the technology of warfare applied at the beginning of World War I manifested many of the tactics and weapons warring Americans crowded into the brisk fight on Mobile Bay, the last major naval battle of the Civil War, and the Mobile Campaign, the last major military battle of the Civil War. Yankee (and Southern) ingenuity wrote a new chapter on the efficacious ways of destroying an adversary, and Mobile provided the final page.

Appendix

Comparative Naval Strength: Battle of Mobile Bay

Union Squadron

Monitors — Starboard Column

Tecumseh	1,034 tons	2 guns (15-inch)
Manhattan	1,034 tons	2 guns (15-inch)
Winnebago	970 tons	4 guns (11-inch)
Chickasaw	970 tons	4 guns (11-inch)

Wooden Gunboats — Port Column

Brooklyn	2,070 tons	24 guns
Octorara	829 tons	6 guns
Hartford	2,900 tons	24 guns
Metacomet	974 tons	9 guns
Richmond	2,700 tons	20 guns
Port Royal	805 tons	8 guns
Lackawanna	1,533 tons	14 guns
Seminole	801 tons	8 guns
Monongahela	1,378 tons	8 guns
Kennebec	507 tons	5 guns
Ossipee	1,240 tons	11 guns
Itasca	507 tons	6 guns
Oneida	1,032 tons	9 guns
Galena	738 tons	10 guns
Total		174 guns

Confederate Squadron

Tennessee	1,273 tons	6 guns (7-inch and 4.6-inch)
Selma	unknown	4 guns

Gaines	unknown	6 guns
Morgan	unknown	6 guns
Total		22 guns

Most of the Union's large wooden gunboats carried 9-inch smoothbores, although the *Monongahela* had two 11-inch smoothbores. The smaller Union gunboats carried a mixture of 9-inch smoothbores and 32-pounders.

The *Tennessee*'s guns were all rifled. Guns on the Confederate wooden gunboats ranged from 9-inch guns down to 32-pounder smoothbores. The batteries were quite mixed on every vessel.

For more detailed information, refer to *ORN*, Series II, Vol. I, *Statistical Data of Union and Confederate Ships*.

Although not directly committed to the Battle of Mobile Bay, Farragut's fleet included the wooden gunboats *Sebago, Genesee, Pembina,* and *Bienville*, which ineffectively engaged Fort Morgan from the rear, and the five light gunboats *Stockdale, Estrella, Narcissus, J. P. Jackson,* and *Conemaugh*, which covered General Granger's landing on Dauphin Island.

Buchanan's squadron also included the ironclads *Baltic* and *Nashville* and the floating steam batteries *Huntsville* and *Tuscaloosa*. These vessels were useless in the bay.

Mobile Campaign: Union and Confederate Forces

Union Army: Maj. Gen. Edward R. S. Canby's Forces

Engineer Brigade: Brig. Gen. Joseph Bailey

96th U.S. Colored Troops: Col. John C. Cobb; 97th U.S. Colored Troops: Lt. Col. George A. Harmount, Col. George D. Robinson; 1st Company of Pontoniers: Capt. John J. Smith.

Siege Train: Brig. Gen. James Totten

1st Indiana Heavy Artillery: Col. Benjamin F. Hays (Companies B, C, H, I, K, L, and M); New York Light Artillery, 18th Battery: Capt. John J. Smith.

XIII Army Corps: Maj. Gen. Gordon Granger

Mortar Batteries

6th Michigan Heavy Artillery, Co. A: Capt., Seldon F. Craig; Co. K: Lt. Charles W. Wood.

First Division: Brig. Gen. James C. Veatch

First Brigade: Brig. Gen. James R. Slack

99th Illinois (5 companies): Lt. Col. Asa C. Matthews; 47th Indiana: Lt. Col. John A.

McLaughlin; 21st Iowa: Col. Salue G. Van Auda; 29th Wisconsin: Lt. Col. Bradford Hancock.

Second Brigade: Brig. Gen. Elias S. Dennis

8th Illinois: Col. Josiah A. Sheetz; 11th Illinois: Col. James H. Coates; 46th Illinois: Col. Benjamin Dornblaser.

Third Brigade: Lt. Col. William B. Kinsey

29th Illinois: Lt. Col. John A. Callicott; 30th Missouri (4 companies): Lt. Col. William T. Wilkerson; 161st New York: Maj. Willis E. Craig; 23rd Wisconsin: Maj. Joseph E. Greene.

Artillery: Capt. George W. Fox

Massachusetts Light, 4th Battery (D): Lt. George W. Taylor; Massachusetts Light, 7th Battery (G): Capt. Newman W. Storer.

Second Division: Brig. Gen. Christopher C. Andrews

First Brigade: Col. Henry Bertram

94th Illinois: Col. John McNulta; 19th Iowa: Lt. Col. John Bruce; 23rd Iowa: Col. Samuel L. Glasgow; 20th Wisconsin: Lt. Col. Henry A. Starr; 1st Missouri Light Artillery, Battery F: Capt. Joseph Foust.

Second Brigade: Col. William T. Spicely

76th Illinois: Col. Samuel T. Busey, Lt. Col. Charles C. Jones; 97th Illinois: Lt. Col. Victor Vifquain; 24th Indiana: Lt. Col. Francis A. Sears; 69th Indiana (4 companies): Lt. Col. Oran Perry, Capt. Lewis K. Harris.

Third Brigade: Col. Frederick W. Moore

37th Illinois: Col. Charles Black; 20th Iowa: Lt. Col. Joseph B. Leake; 34th Iowa: Col. George W. Clark; 83rd Ohio: Lt. Col. William H. Baldwin; 114th Ohio: Col. John H. Kelly.

Artillery

Connecticut Light, 2nd Battery: Capt. Walter S. Hotchkiss; Massachusetts Light, 15th Battery: Lt. Albert Rowse

Third Division: Brig. Gen. William P. Benton

First Brigade: Col. David P. Grier

28th Illinois: Lt. Col. Richard Ritter, Maj. Hinman Rhodes; 77th Illinois: Lt. Col. John B. Reid; 96th Ohio (5 companies): Lt. Col. Albert H. Brown; 35th Wisconsin: Col. Henry Orff.

Second Brigade: Col. Henry M. Day

91st Illinois: Lt. Col. George A. Day; 50th Indiana (5 companies): Lt. Col. Samuel T. Wells; 29th Iowa: Col. Thomas H. Benton, Jr.; 7th Vermont: Col. William C. Holbrook.

Third Brigade: Col. Conrad Krez

33rd Iowa: Col. Cyrus H. Mackey; 77th Ohio: Lt. Col. William E. Stevens; 27th Wisconsin: Capt. Charles H. Cunningham; 28th Wisconsin: Lt. Col. Edmund B. Gray.

Artillery

New York Light, 21st Battery: Capt. James Barnes; New York Light, 26th Battery: Lt. Adam Beattie.

XVI Army Corps: Maj. Gen. Andrew J. Smith

Pontoniers, 114th Illinois: Maj. John M. Johnson.

First Division: Brig. Gen. John McArthur

First Brigade: Col. William L. McMillen

33rd Illinois: Col. Charles E. Lippincott; 26th Indiana: Col. John G. Clark; 93rd Indiana: Col. De Witt C. Thomas; 10th Minnesota: Lt. Col. Samuel P. Jennison; 72nd Ohio: Lt. Col. Charles G. Eaton; 95th Ohio: Lt. Col. Jefferson Brumback.

Second Brigade: Col. Lucius F. Hubbard

47th Illinois: Maj. Edward Bonham, Col. David W. Magee; 5th Minnesota: Lt. Col. William B. Gere; 9th Minnesota: Col. Josiah F. Marsh; 11th Missouri: Maj. Modesta J. Green; 8th Wisconsin: Lt. Col. William B. Britton.

Third Brigade: Col. William R. Marshall

12th Iowa: Maj. Samuel G. Knee; 35th Iowa: Lt. Col. William B. Keeler; 7th Minnesota: Lt. Col. George Bradley; 33rd Missouri: Lt. Col. William H. Heath.

Artillery

Indiana Light, 3rd Battery: Capt. Thomas J. Ginn; Iowa Light, 2nd Battery: Capt. Joseph R. Reed.

Second Division: Brig. Gen. Kenner Garrard

First Brigade: Col. John I. Rinaker

119th Illinois: Col. Thomas J. Kinney; 122nd Illinois: Lt. Col. James F. Drish, Maj. James F. Chapman; 89th Indiana: Lt. Col. Hervey Craven; 21st Missouri: Capt. Charles W. Tracey.

Second Brigade: Brig. Gen. James I. Gilbert

117th Illinois: Col. Risdon M. Moore; 27th Iowa: Maj. George W. Howard; 32nd Iowa: Lt. Col. Gustavus A. Eberhart; 10th Kansas (4 companies): Lt. Col. Charles S. Hills; 6th Minnesota: Lt. Col. Hiram P.Grant.

Third Brigade: Col. Charles L. Harris

58th Illinois (4 companies): Capt. John Murphy; 52nd Indiana: Lt. Col. Zalmon S. Main; 34th New Jersey: Col. William H. Lawrence; 178th New York: Lt. Col. John B. Gandolfo; 11th Wisconsin: Maj. Jesse S. Miller.

Third Division: Brig. Gen. Eugene A. Carr

First Brigade: Col. Jonathan B. Moore

72nd Illinois: Lt. Col. Joseph Stockton; 95th Illinois: Col. Leander Blanden; 44th Missouri: Capt. Frank G. Hopkins; 33rd Wisconsin: Lt. Col. Horatio H. Virgin.

Second Brigade: Col. Lyman W. Ward

40th Missouri: Col. Samuel A. Holmes; 49th Missouri: Col. David P. Dyer; 14th Wisconsin: Maj. Eddy F. Ferrie.

Third Brigade: Col. James L. Geddes

81st Illinois: Lt. Col. Andrew W. Rogers; 108th Illinois: Col. Charles Turner; 124th Illinois: Bvt. Col. John H. Howe; 8th Iowa: Lt. Col. William B. Bell.

Artillery Brigade: Capt. John W. Lowell

Illinois Light, Cogswell's battery: Lt. William R. Etling; 2nd Illinois Light, Battery G: Lt. Perry Wilch; Indiana Light, 1st Battery: Capt. Lawrence Jacoby; Indiana Light, 14th Battery: Capt. Francis W. Morse; Ohio Light, 17th Battery: Capt. Charles S. Rice.

Column from Pensacola Bay: Maj. Gen. Frederick Steele

First Division: Brig. Gen. John P. Hawkins

First Brigade: Brig. Gen. William A. Pile

73rd U.S. Colored Troops: Lt. Col. Henry C. Merriam; 82nd U.S. Colored Troops: Col. Ladislas L. Zulavsky; 86th U.S. Colored Troops: Lt. Col. George E. Yarrington.

Second Brigade: Col. Hiram Scofield

47th U.S. Colored Troops: Lt. Col. Ferdinand E. Peebles; 50th U.S. Colored Troops: Col. Charles A. Gilchrist; 51st U.S. Colored Troops: Col. A. Watson Webber.

Third Brigade: Col. Charles Drew

48th U.S. Colored Troops: Col. Frederick M. Crandal; 68th U.S. Colored Troops: Col. J. Blackburn Jones, Lt. Col. Daniel Densmore; 76th U.S. Colored Troops: Maj. William E. Nye.

Cavalry

Lucas Division: Brig. Gen. Thomas J. Lucas

First Brigade: Col. Morgan H. Chrysler

1st Louisiana: Lt. Col. Algernon S. Badger; 31st Massachusetts (mounted infantry): Lt. Col. Edward P. Nettleton; 2nd New York Veteran: Col. Morgan H. Chrysler, Lt. Col. Asa L. Gurney.

Second Brigade: Lt. Col. Andrew B. Spurling

1st Florida: Capt. Francis Lyons; 2nd Illinois: Maj. Franklin Moore; 2nd Maine: Maj. Charles A. Miller.

Artillery

Massachusetts Light, 2nd Battalion (B): Capt. William Marland.

First Division: Brig. Gen. Joseph F. Knipe

First Brigade: Col. Joseph Karge

12th Indiana: Maj. William H. Calkins; 2nd New Jersey: Lt. Col. P. Jones Yorke; 4th Wisconsin: Col. Webster P. Moore.

Second Brigade: Col. Gilbert M. L. Johnson

10th Indiana: Maj. George R. Swallow; 13th Indiana: Lt. Col. William T. Pepper; 4th Tennessee: Lt. Col. Jacob M. Thornburgh.

Artillery

Ohio Light, 14th Battery: Capt. William C. Myers.

District of South Alabama: Brig. Gen. T. Kilby Smith

Dauphin Island: Lt. Col. Byron Kirby

3rd Michigan Cavalry (6 companies): Capt. Eli D. Grinder; 6th Michigan Heavy Artillery: Capt. Seymour Howell (Companies C, E, F, H, and I).

Mobile Point: Lt. Col. Charles E. Clarke

1st Michigan Light, Battery G: Lt. George L. Stillman; 6th Michigan Heavy Artillery: Maj. Harrison Soule (Companies B, D, and G).

Canby's force for the Mobile Campaign totaled about 45,200 effectives, although he referred to this strength as "a little less than 50,000." His numbers are documented in *ORA*, Series I, vol. XLIX, part 1, page 92. (The organization of the command shown above appears on pages 105–9).

Confederate Army: Maj. Gen. Dabney H. Maury's Forces

Thomas Brigade: Brig. Gen. Bryan M. Thomas

1st Alabama Reserves: Col. Daniel E. Huger; 2nd Alabama Reserves: Lt. Col. Junius A. Law; 21st Alabama: Lt. Col. James M. Williams.

Gibson's Brigade: Brig. Gen. Randall L. Gibson

1st , 16th, and 20th Louisiana: Lt. Col. Robert H. Lindsay; 25th Louisiana and 4th Louisiana Battalion: Col. Francis C. Zacharie; 4th, 13th, 19th and 30th Louisiana: Maj. Camp Flournoy; Battalion Sharpshooters: Col. Francis L. Campbell.

Taylor's Command: Col. Thomas H. Taylor

City Battalion (4 companies): Maj. William Hartwell; Pelham Cadets Battalion: Capt. P. Williams, Jr.

Holtzclaw's Brigade: Brig. Gen. James T. Holtzclaw

18th Alabama: Capt. A. C. Greene; 32nd and 58th Alabama: Col. Bushrod Jones; 36th Alabama: Col. Thomas H. Herndon; 38th Alabama: Capt. Charles E. Bussey.

Sappers and Miners: Capt. L. Hutchinson

Hutchinson's Company: Lt. R. Middleton; Vernon's Company: Lt. J. Armstrong.

French's Division: Brig. Gen. Francis M. Cockrell

Cockrell's Brigade: Col. James McCown

1st and 3rd Missouri (dismounted cavalry): Capt. Joseph H. Neal; 1st and 4th Missouri: Capt. Charles L. Edmondson; 2nd and 6th Missouri: Lt. Col. Stephen Cooper; 3rd and 5th Missouri: Capt. Benjamin E. Guthrie; Steede's Mississippi cavalry battalion: Maj. Abner C. Steede; Abbay's Battery: Capt. George F. Abbay.

Ector's Brigade: Col. David Coleman

29th North Carolina: Capt. John W. Gudger; 39th North Carolina: Maj. Paschal C. Hughes; 9th Texas: Lt. Col. Miles A. Dillard; 10th Texas Cavalry (dismounted): Capt. Jacob Ziegler; 14th Texas Cavalry (dismounted): Lt. Col. Abram Harris; 32nd Texas Cavalry (dismounted): Capt. Nathan Anderson.

Sears' Brigade: Col. Thomas N. Adair

4th Mississippi: Maj. Thomas P. Nelson; 7th Mississippi (battalion): Capt. Samuel D. Harris; 35th Mississippi: Capt. George W. Oden; 36th Mississippi: Lt. Col. Edward Brown; 39th Mississippi: Capt. C. W. Gallaher; 46th Mississippi: Capt. J. A. Barwick.

Clanton's Brigade: Brig. Gen. James H. Clanton

3rd Alabama Reserves: Maj. Strickland; 6th Alabama Cavalry: Lt. Col. Washington T. Lary; 8th Alabama Cavalry: Lt. Col. Thomas L. Faulkner; Keyser's Detachment: Capt. Joseph C. Keyser.

Armistead's Cavalry Brigade: Col. Charles G. Armistead

8th Alabama: Col. Charles P. Ball; 16th Confederate: Lt. Col. Philip B. Spence; Lewis' Battalion: Maj. William V. Harrell.

Maury's Command: Col. Henry Maury

15th Confederate: Col. Henry Maury; Tobin's Battery: Capt. Thomas F. Tobin.

Artillery Reserves, Etc.

Left Wing, Defenses of Mobile: Col. Charles A. Fuller

Artillery: Maj. Henry A. Clinch

1st Louisiana, Company C: Capt. John H. Lamon; 1st Louisiana, Company I: Capt. Edward G. Butler; Coffin's (Virginia) Artillery: Lt. J. B. Humphreys; State Reserves:

Capt. William H. Homer, Lt. R. H. Bush; Barry's Battery: Lt. Richard L. Watkins; Young's Battery: Capt. Alfred J. Young.

Batteries: Lt. Col. L. Hoxton

Dent's Battery: Capt. Staunton H. Dent; Douglas' Battery: Lt. Ben Hardin; Eufaula Battery: Lt. William H. Woods; Fenner's Battery: Lt. W. T. Cluverius; Garrity's Battery: Capt. James Garrity; Rice's Battery: Capt. T. W. Rice; Thrall's Battery: Capt. James C. Thrall.

Right Wing, Defenses of Mobile: Col. Melancthon Smith

Trueheart's Battalion: Capt. Charles L. Lumsden

Lovelace's Battery: Lt. William M. Selden; Lumsden's Battery: Lt. A. C. Hargrove.

Gee's Battalion: Maj. James T. Gee

Perry's Battery: Capt. Thomas J. Perry; Phelan's Battery: Capt. John Phelan; Turner's Battery: Capt. William B. Turner; 1st Alabama Artillery (detachment): Lt. P. Lee Hammond.

Cobb's Battalion: Capt. Cuthbert H. Slocomb

Phillips' Battery: Capt. J. W. Phillips; Ritter's Battery: Capt. William L. Ritter; Slocomb's Battery: Lt. J. Adolph Chalaron.

Grayson's Battalion: Capt. John B. Grayson

Cowan's Battery: Capt. James J. Cowan; Culpeper's Battery: Lt. J. L. Moses; Tarrant's Battery: Capt. Edward Tarrant; Winston's Battery: Capt. William C. Winston.

Batteries, Etc.: Col. William E. Burnet

Battery McIntosh: Maj. W. C. Capers

1st Louisiana Artillery: Companies A and D; 1st Mississippi Artillery: Company L.

Battery Tilghman

Green's (Kentucky) Battery: Lt. H. S. Quisenberry.

Picket Fleet

1st Mississippi Artillery (4 company): Maj. Jeff L. Wofford.

Battery Gladden: Capt. Richard C. Bond

2nd Alabama Artillery: Companies C and E; 1st Louisiana Artillery: Companies B and G.

Battery Missouri: Capt. James Gibney

22nd Louisiana Regiment: Companies E and K; Holmes' light battery.

Battery Buchanan

Crew Gun-Boat Gaines: Capt. P. U. Murphy, CSN; 3rd Missouri Light Artillery: Lt. T. B. Catron.

The organization of troops in the District of the Gulf is listed in *ORA*, series I, vol. XLIX, part 1, pp. 1046–48. Maury's organization consisted of about 12,000 troops with some 6,000 under General Liddell on the Eastern Shore and the balance in and around Mobile and generally subject to his orders. Maury moved regiments and batteries around within the district to meet Federal threats, creating variations within the command structure.

Notes

Introduction

1. Patricia L. Faust, ed., *Historical Times Illustrated Encyclopedia of the Civil War* (New York, 1986), pp. 662–63, hereafter cited as Faust, *Historical Times*. Although many of Scott's subordinates considered him a superannuated bureaucrat and disregarded his advice, his strategy eventually proved to be fundamentally sound.

2. Gideon Welles, *Diary of Gideon Welles*, vol. 1 (Boston, 1911), pp. 84–85, hereafter cited as Welles, *Diary*. John Niven, *Gideon Welles: Lincoln's Secretary of War* (New York, 1973), pp. 389–90, hereafter cited as Niven, *Welles*.

3. James R. Soley, *The Blockade and the Cruisers* (New York, 1890), pp. 111–14, hereafter cited as Soley, *Blockade*.

4. Richard S. West, Jr., *Mr. Lincoln's Navy* (New York, 1957), p. 305, hereafter cited as West, *Mr. Lincoln's Navy*. Note: Galveston was occupied on October 5, 1862, by a naval force under Comdr. W. B. Renshaw, USN, and recaptured on January 1, 1863, by Gen. John B. Magruder (CSA) in a surprise attack. The Confederacy retained possession of the port until June 2, 1865.

5. United States Navy Department, *Official Records of the Union and Confederate Navies in the War of the Rebellion*, 30 vols. (Washington, D.C., 1906). Welles to Farragut, January 20, 1862, *ORN*, vol. I, series 18, pp. 7–8, hereafter cited as *ORN*, with volume, series, and page shown as I, 18:7–8.

6. Farragut to Welles, September 8, 1862, ibid., p. 431. Guns had been mounted on the CSS *Florida*, but they could not be fired.

7. Hitchcock to Fox, July 31, 1862, and Farragut to Welles, August 20, 1862, *ORN*, I, 19:102–3, 164. Records state that the Confederates had two or three gunboats and the ram *Baltic*.

8. Faust, *Historical Times*, p. 86.

9. Welles, *Diary*, I:19.

10. Charles Lee Lewis, *Admiral Franklin Buchanan: Fearless Man of Action* (Baltimore, 1929), pp. 157–73, hereafter cited as Lewis, *Buchanan*.

11. Faust, *Historical Times*, p. 254. Unlike Buchanan, many biographies have been written about Farragut, but the best genealogical information is in Loyall Farragut's *The Life and Letters of David Glasgow Farragut, First Admiral of the United States Navy* (New York, 1879), hereafter cited as Loyall Farragut, *The Life*. Note: Virginia seceded on April 17, 1861.

12. Charles Lee Lewis, *David Glasgow Farragut, Our First Admiral* (Annapolis, Md., 1943), p. 146, hereafter cited as Lewis, *Farragut*. Document located in Ellsworth Eliot, Jr., Collection, Farragut to his wife, October 10, 1862. Lewis's

work on Farragut remains the most thoroughly researched and documented biography on the life of the admiral.

13. Mallory to Buchanan, August 26, 1862, *ORN*, I, 7:62. On April 28, 1862, Buchanan had written Mallory suggesting that Commodore Josiah Tattnall's name, by virtue of seniority and years of close friendship, be placed at the head of the Admirals List. Mallory saw the fighter in Buchanan and could find no good reason to change his mind. Tattnall had been criticized for blowing up the *Virginia* to keep it out of Union hands and had only recently been exonerated by a court of inquiry.

14. Farragut to Butler, August 31, 1862, *ORN*, I, 19:172. As military governor of Louisiana, Butler earned the nickname "Beast" for his brutal administrative policies.

15. Welles to Farragut, August 19, 1862, *ORN*, I, 19:161–62.

16. The Grenada *Appeal*, July 28, 1862. Farragut Papers, September 15, 1862, ibid., pp. 105, 208.

17. Frank L. Owsley, *King Cotton Diplomacy* (Chicago, date not set), pp. 260, 389. Owsley covers blockade-running through Mobile on pages 238–39 and 251–57.

18. Farragut to Welles, September 8, 1862, *ORN*, I, 1:431.

19. Fox to Farragut, September 9, 1862, *ORN*, I, 19:184–85.

20. Farragut to Butler, September 26, 1862, *ORN*, I, 19:240.

21. Correspondence of Gustavus Vasa Fox, I, 318–20, Farragut to Fox, October 11, 1862.

22. Farragut to Butler, October 14 and 23, 1862, *ORN*, I, 19:300, 313.

23. Lincoln to Farragut, November 11, 1862, *ORN*, I, 19:342. Loyall Farragut, *The Life*, pp. 298–303.

24. Loyall Farragut, *The Life*, p. 297. Loyall remained with his father for several months before joining Adm. David D. Porter in the Mississippi Squadron.

25. Forney to Pemberton, October 18, 1862, *ORN*, I, 19:791. Forney to Cooper, October 18, 1862, United States War Department, *The War of the Rebellion: A Compilation of the Official Records of the Union and Confederate Armies* (Washington, D. C., 1886), series I, vol. 15, p. 833, hereafter cited as *ORA*.

26. J. Thomas Scharf, *History of the Confederate States Navy* (New York, 1886), p. 536, hereafter cited as Scharf, *History*.

27. Pemberton to Forney, December 14, 1862, *ORA*, I, 15:899.

28. Cooper to Buckner and Cooper to Maury, April 27, 1863, *ORA*, I, 15:1055–56.

Chapter 1

1. Faust, *Historical Times*, pp. 664–65.

2. Cooper to Maury, April 27, 1863, and Maury to Cooper, June 22, 1863, *ORA*, I, 15:1056;I, 26, pt. 2, p. 74.

3. Maury to Cooper, June 22, 1863, *ORA*, I, 26: pt. 2, p. 74. The *Alabama* referred to by Maury was a blockade-runner and not the famous commerce raider.

4. Loyall Farragut, *The Life*, p. 294.

5. Hitchcock memorandum to Jenkins, February 24, 1863, *ORN*, I, 19:627–28. At this time only the *Tennessee* and the two floating batteries were near enough complete to be towed from Selma to Mobile for completion. Another 15 months passed before the *Tennessee* took station on Mobile Bay.

6. Ibid. Ship's Island lay off the coast of Mississippi and served the Union navy as a small supply center.

7. Lewis, *Buchanan*, pp. 205–06. Among the officers assigned to the mission was Capt. Julius E. Meiere, Buchanan's son-in-law. See also *ORN*, I, 19:629, where Hitchcock reports that the *Alice* slipped out in the fog with five hundred bales of cotton.

8. Hitchcock to Jenkins, February 24, 1863, *ORN,* I, 19:628. Milton F. Perry, *Infernal Machines* (Baton Rouge, 1965), pp. 96–97, hereafter cited as Perry, *Infernal Machines.* Who deserves credit for dubbing submarines, mines, torpedoes, or any hidden explosive device as "infernal machines" is not known, but the first reference in the official records was made by Acting Master William Budd on July 8, 1861. See Budd to Rowan, July 8, 1861, *ORN,* I, 4:566–67. This crude device consisted of two barrels tied by a rope and floated down the Potomac River in the hope that the current would carry the explosives into a Union vessel. As the war progressed, torpedo and mine technology developed at a rapid rate and Mobile Bay eventually became a site for testing or using nearly every new improvement.

9. Maury Papers, Manuscript Division, Library of Congress. McClintock to Maury, vol. 46, undated, cited hereafter as Maury Papers. In 1879 a small submarine was discovered near New Orleans by a channel dredge whose crew pulled it ashore, but it lay in the mud for another generation. Eventually the submarine was cleaned up and placed on the bank of Bayou Teche at the Louisiana State Home for Confederate Veterans. Today the vessel can be seen in Jackson Square, New Orleans, outside the Louisiana State Museum. J. E. Kloeppel, writing for *Civil War Times Illustrated* in September 1989, states that the sub at Jackson Square is not *Pioneer* but a smaller experimental model possibly designed by another individual.

10. McClintock to Maury, no date, Maury Papers. W. A. Alexander, "Thrilling Chapter in the History of the Confederate States Navy. Work of the Submarine Boats," *Southern Historical Society Papers,* XXX (1902), p. 165, hereafter cited as Alexander, "Thrilling Chapter." Gordon Levey, "Torpedo Boats at Louisiana Soldier's Home," *Confederate Veteran,* XVII (1900), p. 459, hereafter cited as Levey, "Torpedo Boats." William Robinson, Jr., *The Confederate Privateers* (New Haven, 1928), pp. 174–6, hereafter cited as Robinson, *Confederate Privateers.* Perry, *Infernal Machines,* pp. 96–97. Although the name of the submarine is not positively known, other historians have referred to the vessel as *Pioneer II.*

11. Caldwell Delaney, *The Story of Mobile* (Mobile, 1981), pp. 124–25, hereafter cited as Delaney, *Story of Mobile.*

12. Alexander, "Thrilling Chapter," p. 167. Perry, *Infernal Machines,* pp. 98–99.

13. Hitchcock to Jenkins, March 3, 1863, *ORN,* I, 19:648. Hitchcock's memorandums worried his superiors and suggested that the commodore could not cope with his problems.

14. E. Willis, "Torpedoes and Torpedo Boats and Their Bold and Hazardous Expeditions" (Manuscript Division, Library of Congress); *ORN,* I, 15:332–35; Levey, "Torpedo Boats," p. 459; Robinson, *Confederate Privateers,* pp. 176–77; Perry, *Infernal Machines,* p. 99.

15. Hitchcock to Welles, March 25, 1863, *ORN,* I, 20:100.

16. Welles to Hitchcock, April 16, 1863, and Hitchcock to Welles, April 18 and 22, 1863, *ORN,* I, 20:141, 144, 145.

17. Faust, *Historical Times,* p. 314.

18. Goldsborough to Welles, March 25, 1863, April 24, 1863, and May 7, 1863, *ORN,* I, 20:99, 161, 171.

19. Goldsborough to Welles, May 8, 1863, *ORN,* I, 20:171. Note: Many Northern shippers continued to deal with the South and financed blockade-runners to deliver their goods. Huge profits were to be made in the trade, and the cost of the vessel could be recovered in one or two successful voyages.

20. Farragut to Marvin, May 20, 1863, ibid.

21. Statistical Data of U.S. Ships, *ORN,* II, 1:96.

22. Mayo to Goldsborough and Goldsborough to Farragut, May 15 and 18, 1863, *ORN,* I, 20:193–94, 277–78.

23. De Bow, Fenner, and Bensadon to Buchanan, May 20, 1863, ibid., pp. 826–27.

24. Farragut to Goldsborough, May 25, 1863, ibid., pp. 275–76. Note: Farragut's sister lived near Pascagoula and had frequently applied to her brother for favors. Despite the close relationship, Farragut remained unyielding even to close family members.

25. Dabney H. Maury, *Recollections of a Virginian in the Mexican, Indian and Civil War* (New York, 1897), pp. 193–94, hereafter cited as Maury, *Recollections*.

26. Farragut to Welles and General Orders No. 3 by W. D. Smith, May 22, 1863, *ORN*, I, 20:273. The cause of yellow fever had not yet been traced to mosquitoes.

27. Miller to Goldsborough, September 1, 1863; Bell to Goldsborough, September 3, 1863; Bell to Goldsborough, September 5, 1863, ibid. pp. 504–05, 509, 582–83.

28. Welles to Bell, Welles to Goldsborough, Welles to Jenkins, September 23, 1863, and Thatcher to Bell, September 24, 1863, all in ibid., pp. 600–01.

29. Bell to Welles and Thatcher to Bell, October 8 and 15, 1863, ibid., pp. 617, 628–29.

30. Farragut to Bell, July 29, 1863, ibid., pp. 424–25.

31. Bell to Farragut, December 4, 1863, ibid., p. 708.

Chapter 2

1. Abstract Statement of J. W. Porter to Rear Admiral Farragut, September 29, 1862, *ORN*, I, 19:198–200.

2. Ibid.

3. William N. Still, Jr., *Iron Afloat: The Story of the Confederate Ironclads* (University of South Carolina, 1989), p. 190, hereafter cited as Still, *Iron Afloat*.

4. Ibid.

5. Dabney H. Maury, *Southern Historical Society Papers*, vol. V, p. 4, hereafter cited as Maury, *SHSP*. Maurice Melton, *The Confederate Ironclads* (New York, 1968), p. 204, hereafter cited as Melton, *Confederate Ironclads*. Note: After Buchanan had been wounded during the battle between the *Virginia* (*Merrimack*) and the *Monitor*, Catesby ap Jones commanded the *Virginia* the second and last day of that battle.

6. Melton, *Confederate Ironclads*, p. 205. Note: McBlair had been associated with the building of the CSS *Arkansas*, which he later commanded without distinction.

7. Still, *Iron Afloat*, p. 190. Farrand was placed in charge of all shipbuilding in Alabama but reported to Buchanan. Farrand's orders from Mallory are located in the National Archives, Record Group 45 (on microfilm).

8. Survey report by Rear Adm. H. K. Thatcher, *ORN*, I, 22:225–26. In 1861 the Alabama state legislature funded an ironclad that is believed to be the *Nashville*.

9. Mallory to Davis, November 5, 1864, *ORN*, II, 2:744.

10. Still, *Iron Afloat*, p. 191, taken from Buchanan's Letterbook, October 15, 1862.

11. Ibid., n. 12, McRae to Harris, October 31, 1862, McRae Collection.

12. John L. Porter's report of vessels under construction, November 1, 1864, *ORN*, I, 21:600. Still, *Iron Afloat*, p. 192. National Archives, Record Group 45.

13. Several ironclad rams were under construction in Europe, utilizing the latest British and French technology. Only one vessel ever reached North America, the CSS *Stonewall*, but by then the war had ended.

14. Lewis, *Buchanan*, p. 208, n. 1.

15. Montgomery *Daily Advertiser*, March 8, 1863. Still, *Iron Afloat*, p. 193.

16. Lewis, *Buchanan*, p. 208, n. 2. James D. Johnston's address delivered before the Georgia Historical Society. Copy in National Archives, Record Group 45.

17. Johnson and Buel, eds., *Battles and Leaders*, "The Ram *Tennessee* at Mobile Bay," by James D. Johnston, vol. 4, p. 401, hereafter cited as Johnson, *B & L*. See also Delaney, *Story of Mobile*, p. 127. Several other descriptions exist describing the specifications of the *Tennessee*. Those used by the author are derived from authoritative sources.

18. Jones to Buchanan, December 17, 1863, *ORN*, I, 20:857.

19. Jones to Buchanan, December 24, 1863, ibid., p. 858.

20. Jones to Brooke, January 6, 1864, ibid., 21:858–59.

21. Walter W. Stephen, "The Brooke Guns at Selma," *Alabama Historical Quarterly*, XX (1958), 462–75.

22. Lewis, *Buchanan*, p. 217. From an address delivered to the Georgia Historical Society. Stephen, "The Brooke Guns at Selma," p. 465. Buchanan to Mallory, Buchanan Letterbook, October 1, 1863.

23. Statistical Data of Confederate Ships, *ORN*, II, 1:268. James M. Merrill, *The Rebel Shore: The Story of Union Sea Power in the Civil War* (Boston, 1957) p. 181, hereafter cited as Merrill, *Rebel Shore*. The Union navy appraised the value of the vessel at $883,000.

24. Maury, *SHSP*, V, p. 44; Still, *Iron Afloat*, pp. 191–92; Melton, *Confederate Ironclads*, p. 209; Lewis, *Buchanan*, p. 218. Note: After removing the engines from the *Alonzo Child*, the Confederates had sunk the vessel at Snyder's Bluff on the Yazoo as a river obstruction. There is some doubt that the *Tennessee*'s engines came from the *Alonzo Child*, since those engines were being removed at about the same time as the *Tennessee*'s were being installed. If so, it is not clear who provided the *Tennessee*'s machinery.

25. Buchanan to Mitchell, June 22, 1863, Mitchell Papers. Still, *Iron Afloat*, p. 197. A little later, and especially after the war, Buchanan gave high praise to his Tennesseeans.

26. Buchanan to Jones, May 7, 1864, *ORN*, I, 21:896–97.

27. Still, *Iron Afloat*, p. 193.

28. Buchanan to Mallory, September 20, 1863, Buchanan Letterbook. Buchanan to Mitchell, June 13, 1863, Mitchell Papers.

29. Ibid.

30. Buchanan to Mallory, October 1, 1863, Buchanan Letterbook; Buchanan to Farrand, December 1, 1863, National Archives, Record Group 45; Buchanan to Mitchell, January 26, 1864, Mitchell Papers; Still, *Iron Afloat*, p. 194.

31. Still, *Iron Afloat*, p. 93.

Chapter 3

1. Porter to Welles, December 17, 1862, *ORN*, I, 19:544–45.

2. Hitchcock to Jenkins, *ORN*, I, 19:629–33.

3. During the Civil War, all underwater exploding devices were called torpedoes or infernal machines. Technically, stationary or floating explosives were not torpedoes but varieties of mines. Explosives carried underwater by vessels were torpedoes. Because all underwater explosives were referred to as torpedoes during the Civil War, I have chosen to do the same.

4. Diana Fontaine Maury Corbin, *A Life of Matthew Fontaine Maury* (London, 1888), p. 192, hereafter cited as Corbin, *Maury*.

5. Richard L. Maury, "Notes by Colonel Richard L. Maury," *SHSP,* XXXI (1903), pp. 326–28. Corbin, *Maury,* pp. 189–201.

6. Tom H. Wells, *The Confederate Navy: A Study in Organization* (University, Ala., 1971), pp. 58–61, hereafter cited as Wells, *Confederate Navy.*

7. The most comprehensive work on torpedoes and mines is Perry, *Infernal Machines.*

8. W. R. King, *Torpedoes: Their Invention and Use, from the First Application to the Art of War to the Present Time* (Washington, D.C.: 1866), pp. 14–15, hereafter cited as King, *Torpedoes.* Royal B. Bradford, *History of Torpedo Warfare* (Newport, R.I., 1882), p. 52, hereafter cited as Bradford, *History.* Land mines with Rains fuses recovered near Mobile as late as 1960 were still considered dangerous.

9. J. S. Barnes, *Submarine Warfare* (New York, 1869), p. 63, hereafter cited as Barnes, *Submarine Warfare.* Bradford, *History,* p. 55. Perry, *Infernal Machines,* p. 38.

10. Bradford, *History,* p. 66. Barnes, *Submarine Warfare,* p. 69. King, *Torpedoes,* p. 10.

11. Caldwell to Farragut, January 19, 1863, *ORN,* I, 19:543–44. Although Caldwell did not know it, he had found a Brown-McDaniel-Ewing-Kennon torpedo, the design that had destroyed the *Cairo.*

12. Smith to Farragut, February 28, 1862, ibid., pp. 640–41.

13. Barnes, *Submarine Warfare,* pp. 71–73.

14. Buchanan to Harrison, May 25, 1863, *ORN,* I, 20:828. Ledbetter Report of Mobile Defenses, May 31, 1863, *ORA,* I, XXVI, pt. 2, pp. 226–28.

15. Ledbetter Report of Mobile Defenses for September 1863, *ORA,* I, XXVI, pt. 2, pp. 274–75.

16. Gray to Echols, April 16, 1864, *ORN,* I, 16:425. This cable had been purchased and shipped from London by Matthew Fontaine Maury.

17. Rains to Seddon, August 15, Barrett to Andrews, August 20, and Maury's endorsement, September 26, 1864, *ORN,* I, 21:567, 569–70.

18. Abstract log, USS *Gertrude,* *ORN,* I, 21:63–64. I cannot identify origin of this design from the description given.

19. Farragut to Welles, May 25, 1864, *ORN,* I, 21:298. There is no record of the *Tennessee* carrying a spar torpedo.

20. Perry, *Infernal Machines,* pp. 199–201. Perry's appendix lists all the Union vessels damaged by torpedoes by date, tonnage, location and severity.

Chapter 4

1. Scharf, *History,* pp. 551–52. Fort Morgan was built on the site once occupied by Fort Bowyer, which on September 15, 1814, repelled an attack by the British fleet. See Delaney, *Story of Mobile,* pp. 62–63. After French domination of Mobile Bay, the *e* was dropped from Dauphine Island.

2. Faust, *Historical Times,* p. 276. Delaney, *Story of Mobile,* pp. 111–13. After the war, Fort Morgan was refurbished and continued in military use for many years. Today it survives under the care of the National Park Service.

3. Moore to President James Buchanan, January 4, 1861, *ORA,* I, 1:327–30. Doris Rich, *Fort Morgan and the Battle of Mobile Bay* (Foley, Ala., 1972), p. 11, hereafter cited as Rich, *Fort Morgan.*

4. Faust, *Historical Times,* p. 360.

5. Ibid., p. 553.

6. Scharf, *History,* p. 552.

7. Jenkins to Welles, January 15, 1864, *ORN,* I, 21:35–36.

8. Hitchcock to Jenkins, February 25, 1863, *ORN,* I, 19:628–29.

9. Canby to Halleck, August 24, 1864, *ORN,* I, 21:539.

10. Mark M. Boatner, III, *The Civil War Dictionary* (New York, 1959), p. 13, hereafter cited as Boatner, *Dictionary.* Page to Maury and Maury to Seddon, August 8, 1864, *ORN,* I, 21:561–62. John Kent Folmar, ed., *From That Terrible Field: Civil War Letters of James M. Williams, Twenty-First Alabama Infantry Volunteers* (University, Ala., 1981), p. 169, hereafter cited as Folmar, *From That Terrible Field.*

11. Scharf, *History,* pp. 552–53. Pomeroy to de Krafft, August 6, 1864, *ORN,* I, 21:504–5. There is little consistency in the number of guns reported in each fort. See also Williams to Garner, August 7, 1864, in ibid., pp. 560–61. Canby claimed the capture of 18 guns, but his report does not coincide with de Krafft's inventory after the fort had been evacuated.

12. Myer to Farragut, July 9, 1864, *ORN,* I, 21:371–72.

13. Powell to Croom and Randolph to Forney, July 1 and 5, 1862, *ORA,* I, 15: 112–15, 116–17.

14. Williams to Garner and Maury to Seddon, August 7, 1862, *ORN,* I, 21:560–62. Folmar, *From That Terrible Field,* p. 136. Williams was reinstated and eventually returned to the 21st Alabama and commanded the regiment at Spanish Fort.

15. Jenkins to Bell, January 15, 1864, *ORN,* I, 21:34–36. Delaney, *Confederate Mobile* (Mobile, 1971), pp. 98–103, hereafter cited as Delaney, *Confederate Mobile.* This work consists of photographs and maps that show the exact locations of the various batteries.

16. Jenkins to Bell, ibid., p. 36. Delaney, *Confederate Mobile,* pp. 78–91, 110. See also Marchand to Farragut, February 18, 1864, *ORN,* I, 21:106–7, which summarizes information obtained from four deserters.

17. Marchand to Farragut, February 18, 1864, *ORN,* I, 21:105–6.

18. Farragut to Banks and Farragut to Welles, February 11 and 28, 1864, ibid., pp. 91–92, 96–97. Loyall Farragut, *The Life,* p. 392. Folmar, *From That Terrible Field,* pp. 128–29.

19. Maury to Seddon and Maury to Polk, February 15 and 20, 1864, *ORN,* I, 21:103–4, 104–05.

20. Maury to Seddon and Sims to Jones, February 15, 18, 19, and 20, and March 5 and 20, 1864, ibid., pp. 103–05, 880–81, 885–86.

21. Lieutenant Colonel Williams had difficulty with shells produced at Selma. Many either failed to explode or exploded prematurely. Williamson to Garner, *ORN,* I, 21:881.

Chapter 5

1. Mobile *Tribune,* April 10, 1863. Scharf, *History,* p. 537.

2. Ibid. See also extract of Secretary Mallory's report in *ORN,* I, 20:809.

3. Farragut to Watters, June 16, 1863, extract from Secretary Mallory's report, *ORN,* I, 20:302, 828. Scharf, *History,* pp. 538–39. Duke's mission may have been fitted out by Mobile citizen Junius Buttner.

4. Farragut to Commanding Officer, June 22, 1863, *ORN,* I, 20:308–09.

5. Bell to Macomb, August 22, 1863, Farragut to Jenkins, January 30, 1864, and Marchand to Farragut, February 18, 1864, *ORN,* I, 20:476–77 and 21:65, 106.

6. Buchanan to Baker, April 21, 1864, *ORN,* I, 21:915.

7. Scharf, *History,* p. 540.

8. Buchanan to Baker, April 20 and 21, 1864, *ORN*, I, 21:915. Scharf, *History*, pp. 540–41.

9. Baker to Buchanan, April 29, 1864, *ORN*, I, 21:916–17. Scharf, *History*, pp. 542–43.

10. Scharf, *History*, p. 543.

11. Mallory to Baker and Bragg to Mallory, September 26, 1864, *ORN*, I, 21:922.

12. Farrand to Baker, October 6, 1864, ibid., p. 923.

13. Baker to Mallory, November 1 and 9, 1864, ibid., pp. 925–26, 926–27.

14. Mallory to Baker, November 24, 1864, ibid., p. 928.

15. Garner to Moore and Maury to Moore, December 6 and 10, 1864, ibid., pp. 932, 933. See chapter 11.

16. Scharf, *History*, p. 545, n. 1.

17. Hitchcock to Jenkins, February 25, 1863, *ORN*, I, 19:631.

18. Buchanan to Swain, November 9, 1863, *ORN*, I, 20:848.

19. Bell to Thatcher and Bell to Greene, November 25, 1863, Bell's Report of Confederate Strength, December 1, 1863, and Marchand to Farragut, February 18, 1864, *ORN*, I, 20:696, 697, 705, and 21:106.

20. Still, *Iron Afloat*, p. 203; *ORN*, I, 21:935.

21. *Journal of Engineer John C. O'Connell, CSN, and Journal of Pvt. Charles Brother, USMC,* in *Two Naval Journals: 1864 at the Battle of Mobile Bay*, ed. C. Carter Smith, Jr. (Birmingham, 1864), p. 2, hereafter cited as *Two Naval Journals.*

22. Page to Jones, June 26, 1864, and log of the *Tennessee, ORN*, I, 21:903–4, 935. Lewis, *Buchanan*, p. 223. Still, *Iron Afloat*, p. 203.

Chapter 6

1. Farragut to Palmer, *ORN*, I, 20:77.

2. Farragut to Welles, May 12, 1863, ibid., pp. 179–80.

3. Loyall Farragut, *The Life*, p. 366.

4. Welles to Farragut and Farragut to Welles, May 12 and 28, 1863, ibid., pp. 182, 277.

5. Farragut to Porter, July 15, 1863, Farragut to Jenkins, July 20, 1863, Farragut to Bell, July 28 and 29, 1863, Bell to Weaver, August 15, 1863, Bell to Welles, August 19, 1863, ibid., pp. 393, 401, 423–24, 424–25, 461–62, 467–68.

6. Bell to Welles, August 19, 1863, and Bell to Mullany, August 22, 1863, Goldsborough to Bell, August 24, 1863, ibid., pp. 469, 475, 481.

7. Palmer to Welles, Farragut to Welles, August 10, 1863, ibid., pp. 442, 443. Loyall Farragut, *The Life*, pp. 384–85.

8. Farragut to Welles, October 6, 1863, Welles to Farragut, October 7, 1863, ibid., p. 613.

9. Farragut to Bell, October 15, 1863, ibid., pp. 629, 630. Correspondence of Gustavus Vasa Fox, I, pp. 337, 338.

10. Farragut to Welles, November 20, 1863, *ORN*, I, 20:691.

11. Farragut to Welles, January 5, 1864, Farragut to Drayton, February 7, 1864, and log of the *Hartford, ORN*, I, 21:14, 74, 796. Faust, *Historical Times*, p. 226. Loyall Farragut, *The Life*, p. 390.

12. Hurlbut to Welles, December 30, 1863, Welles to Farragut, January 2, 1864, *ORN*, I, 21:4–5.

13. Bell to Goldsborough, September 14, 1863, *ORN*, I, 20:590.

14. Bell to Welles, January 14, 1864, Bell to Porter, January 15, 1864, *ORN*, I, 21:31–32.

15. Farragut to Welles, January 20, 1864, ibid., p. 45. Correspondence of Gustavus Vasa Fox, I, pp. 341–42.

16. Farragut to Porter, January 17, 1864, Farragut to Welles, January 20, 1864, *ORN*, I, 21:39–40, 45–46.

17. Jenkins' report on the defenses of Mobile, January 15, 1864, ibid., p. 35–36.

18. Bell to Farragut, January 18, 1864, Farragut to Welles, January 22, 1864, ibid., pp. 43, 52–53.

19. Letters of Capt. Percival Drayton, pp. 43–44. Farragut to Welles, *ORN*, I, 21:96–97.

20. Farragut to Jenkins, March 1, 1864, Farragut to Banks, March 2, 1864, Farragut to Palmer, March 6, 1864, Farragut to Welles, March 9, 1864, *ORN*, I, 21:98, 122, 127–28, 130–31. Loyall Farragut, *The Life*, pp. 392–93. Correspondence of Gustavus Vasa Fox, I, pp. 347–348.

21. Farragut to Welles, March 15, April 20, and May 3, 1864, and Farragut to Banks, May 6, 1864, *ORN*, I, 21:141, 196–97, 235–36, 244. Loyall Farragut, *The Life*, pp. 395–96.

22. Farragut to Welles, May 3, 1864, *ORN*, I, 21:242.

23. Farragut to Welles, May 9, 1864, ibid., pp. 267–68.

24. Farragut to Marchand, May 10, 1864, ibid., p. 270.

25. Drayton to Jenkins, May 13, 1864, ibid., pp. 273–74.

26. Johnson, *B & L*, p. 402. Farragut to Welles, May 17, 1864, Alden to Welles, May 22, 1864, and log of the *Tennessee*, *ORN*, I, 21:282–83, 293, 935. Lewis, *Farragut*, p. 243.

27. Farragut to Gibson, Farragut to Smith, May 21, 1864, *ORN*, I, 21:291. Loyall Farragut, *The Life*, p. 400. Farragut exaggerated Buchanan's strength. Buchanan had three wooden gunboats and the ram.

28. Farragut to Welles, May 25, 1864, Farragut to Bailey, May 26, 1864, *ORN*, I, 21:298, 299.

29. Welles to Nicholson, June 7, 1864, Welles to Farragut , June 25, 1864, ibid., pp. 323, 344.

30. Statistical Data of U.S. Ships, *ORN*, II, 1:133.

31. Ibid., pp. 133, 220–21. Welles to Farragut, June 25, 1864, p. 344.

32. Welles to Porter, June 9, 1864, *ORN*, I, 26:379–80.

33. Porter to Welles, June 13, 1864, Welles to Porter, June 25, 1864, ibid., pp. 388, 438. A known fact was Porter's envy of Farragut's feats. Some authorities speculate that Porter purposely withheld resources Farragut sorely needed. Porter had just returned from a military debacle on the Red River, giving credence to the opinion that he may have wished a disaster on Farragut.

34. Statistical Data of U.S. Ships, *ORN*, II, 1:56, 240.

35. Sherman to Canby, Sherman to Smith, *ORN*, I, 21:317. Sherman wrote from Allatoona Creek just prior to the battle of Kennesaw Mountain. His strategy coincided with General Grant's, who had proposed to attack Mobile after Vicksburg fell but was unable to obtain approval for the plan.

36. Order of Rear Admiral Farragut, June 14, 1863, ibid., p. 336.

37. Buchanan to Jones, June 14, 1864, ibid., p. 902.

38. Faust, *Historical Times*, p. 111. Drayton, Percival, *Naval Letters from Captain Percival Drayton, 1861–1865* (New York, 1906), pp. 58–60, hereafter cited as Drayton, *Letters*. Lewis, *Farragut*, p. 248.

39. Canby to Halleck, June 18, 1864, *ORN*, I, 21:339.

40. Farragut to Welles, July 15, 1864, and log of the *Hartford*, *ORN*, I, 21:374–75, 799. Drayton, *Letters*, pp. 63, 64. Lewis, *Farragut*, pp. 252–53.

41. Farragut to Welles, July 15, 1864, *ORN*, I, 21:374–75.

42. General Orders No. 10 from Farragut to commanders, July 12, 1864, *ORN*, I, 21:397–98.

43. Farragut to Palmer, ibid., pp. 378–79.

44. Canby to Sherman, July 20, 1864, Farragut to Canby, July 25, 1864, Farragut to Welles, July 26, 1864, Canby to Farragut, July 26, 1864, Canby to Farragut, July 29, 1864, ibid., pp. 380, 386, 387, 388, 390.

45. Farragut to Welles, July 26, 1864, Craven to Welles, July 29, 1864, Farragut to Welles, July 30, 1864. Log of the *Hartford*, ibid., pp. 387, 390, 799. Tunis A. M. Craven was Capt. Thomas T. Craven's younger brother. Thomas had served under Farragut on the Mississippi and captained the *Brooklyn*. After Thomas was promoted to commodore, Welles sent him to Europe to chase Confederate cruisers.

46. Faust, *Historical Times*, p. 191.

47. General Orders No. 11, Farragut to commaders, July 29, 1864, *ORN*, I, 21:398.

48. Fremaux to Maury, June 2, 1864, ibid., p. 900.

49. "Farragut and Mobile Bay — Personal Reminiscences," by Rear Adm. John C. Watson, USN, War Paper No. 98 in MOLLUS, Commandery of the District of Columbia. Also cited in Lewis, *Farragut*, p. 258.

50. Jones to Page, July 25, 1864, *ORN*, I, 21:908.

51. Loyall Farragut, *The Life*, p. 404.

52. Farragut to Smith and Farragut to Jenkins, August 1, 1864, Drayton to Jenkins, August 2, 1864, Farragut to Howison, August 3, 1864, Farragut to Jenkins, August 3, 1864, *ORN*, I, 21:395–96, 399–400, 401, 403.

53. Faust, *Historical Times*, p. 319. Farragut to Jenkins, August 2, 1864, *ORN*, I, 21:401.

54. Farragut to Jenkins, August 3, 1864, ibid., p. 403. Loyall Farragut, *The Life*, p. 405. Drayton, *Letters*, pp. 65, 66.

55. Farragut to Stevens, diagram of line of battle, and log of the *Oneida*, August 4, 1864, *ORN*, I, 21:404–05.

56. Loyall Farragut, *The Life*, pp. 405–06, also cited as in the Ellsworth Eliot, Jr., Collection in Lewis, *Farragut*, p. 463, n. 41.

Chapter 7

1. McAlester to Delafield, August 17, 1864, log of the *Hartford* and log of the *Manhattan*, August 5, 1864, *ORN*, I, 21:531–33, 799, 824. Loyall Farragut, *The Life*, p. 412. Lewis, *Farragut*, p. 263. Alfred T. Mahan, *Admiral Farragut* (New York and London, 1892), pp. 269, 270, hereafter cited as Mahan, *Farragut*.

2. Loyall Farragut, *The Life*, p. 413. Diagram of battle, Farragut to Welles, August 5 and August 12, 1864, *ORN*, I, 21:404, 405, 416–17, 422, 423.

3. Ibid.

4. Farragut to Welles, August 12, 1864, battle map of Mobile Bay, *ORN*, I, 21:416–17, 600. Loyall Farragut, *The Life*, 412. Lewis, *Farragut*, pp. 264, 464, n. 5, clarifying that Farragut was sipping coffee and not tea, as reported by his son Loyall.

5. Rear Adm. Henry Walke, *Naval Scenes and Reminiscences of the Civil War in the United States on the Southern and Western Waters* (New York, 1877), p. 429.

Rear Adm. Charles E. Clark, *My Fifty Years in the Navy* (Boston, 1917), p. 96. Lewis, *Farragut*, p. 264.

6. Farragut to Welles, August 12, and Kimberly to Drayton, August 8, 1864, log of the *Hartford*, log of the *Chickasaw*, and other related logs, *ORN*, I, 21:417, 428–29, 783, 786, 794, 799, 800, 804, 805, 808, 819–23, 824–28, 830–32, 835, 838, 839, 841, 844, 846–48, 852. Loyall Farragut, *The Life*, p. 414.

7. Foxhall A. Parker, *The Battle of Mobile Bay and the Capture of Forts Powell, Gaines, and Morgan* (Boston, 1878), first read as an address before the Military Historical Society of Massachusetts, December 10, 1877, p. 224, hereafter cited as Parker, *Mobile Bay*.

8. Loyall Farragut, *The Life*, pp. 414–15; Parker, *Mobile Bay*, p. 225. Johnson, *B & L*, IV, pp. 390, 407. J. Crittenden Watson letter of September 6, 1880, *Scribner's Monthly* (June 1881), XXII, p. 306; H. D. Baldwin, "Farragut in Mobile Bay, Recollections of One Who Took Part in the Battle," *Scribner's Monthly* (February 1877), XIII, p. 542. Lewis, *Farragut*, p. 265.

9. Ibid.

10. William F. Hutchinson, M.D., *The Bay Fight: A Sketch of the Battle of Mobile Bay* (Providence, 1879), p. 14. The author was the Acting Assistant Surgeon on the USS *Lackawanna*.

11. Parker, *Mobile Bay*, pp. 226–27.

12. Perkins to Farragut, August 7, 1864, *ORN*, I, 21:500–01. Mahan, *Farragut*, p. 276.

13. Loyall Farragut, *The Life*, pp. 415–16.

14. Alden to Farragut, August 6, 1864, Denicke to Marston, August 12, 1864, Marston to Christensen, August 10, 1864, *ORN*, I, 21:445, 507–08, 525–26. Johnson, *B & L*, IV, pp. 387–88. Lt. John C. Kinney, "An August Morning with Farragut," *Scribner's Monthly* (June 1881), XXII, pp. 199–208. Loyall Farragut, *The Life*, p. 416. Lewis, *Farragut*, p. 266.

15. Farragut to Stevens, August 4, 1864, *ORN*, I, 21:404. Alden had stopped the *Brooklyn* before the *Tecumseh* struck the torpedo.

16. Alden to Farragut, August 5, 1864, logs of the *Brooklyn, Hartford, Manhattan, Metacomet, Richmond, ORN*, I, 21:508, 783, 799–800, 824, 828, 846. Johnson, *B & L*, IV, pp. 388, 399, footnote. The various logs report different time for the sinking of the *Tecumseh*. The *Brooklyn* reports the sinking at 7:25 A.M.; the *Hartford* at 7:40 A.M.

17. Loyall Farragut, *The Life*. Parker, *Mobile Bay*, p. 227.

18. Alden to Farragut and Farragut to Alden, August 5, 1864, *ORN*, I, 21:508.

19. Johnston to Buchanan, August 13, 1864, *ORN*, I, 21:579. Parker, *Mobile Bay*, pp. 227–28. Johnson, *B & L*, IV, pp. 388, 403.

20. Johnson, *B & L*, pp. 388–89. Parker, *Mobile Bay*, p. 228. Loyall Farragut, *The Life*, p. 425. W. F. Hutchinson in *The Bay Fight: A Sketch of the Battle of Mobile Bay* (Providence, R.I., 1879), p. 18, states that Craven was partially out of the monitor when the pilot grasped him by the leg and cried, "Let me get out first, Captain, for God's sake; I have five little children!" Craven drew back, saying, "Go on, sir," gave up his place, and went down with the ship.

21. Jouett to Farragut, August 8, 1864, Langley and Cottrell to Farragut, August 6, 1864, Roster of Officers and Men of the *Tecumseh*, *ORN*, I, 21:442, 490–91, 492. Parker, *Mobile Bay*, p. 231. Lewis, *Farragut*, p. 268.

22. Johnson, *B & L*, IV, p. 408. Nashville *Daily Amercian*, September 13, 1877. Parker, *Mobile Bay*, p. 231.

23. Farragut to Alden, August 5, and Alden to Farragut, August 8, 1864, *ORN*, I, 21:508, 445.

24. Alden to Farragut, August 6, 1864, log of the *Brooklyn*, *ORN* I, 21:445–46, 783. Loyall Farragut, *The Life*, p. 416. Parker, *Mobile Bay*, pp. 229–30. Johnson, *B & L*, IV, pp. 389–91; Lewis, *Farragut*, pp. 268–69.

25. Johnson, *B & L*, IV, pp. 389–90.

26. Loyall Farragut, *The Life*, p. 544.

27. Johnson, *B & L*, IV, 390–91. Parker, *Mobile Bay*, p. 230. Loyall Farragut, *The Life*, pp. 416–17. There is no record of Farragut's quote in the Official Records. The earliest source seems to be Foxhall Parker. In Charles Lee Lewis' excellent biography of David Glasgow Farragut, his note 40 on page 469 lists many different variations to these famous words from a number of different sources.

28. Thom Williamson, Jr., *U.S. Naval Institute Proceedings* (November 1939), LXV, 1676. Williamson's statement may have been borrowed from Foxhall Parker, as Williamson was supposed to be on the *Manhattan* and Farragut was probably still in the rigging.

29. Clarence E. Macartney, *Mr. Lincoln's Admirals* (New York, 1956), pp. 68–69. In Farragut's official report, he never mentioned Alden's actions as cowardly, but he privately blamed himself for not putting the flagship in the lead.

30. Myer to Farragut, August 9, 11, and 13 and Farragut to Welles, August 12, 1864, *ORN*, I, 21:371, 372, 374, 417. Johnson, *B & L*, IV, pp. 391, 409. Daniel B. Conrad, "Capture of the C.S. Ram *Tennessee* in Mobile Bay, August, 1864," *Southern Historical Society Papers*, XIX, 81. Drayton *Letters*, pp. 67–68. Lewis, *Farragut*, p. 269.

31. Johnson, *B & L*, IV, p. 391. Conrad, "Ram *Tennessee*," 471. Parker, *Mobile Bay*, pp. 232–33. Lewis, *Farragut*, p. 270.

32. Scharf, *History*, p. 562, footnote. Lewis, *Buchanan*, pp. 230–31.

33. Alden to Farragut, *ORN*, I, 21:445.

34. Parker, *Mobile Bay*, p. 233.

35. Johnson, *B & L* IV, p. 393.

36. Ibid.

37. Alden to Farragut, August 6, 1864, and log of the *Brooklyn*, *ORN*, I, 21:445, 783.

38. Johnson, *B & L*, IV, p. 393. Log of the *Richmond*, p. 847.

39. Logs of the *Lackawanna, Monongahela*, and *Kennebec*, *ORN*, I, 21:808, 831, 806. Lewis, *Buchanan*, pp. 231, 232.

40. Huntington to Farragut, August 6, 1864, and logs of the *Galena, Ossipee*, and *Oneida*, *ORN*, I, 21:479, 794, 838, 841. Lewis, *Farragut*, p. 271.

41. Farragut to Welles, August 12, and Jouett to Farragut, August 8, 1864, and logs of the *Hartford* and *Metacomet*, *ORN*, I, 21:417, 442, 800, 828. Parker, *Mobile Bay*, p. 234. Lewis, *Buchanan*, pp. 232–33.

42. Bennett to Mallory, August 8, and December 23, 1864, *ORN*, I, 21:588–90, 591–92.

43. Harrison to Mallory, August 10, and Harrison to Buchanan, October 1, 1864. Logs of the *Kennebec* and *Port Royal*, *ORN*, I, 575, 583–85, 806, 844. Charleston *Mercury*, August 17, 1864.

44. Murphey to Buchanan, August 15, and Jouett to Farragut, August 8, 1864, *ORN*, I, 21:442–43, 587–88.

45. James M. Morgan and John P. Marquand, *Prince and Boatswain: Sea Tales from the Recollection of Rear Admiral Charles E. Clark* (Greenfield, Mass., 1915), see chapter on Jouett; Lewis, *Farragut*, p. 272.

46. Conrad, "Ram *Tennessee*," 81. Buchanan to Mallory, August 25, 1864, Johnson to Buchanan, August 13, 1864, *ORN*, I, 21:576, 579.
47. Page to Maury, August 6, 1864, ibid., pp. 557–58.
48. Page to Maury, August 6, and Whiting to Maury, October 4, 1864, *ORN*, I, 21:557–58, 598. Maury endorsement of Lt. F. S. Barrett's report, August 20, 1864, *ORA*, I, 39, pt. 2, pp. 786–87. Johnson, *B & L*, IV, p. 409. Lewis, *Farragut*, p. 272.
49. Mahan, *Farragut*, pp. 288–89.

Chapter 8

1. *Two Naval Journals*, p. 6.
2. Loyall Farragut, *The Life*, p. 422. Conrad, "Ram *Tennessee*," pp. 45–75.
3. Conrad, "Ram *Tennessee*," p. 76. Lewis, *Buchanan*, p. 234.
4. Ibid., p. 75.
5. Ibid., p. 80. See also Dr. Conrad's "What a Fleet Surgeon Saw of the Fight in Mobile Bay," *The United Service: A Monthly Review of Military and Naval Affairs* (September 1892), VII, pp. 261–70. (*Merrimack* is often spelled *Merrimac*.)
6. Johnson, *B & L*, IV, pp. 394–95.
7. Lewis, *Farragut*, p. 274, cites the notebook of Farragut in manuscript, owned by George T. Keating. Mahan, *Farragut*, p. 281, states that Farragut said to Drayton: "As soon as the people have had their breakfasts, I am going for her."
8. Johnson, *B & L*, IV, p. 407.
9. Log of the *Monongahela*, Farragut to Alden, August 5, 1864, *ORN*, I, 21:509, 831. Loyall Farragut, *The Life*, p. 424.
10. Mahan, *Farragut*, p. 285, quoted from Palmer's diary.
11. Johnson, *B & L*, IV, p. 395. Farragut to Welles, August 12, 1864, *ORN*, I, 21:418.
12. Parker, *Mobile Bay*, p. 235.
13. Batcheller to Strong, August 5, Strong to Farragut, August 6, Farragut to Welles, August 12, 1864, Buchanan to Mallory, August 25, 1864, and log of the *Monongahela*, *ORN*, I, 21:418, 472, 473, 577, 831. Parker, *Mobile Bay*, p. 235.
14. Marchand to Farragut and enclosed damage report, August 5, Farragut to Welles, August 12, 1864, and log of the *Lackawanna*, *ORN* I, 21:418, 465–66, 466–67, 808.
15. Mahan, *Farragut*, p. 272. Johnson, *B & L*, IV, p. 407. Watson, MOLLUS, December 16, 1916, No. 98. Lewis, *Farragut*, p. 276.
16. Johnson, *B & L*, IV, p. 396. Kinney, *Scribner's Monthly*, XXII (June 1881).
17. Johnson, *B & L*, IV, p. 396. Lewis, *Farragut*, p. 276.
18. Drayton to Farragut, August 6, 1864, *ORN*, I:21:426; Johnson, *B & L*, IV, p. 396. Macartney, *Mr Lincoln's Admirals*, p. 72.
19. Conrad, "What a Fleet Surgeon Saw," p. 265; Lewis, *Farragut*, p. 276.
20. Marchand to Farragut, August 5, and Farragut to Welles, August 12, 1864, ibid., pp. 418, 466.
21. Loyall Farragut, *The Life*, p. 426.
22. Johnson, *B & L*, IV, 397.
23. Ibid.
24. Conrad, "Ram *Tennessee*," p. 76.
25. Parker, *Mobile Bay*, p. 236. Farragut to Welles, August 12 and September 27, Nicholson to Farragut, August 6, 1864, *ORN*, I, 21:418, 493, 664; Lewis, *Buchanan*, pp. 235–36.
26. Perkins to Farragut, October 13, 1864, *ORN*, I, 21:681.

27. Conrad, "Ram *Tennessee*," pp. 76–77. Johnson, *B & L*, IV, p. 404.

28. Ibid., pp. 77–78, 82. Buchanan had been wounded by a fragment of iron, either a piece of solid shot, or part of the plating of the ram, which fractured the large bone of the leg, comminuting it, and the splintered ends protruded through the muscles and the skin.

29. Johnson, *B & L*, IV, p. 404. Because the *Hartford* struck the ram on the port bow, the vessel reported by Johnston was probably the *Lackawanna*, which struck amidships, and not the flagship.

30. Conrad, "Ram *Tennessee*," p. 78. Lewis, *Buchanan*, p. 238.

31. Johnson, *B & L*, IV, pp. 398, 404.

32. Johnson to Buchanan, August 13, 1864, *ORN*, I, 21:580–81. See also Johnston, *B & L*, IV, p. 404, where Johnston gives a slightly different account of the surrender.

33. Johnson, *B & L*, IV, p. 404. Le Roy to Farragut, August 6, 1864, *ORN*, I, 21:475–76. Lewis, *Farragut*, p. 472, n. 27, quotes Adm. Charles E. Clark, USN, as follows: "Le Roy . . . was a perfect example of a gentleman of the old school. Once, when he was about to ram an enemy's ship, an officer remarked to another standing near him: 'There goes Lord Chesterfield at the Reb. I'll wager he's getting ready to apologize now for being obliged to hit him so hard.'"

34. Buchanan to Mallory, August 25, and postscript dated September 17, Farragut to Welles, August 12, Perkins to Farragut, August 7, 1864, and logs of the *Ossipee* and *Hartford*, *ORN*, I, 21:578, 418, 500–501, 842, 800.

35. Conrad, "What a Fleet Surgeon Saw," p. 267. The flag of the *Tennessee* is in the Naval Historical Foundation, Navy Department, donated by Mrs. Larz Anderson, daughter of Commodore George H. Perkins. Buchanan's sword was presented to the U.S. Naval Academy Museum on May 10, 1924, by Ensign Franklin Buchanan Sullivan, USN.

36. Johnson, *B & L*, IV, pp. 404–5.

37. Conrad, "What a Fleet Surgeon Saw," p. 267.

38. Loyall Farragut, *The Life*, p. 427, quotes directly from the diary of Surgeon Palmer.

39. Ibid., pp. 427–28, see also footnote.

40. Farragut to Welles, Farragut to Page, Page to Farragut, August 5, 1864, log of the *Metacomet*, *ORN*, I, 21:406, 424, 425, 828.

41. James M. Morgan and John P. Marquand, *Prince and Boatswain: Sea Tales from the Recollection of Rear Admiral Charles E. Clark* (Greenfield, MA, 1915), p. 105, hereafter cited as Morgan and Marquand, *Prince and Boatswain*, p. 105. Lewis, *Farragut*, p. 280.

42. Buchanan to Mallory, with enclosure from Surgeon Conrad, August 25, 1864, *ORN*, I, 21:578–79. Lewis, *Buchanan*, p. 239.

43. Bennett to Mallory, August 8, 1864, *ORN*, I, 21:590.

44. Harrison to Buchanan, October 1, 1864, ibid., pp. 584–85.

45. Farragut to Welles, August 8, 1864, *ORN*, I, 21:406–07. Lewis, *Farragut*, p. 280, n. 37. Johnson, *B & L*, IV, pp. 399, editor's note. For details of Union losses by vessel, see *ORN*, I, 21:406–13.

46. Farragut to Welles, August 8, and Drayton to Farragut, August 6, 1864, *ORN*, I, 21:406–07, 425–28.

47. Burcham to Drayton, August 8, 1864, ibid., pp. 433–34.

48. Thomas to Lull, August 5, 1864, ibid., pp. 449–50.

49. Ibid., passim. A brief summary report of damages also appears in Lewis, *Buchanan*, pp. 239–40, and Lewis, *Farragut*, pp. 280–81.

50. Jenkins et al. to Farragut, August 13, 1864, *ORN*, I, 21:547–50.

51. Palmer et al. to Farragut, September 12, 1864, ibid., pp. 550–51 and passim. Statistical Data of Confederate Ships, *ORN*, II, 1:268.

52. Granger to Canby, August 5, 1864, *ORN*, I, 21:520.

53. Parker, *Mobile Bay*, pp. 234–35.

54. F. T. Miller and James Barnes, *Photographic History of the Civil War*, vol. VI, p. 149.

55. Mahan, *Farragut*, p. 288. Early in his naval career Midshipman Farragut had served under Capt. David Porter on the U.S. frigate *Essex*, the most famous Union commerce raider in the War of 1812. The *Essex* was finally captured by two British frigates after a bloody engagement.

56. Farragut to Welles, August 12, 1864, *ORN*, I, 21:416.

57. Conrad, "Ram *Tennessee*," p. 80. Granger's total force numbered about 2,400.

58. Loyall Farragut, *The Life*, pp. 422–23.

59. General Orders No. 12, *ORN*, I, 21:438.

60. Macartney, *Mr. Lincoln's Admirals*, pp. 74–75.

61. Butler to Lincoln, August 8, 1864, *ORN*, I, 21:440.

62. Welles, *Diary*, vol. 2, p. 100.

63. Welles to Farragut, August 15, 1864, ibid., pp. 542–43.

64. Lincoln's message, order, and proclamation were issued on September 3, 1864, and jointly included the victories at Mobile Bay by Farragut and Canby and the surrender of Atlanta to General Sherman, ibid., pp. 543–44.

Chapter 9

1. Maury to Seddon, August 5, 1864, *ORN*, I, 21:556.

2. Gilmer to Maury, August 5, 1864, ibid., pp. 556–57.

3. Davis to Maury, August 5, 1864, ibid., p. 557.

4. Farragut to de Krafft, July 28, 1864, *ORN*, I, 21:388.

5. De Krafft to Farragut, August 6, 1864, ibid., pp. 502–03.

6. Perkins to Farragut, August 7, 1864, log of the *Chickasaw*, Williams to Garner, August 7, 1864, ibid., pp. 500–01, 560, 786–87.

7. Williams to Garner, August 7, 1864, ibid., p. 560.

8. Ibid., pp. 560–61.

9. Maury endorsement, August 8, Maury to Cooper, August 9, and Maury to Seddon, August 12, 1864, ibid., pp. 561, 564, 566. Williams was later reinstated and commanded the 21st Alabama at Spanish Fort.

10. Maury to Cooper, August 9, 1864, ibid., p. 564. The Official Records do not contain an actual copy of this order.

11. Maury to Seddon, August 7, and Page to Maury, August 8, 1864, ibid., pp. 559, 561.

12. Page to Maury, August 8, 1864, ibid., p. 561.

13. Maury to Seddon, August 8, 1864, ibid., pp. 561–62.

14. Ibid., August 9, 1864, p. 558.

15. Log of the *Hartford*, ibid., p. 801.

16. De Krafft to Farragut, and Pomeroy to de Krafft, August 6, Canby to Halleck, August 9, 1864, ibid., pp. 503, 504–05, 524.

17. Canby to Halleck, August 6, and Granger to Christensen, August 5, 1864, ibid., pp. 519, 520.

18. Granger to Canby, August 5, 1864, ibid., pp. 520–21.

19. Perkins to Farragut, August 7, 1864, log of the *Chickasaw*, ibid., pp.

500–01, 787. Joseph T. Woods, *Services of the 96th Ohio Volunteers* (Toledo, 1874).

20. Farragut to Welles and Anderson to Farragut, August 8, 1864, ibid., p. 414.

21. Scharf, *History*, claims that Farragut invited Anderson to come on board the *Hartford* with the purpose of persuading the colonel to surrender. There is no evidence to support this claim.

22. Farragut and Granger to Anderson, August 7, 1864, ibid., p. 415.

23. Scharf, *History*, pp. 584–85. Farragut to Welles, August 12, 1864, log of the *Hartford, ORN*, I, 21:414, 801.

24. Granger to Christensen and Farragut to Welles, August 8, 1864, log of the *Hartford, ORN*, I, 21:524–25, 414, 801. Confederate officers had the option of surrendering their swords to either branch of the service; all but one presented them to Drayton of the navy.

25. Maury to Seddon, August 12, 1864, ibid., p. 566. William H. Bentley, *History of the 77th Illinois Volunteer Infantry* (Peoria, Ill., 1883), p. 323, hereafter cited as Bentley, *77th Illinois*.

26. Ibid.

27. Farragut to Canby, August 9, 1864.

28. Maury to Cooper, August 9, 1864, ibid., pp. 563–64.

29. Farragut to Canby, August 16, 1864, ibid., pp. 529–30.

30. Farragut and Granger to Page, August 30, 1864, log of the *Hartford*, ibid., pp. 572–73, 801. Johnson, *B & L*, IV, p. 409. Scharf, *History*, p. 585.

31. Page to Farragut and Granger, August 9, 1864, *ORN*, I, 21:563. Johnson, *B & L*, IV, p. 409.

32. Johnson, *B & L*, IV, p. 409.

33. Ibid., p. 410. Page to Maury, August 30, 1864, Farragut to Welles, August 23, 1864, and log of the *Hartford, ORN*, I, 21:573, 802.

34. Log of the *Hartford, ORN*, I, 21:802; Lewis, *Farragut*, p. 288, n. 33, quotes Farragut's diary, owned by George T. Keating.

35. Page to Maury, August 30, 1864, log of the *Manhattan, ORN*, I, 21:826.

36. Loyall Farragut, *The Life*, p. 463.

37. Lurton D. Ingersoll, *Iowa and the Rebellion* (Philadelphia, 1867), pp. 634–35, hereafter cited as Ingersoll, *Iowa Infantry*.

38. Ibid., p. 635.

39. Page to Maury, August 30, 1864, *ORN*, I, 21:573.

40. Farragut to Welles, August 23, 1864, *ORN*, I, 21:535.

41. Ingersoll, *Iowa Infantry*, p. 635.

42. Farragut to Welles, August 23, Page to Maury, August 30, 1864, log of the *Hartford, ORN*, I, 21:535–36, 573–74, 802; Johnson, *B & L*, IV, p. 410; Loyall Farragut, *The Life*, p. 467.

43. Page to Maury, August 30, 1864, *ORN*, I, 21:574. Johnson, *B & L*, IV, p. 410.

44. Drayton and Arnold to Page and Page to Drayton and Arnold, August 23, 1864, log of the *Hartford*, ibid., pp. 537, 538, 803. Ingersoll, *Iowa Infantry*, p. 635. In Johnson, *B & L*, IV, p. 410, the general writes that he displayed the white flag at 6:00 A.M. It is quite possible that the flag was not seen by Union forces or reported to higher authorities until 6:30 A.M. Bentley, *77th Illinois*, p. 324.

45. Page to Maury, August 30, and Canby to Halleck, August 24, 1864, *ORN*, I, 21; and Johnson, *B & L*, IV, p. 409, refers to a garrison of "400 effectives." Other accounts range from 600 prisoners to 780. See *ORA*, I, 39, pt. 1, pp. 404, 419–20,

439; and Johnson, *B & L*, IV, p. 400, statistics. Charles Stewart Papers, Civil War Times Illustrated Collection, Carlisle Barracks.

46. Farragut to Welles, August 25, 1864, *ORN*, I, 21:536. Joseph T. Woods, *Services of the 96th Ohio Volunteers* (Toledo, 1874), pp. 93–94, hereafter cited as Woods, *96th Ohio.*

47. Farragut to Canby, August 26, 1864, ibid., pp. 541–42.

48. Lewis, *Farragut*, p. 290, note 48, cites Farragut's notebook, owned by George T. Keating.

49. Commission's report, *ORA*, I, 39, pt. 1, p. 405.

50. Proclamation by Lincoln, September 3, Welles to Farragut, September 5, and Farragut to Granger, September 19, 1864, *ORN*, I, 21:544, 545.

51. C. S. Alden, *George H. Perkins, USN, His Life and Letters* (Boston, 1914), pp. 202–3. Lewis, *Farragut*, pp. 290–91.

52. Farragut to Welles, August 27, 1864, *ORN*, I, 21:612.

53. Farragut to Canby, September 5, 1864, ibid., p. 626.

54. Farragut to Welles, September 19, 1864, ibid., pp. 545–46.

55. Welles, *Diary*, vol. 2, pp. 124, 127–28.

56. Welles to Farragut, September 5, 1864, Naval Records and Library, Navy Department.

57. Correspondence of Gustavus Vasa Fox, I, pp. 345–51; Lewis, *Farragut*, p. 300.

58. Welles, *Diary*, vol. 2, p. 232.

59. Canby to Farragut, October 28, 1864, *ORN*, I, 21:718.

60. Sherman to Grant, November 3, 1864, ibid., p. 719.

61. Welles to Farragut, November 9, and Farragut to Welles, November 22, 1864, ibid., pp. 724, 735.

62. Maury's Report, Mobile *Times*, March 11, 1866. C. C. Andrews, *History of the Campaign of Mobile* (New York, 1867), p. 20, hereafter cited as Andrews, *Mobile.*

Chapter 10

1. Scharf, *History*, p. 592.

2. Farragut to Welles, August 16, and Butler to Fox, August 17, 1864, *ORN*, I, 21:529, 530. Scharf, pp. 592, 593. Richmond *Sentinel*, August 17, 1864.

3. Wiggin to Farragut, September 13, 1864, *ORN*, I, 21:634.

4. Wiggin to Farragut, September 13, Stone to Durgin, September 11 and 13, 1864, ibid., pp. 634, 635, 636, 637.

5. Maury to S. D. Lee and Maury to Seddon, July 9, 1864, *ORA*, I, 39, pt. 2, pp. 697, 698.

6. Sheliha to Rives, July 9, and Lee to Bragg and Maury to Lee, July 9, 10, and 11, 1864, ibid., pp. 698, 700, 703.

7. Withers to Cooper, July 14, 1864, ibid., p. 712.

8. Maury to Cooper, July 19, 1864, ibid., p. 719. Folmar, *From That Terrible Field*, p. 146.

9. Davis to Bragg, July 20, 1864, ibid., p. 720.

10. Maury to Liddell, August 5, Maury to Seddon, August 7, 1864, ibid., pp. 755, 764.

11. Maury to Cooper, August 13, 1864, ibid., pp. 773–74.

12. Watts to Maury, August 16, 1864, ibid., p. 780.

13. Maury to Seddon, August 19, 1864, ibid., p. 782.

14. Maury to Davis and Maury to Watts, August 28 and Davis to Maury, September 2, 1864, ibid., pp. 801, 802, 812.

15. Maury to Gorgas, November 17, 1864, ibid., p. 821 and passim.
16. Sheilha to Lockett, November 20, and Maury to Watts, November 23, 1864, *ORA*, I, 45, pt. 1, pp. 1230, 1241.
17. Sheliha to Lockett, November 20 and 28, 1864, ibid., pp. 1230–31, 1249–51.
18. McPherson to Sawyer, March 16, 1864, Tate to Polk, March 8, 1864, *ORA*, I, 32, pt. 1, pp. 211–13, 344–45.
19. Maury to Watts, Brent, Adams, and Liddell, December 1, 1864, *ORA*, I, 45, pt. 2, pp. 630, 631.
20. Grierson to Harris, January 14, 1865, *ORA*, I, 45, pt. 1, pp. 844–47, passim. Canby to Halleck, January 8, 1865, *ORA*, I, 41, pt. 2, p. 998, passim. Maury to Gardner, December 3, 1864, *ORA*, I, 45, pt. 2, p. 645.
21. Bertram to Montgomery and Granger to Canby, December 22–23, 1864, *ORA*, I, 45, pt. 1, p. 843. Bertram's statement of enemy strength was grossly exaggerated.
22. Davidson to Christensen, December 13, and Maury to Cooper, December 15, 1864, ibid., pp. 787–89, 789–90.
23. Sheliha's Weekly Reports, December 18 and 25, 1864, *ORA*, I, 45, pt. 2, pp. 707–8, 734–35.
24. Taylor to Brent, January 23, 1865, *ORA*, I, 49, pt. 1, p. 929.
25. Beauregard's Special Field Orders and Hood's farewell address, January 23, 1865, ibid., p. 805.
26. Faust, *Historical Times*, pp. 743–44.
27. Bullock to Maury, January 31, Taylor to Davis and Taylor to Maury, February 1 and 4, 1864, *ORA*, I, 39, pt. 1, pp. 947, 949, 951, 955.
28. Richard Taylor, *Destruction and Reconstruction* (New York, 1879), pp. 207, 218, hereafter cited as Taylor, *Destruction*.

Chapter 11

1. Thomas to Rawlins, June 1, Grant to Halleck and Halleck to Thomas and Allen and Canby, January 26, 1985, *ORA*, I, 39, pt. 1, pp. 342–43, 584, 593.
2. Canby's Official Report, June 1, 1865; Organization of Union Forces, ibid., pp. 92, 105–9. General Granger's Orders No. 1, February 25, 1865, ibid., p. 771.
3. Organization of troops in the District of the Gulf, ibid., pp. 1045–48. Nathaniel C. Hughes, ed., *Liddell's Record: St. John Richardson Liddell, Brigadier General, CSA, Staff Officer and Brigade Commander, Army of Tennessee* (Dayton, 1985) p. 189, hereafter cited as *Liddell's Record*.
4. Deas to Maury, August 2, 1864, and War Department's Special Orders No. 187, *ORA*, I, 39, pt. 2, pp. 748, 767. *Liddell's Record*, p. 196. Faust, *Historical Times*, p. 438.
5. Andrews, *Mobile*, pp. 23–24.
6. Smith to Stanton and Halleck to Smith, February 8, 1865, *ORA*, I, 39, pt. 1, p. 669.
7. Ramsey to Smith and Wilson, February 2; Christensen to Smith, February 27, 1865, ibid., pp. 630, 780. Byron R. Abernethy, ed., *Private Elisha Stockwell, Jr., Sees the Civil War* (Norman, Okla., 1958), pp. 153–55, hereafter cited as Abernethy, *Private Stockwell*.
8. Abernethy, *Private Stockwell*, pp. 156–57.
9. Sketch of Spanish Fort and Fort Blakely, *ORA*, I, 39, pt. 1, pp. 145, 148, 213.
10. Steele to Christensen, April 12, 1865, ibid., p. 279. Andrews, *Mobile*, pp. 96–97.

11. Spurling to Lacey, March 27, 1865, *ORA*, I, 39, pt. 1, pp. 309–10.

12. Liddell to Maury, March 12, and Steele to Christensen, April 12, 1865, *ORA*, I, 39, pt. 1, pp. 279–80, 1052–53.

13. Steele to Christensen, ibid., pp. 280–81. Andrews, *Mobile*, pp. 107–10.

14. Steele to Christensen, April 17, 1865, ibid., pp. 279–82. Liddell to Armistead, March 25, 1865, ibid., pt. 2, p. 1154. Andrews, *Mobile*, pp. 116–20.

15. Benton to Emery, April 12, Veatch to Emery, April 13, Slack to Curtis, April 29, 1865, ibid., pt. 1, pp. 158, 160–61, 216–17.

16. Bernhardt-Campbell Family Papers, Carlisle Barracks Archives, March 21, 1865. Bernhardt's diary is written in German and translated into English. The diary contains numerous sketches made along the march.

17. Andrew F. Sperry, *History of the 33rd Iowa Infantry Volunteer Regiment* (Des Moines, 1866), hereafter cited as Sperry, *33rd Iowa*.

18. Benton to Emery, April 12, and Smith to Osterhaus, May 13, 1865, *ORA*, I, 39, pt. 1, pp. 216–17, 228. Andrews, *Mobile*, p. 35. Bentley, *77th Illinois*, p. 340.

19. Matthews to Massie, April 21, Van Anda and Hadley to Massie, April 20, 1865, *ORA*, I, 39, pt. 1, pp. 165, 169, 170. Andrews, *Mobile*, pp. 35–36.

20. Itinerary, XVI Army Corps, 1st Brigade, 3rd Division, *ORA*, I, 39, pt. 1, pp. 132–33. Andrews, *Mobile*, pp. 36–37. Wales W. Wood, *A History of the Ninety-Fifth Regiment Illinois Infantry Volunteers* (Chicago, 1865), pp. 163–69, hereafter cited as Wood, *95th Illinois*.

21. Granger to Christensen, April 24, and Smith to Osterhaus, May 13, 1865, *ORA*, I, 39, pt. 1, pp. 141, 228–29. Wood, *95th Illinois*, pp. 168–70.

22. Liddell to Spence, Lewis to Tutt, March 25, 1864, *ORA*, I, 39, pt. 2, pp. 1152–53, 1153–54.

23. Liddell to Spence and Liddell to Maury, March 25 and 26, 1865, ibid., pp. 1154, 1155, 1157.

24. Liddell to Gibson, Liddell to Maury, March 25 and 26, 1865, ibid., pp. 1153, 1157. Andrews, *Mobile*, pp. 45–47.

Chapter 12

1. Delaney, *Confederate Mobile,* pp. 304, 306, 307, 309. Some maps will show Spanish Fort on the Blakely River.

2. Ibid., p. 304. Old Spanish Fort had been built about 1780 by Spain for protection against the British, who at that time occupied Pensacola. Mobile then was part of Western Florida, a Spanish colony. Andrews, *Mobile*, pp. 48–49. Richard L. Howard, *History of the 124th Regiment Illinois Infantry* (Springfield, 1880), pp. 295–96, hereafter cited as Howard, *124th Illinois. Liddell's Record,* p. 183.

3. Gibson to Liddell, March 27, 1865, *ORA*, I, 39, pt. 2, pp. 1162, 1164. Abernethy, *Private Stockwell,* p. 161.

4. Gibson to Liddell, ibid., p. 1164.

5. Faust, *Historical Times,* p. 115.

6. Carr to Hough, April 9, Smith to Osterhaus, May 13, 1865, ibid., pt. 1, pp. 228–29, 267. Andrews, *Mobile*, pp. 50–52. Lieutenant Colonel Williams had once earned Maury's disapproval by blowing up and evacuating Fort Powell.

7. McArthur to Hough, April 12, Geddes to Wilson, April 9, Carr to Hough, April 9, 1865, *ORA*, I, 39, pt. 1, pp. 233, 267–68, 275. Andrews, *Mobile*, pp. 52–53.

8. Stephen E. Ambrose, ed., *A Wisconsin Boy in Dixie: The Selected Letters of James K. Newton* (Madison, Wis., 1961), hereafter cited as Ambrose, *Letters.* The

14th Wisconsin had fought at Shiloh, Vicksburg, Franklin, and Nashville and many lesser battles.

9. Carr to Hough, *ORA*, I, 39, pt. 1, p. 267.

10. Bradley to Hoover, Reed to Randall, April 12, Ginn to Randall, April 13, Smith to Osterhaus, May 13, 1865, *ORA*, I, 39, pt. 1, pp. 228–29, 244, 246, 247.

11. David W. Reed, *Campaigns and Battles of the Twelfth Regiment Iowa Veteran Volunteer Infantry* (Evanston, Ill., 1903), p. 228, hereafter cited as Reed, *12th Iowa*.

12. Day to Rouse, April 16, Grier to Rouse, April 11, Veatch to Emery and Benton to Emery, April 12, 1865, *ORA*, I, 39, pt. 1, pp. 156, 217, 220, 222.

13. Bertram to Emery, April 11, Bruce to Rockwell, April 14, Granger to Christensen, April 24, 1865, ibid., pp. 142, 206, 208.

14. Granger to Christensen, April 24, 1865, Smith to Osterhaus, May 13, 1865, ibid., pp. 142, 229.

15. By carefully counting the number of men actually within Spanish Fort at the time of Canby's investment, Gibson had about 2,700 effectives, and this number varied from day to day. See *ORA*, I, 39, pt. 1, pp. 313–19.

16. Faust, *Historical Times*, pp. 309–10.

17. Gibson to Flowerree, April 16, 1865, *ORA*, I, 39, pt. 1, pp. 314–15. Gibson to Liddell, March 27 and 28, 1865, ibid., pt. 2, pp. 1163, 1168.

18. Gibson to Flowerree, April 16, 1865, ibid., p. 314.

19. Smith to Osterhaus, May 13, 1865, ibid., pt. 1, p. 229. Liddell to Garner, May 29, 1865, ibid., pt. 2, p. 1173.

20. Abernethy, *Private Stockwell*, pp. 161–62.

21. Smith to Osterhaus, May 13, 1865, *ORA*, I, 39, pt. 1, p. 229.

22. Moore to Wilson, April 11, Blanden to Carter, April 15 and Ward to Wilson, April 14, 1865, ibid., pp. 270, 273, 274. Andrews, *Mobile*, pp. 62–63.

23. Eugene A. Carr Papers, Carlisle Barracks, April 1, 1865.

24. Day to Rouse, April 10, Benton to Emery, April 12, Holbrook to Washburn, April 17, and Krez to Rouse, April 15, 1865, *ORA*, I, 39, pt. 1, pp. 217, 222, 224, 227.

25. Gibson to Flowerree, April 16, Van Anda to Massie, April 11 and 20, 1865, ibid., pp. 167, 169, 314–15. Andrews, *Mobile*, pp. 66–67.

26. Thatcher to Welles, April 3, and Gillis to Thatcher, March 30, 1865, *ORN*, I, 22:70, 71.

27. Gillis to Thatcher, ibid., p. 71.

28. Liddell to Garner, March 28, 1865, *ORA*, I, 39, pt. 2, p. 1168.

29. Thatcher to Shook, March 30, 1865, *ORN*, I, 22:75.

30. Gamble to Thatcher, March 29, Gifford to Thatcher, April 4, 1865, ibid., pp. 72, 73.

31. Dyer to Thatcher, April 2, and Colby to Dyer, April 2, 1865, ibid., pp. 72–73, 74.

32. Palmer to Canby, March 30, Thatcher to Picket Boats, March 31, Thatcher and Simpson to Crosby, April 2, Canby to Thatcher, and Thatcher to Canby, April 4, Gill and Simpson to Crosby, April 9, 1865, ibid., pp. 75, 76, 78, 80, 81, 87–88.

33. Day to Rouse, April 10, 1865, *ORA*, I, 39, pt. 1, p. 222. Andrews, *Mobile*, pp. 74–76.

34. Howard, *124th Illinois*, pp. 300–02.

35. Gibson to Garner, March 31, 1865, *ORA*, I, 39, pt. 2, p. 1179. Burnet, a Texan, had responsibility for batteries not assigned directly to brigade commanders. Gibson and Burnet had been on a reconnaissance and for some reason, Burnet picked up a rifle, aimed it from behind the breastworks, and took a minié ball in the head.

36. Stearns to Sheldon, and Gibson to Flowerree, *ORA*, I, 39, pt. 1, pp. 224–25, 316.

37. Gibson to Garner, *ORA*, I, ibid., pt. 2, p. 1176.

38. Gibson to Flowerree, March 31, 1865, ibid., p. 1180. Gibson to Flowerree, April 16, 1865, ibid., pt. 1, p. 317.

39. Abernethy, *Private Stockwell*, pp. 166–67.

40. Reed, *12th Iowa*, p. 229.

41. Granger to Christensen, April 24, 1865, *ORA*, I, 39, pt. 1, p. 142.

42. Gibson to Clark, Liddell to Gibson, Gibson to Maury, April 1, 1865, ibid., pt. 2, pp. 1184, 1185, 1186, 1187.

Chapter 13

1. By road from the rear of Spanish Fort, Carr wrote that the marching distance to Fort Blakely was six miles. Carr Papers, April 1, 1865.

2. Steele to Christensen, April 17, 1865, *ORA*, I, 39, pt. 1, pp. 282–83.

3. Faust, *Historical Times*, p. 148.

4. Lewis to Winston, March 29, Lewis to McCown, March 31, and Lewis to Cockrell, April 1, 1865, *ORA*, I, 39, pt. 2, pp. 1178, 1181, 1188.

5. Spurling to Lacey, April 2, 1865, ibid., pt. 1, p. 311.

6. Itinerary, Pensacola Column, Veatch to Emery, April 13, and Steele to Christensen, April 17, 1865, ibid., pp. 136, 159, 283–84.

7. Drew to Ferguson, April 13, 1865, ibid., pp. 295–96.

8. Pile to Ferguson, April 13, 1865, ibid., p. 288.

9. Scofield to Ferguson, April 11, 1865, ibid., p. 290. Hawkins' Division consisted of about 5,000 infantry.

10. Andrews to Emery and Steele to Christensen, April 12, 1865, ibid., pp. 204, 282. Andrews commanded three brigades and normally reported to Granger. During the Mobile Campaign, his force was split. Bertram's 1st Brigade remained with Granger, but Andrews, along with Spicely's 2nd Brigade and Moore's 3rd Brigade joined Steele's Column.

11. Boatner, *Dictionary*, p. 16.

12. Andrews to Emery, April 12, Moore to Monroe, April 10, Spicely to Monroe, April 11, 1865, *ORA*, I, 39, pt. 1, pp. 204, 209, 215. Andrews, *Mobile*, p. 127.

13. Liddell to Maury and to Gibson, April 2, 1865, ibid., pt. 2, pp. 1190, 1191. Andrews, *Mobile*, pp. 128–29.

14. Steele to Christensen, April 17, 1865, *ORA*, I, 39, pt. 1, p. 283. Osterhaus to Smith, Smith to Canby, April 3, 1865, ibid., pt. 2, p. 209. Alfred J. Hill. *History of Company E of the Sixth Minnesota Regiment of Volunteer Infantry* (St. Paul, 1899), p. 32, hereafter cited as Hill, *6th Minnesota*.

15. Andrews to Emery, April 12, 1865, *ORA*, I, 59, pt. 1, p. 204. Andrews, *Mobile*, p. 171.

16. Andrews, *Mobile*, pp. 172–73.

17. Liddell to Myers, April 5, 1865, Liddell correspondence in Andrews, *Mobile*, p. 177. Liddell's correspondence is missing in the Official Records.

18. Murphy to Jackson, April 10, 1865, *ORA*, I, 39, pt. 1, pp. 262–63.

19. Gilbert to Sample, April 10, 1865, ibid., p. 255; Andrews, *Mobile*, p. 179.

20. Steele to Christensen, April 8, and April 17, 1865, *ORN*, I, 22:86, and *ORA*, I, 39, pt. 1, p. 283.

21. Andrews to Emery, April 12, 1865, *ORA*, I, 39, pt. 1, p. 205. Liddell to Maury, April 8, 1865, ibid., pt. 2, p. 1217.

Chapter 14

1. Andrews, *Mobile*, p. 147.
2. Gibson to Maury, April 7 and 8, 1865, *ORA*, I, 39, pt. 2, pp. 1215, 1217.
3. Gibson to Maury and Liddell, April 8, 1865, ibid., pp. 1217, 1218.
4. Canby to War Department, June 1, Granger to Christensen, April 24, and Smith to Osterhaus, May 13, 1865, ibid., pt. 1, pp. 96, 143, 229. Osterhaus to Granger, April 8, 1865, ibid., pt. 2, p. 281. Howard, *124th Illinois*, p. 304.
5. Geddes to Wilson and Bell to Henry, April 9, 1865, *ORA*, I, 39, pt. 1, pp. 275, 277–78. Howard, *124th Illinois*, pp. 305–6.
6. Bell to Henry, *ORA*, I, 39, pt. 1, p. 279, Andrews, *Mobile*, pp. 153–54.
7. Bell to Henry, *ORA*, I, 39, pt. 1, p. 278.
8. Ibid.
9. Ambrose, *Letters*, p. 150.
10. Bell to Henry, *ORA*, I, 39, pt. 1, p. 278. Howard, *124th Illinois*, pp. 306–07.
11. Ambrose, *Letters*, p. 151.
12. Woods, *96th Ohio*, pp. 117–18. Lee surrendered the following day, April 9, although the official surrender took place on April 12.
13. Bruce to Rockwell, April 14, 1865, *ORA*, I, 39, pt. 1, p. 208. Andrews, *Mobile*, p. 156.
14. Bell to Henry, April 9, Gibson to Flowerree, April 16, 1865, *ORA*, I, 39, pt. 1, pp. 278, 316–17.
15. Gibson to Flowerree, April 16, 1865, ibid., p. 317.
16. Andrews, *Mobile*, pp. 161–62.
17. Gibson to Flowerree, April 16, 1865, *ORA*, I, 39, pt. 1, p. 317.
18. Carr to Hough, April 9, Moore to Wilson, April 11, and Blanden to Carter, April 15, 1865, ibid., pp. 267–68, 271–72, 273–74. Ambrose, *Letters*, p. 151. Howard, *124th Illinois*, p. 307.
19. Williamson to Emery, April 12, 1865, *ORA*, I, 39, pt. 1, pp. 150–51.
20. Garrard to Hough, April 11, 1865, ibid., p. 248.
21. Ibid., pp. 248–49.
22. Andrews to Emery, April 12, 1865, ibid., p. 205. Andrews, *Mobile*, p. 192.
23. Liddell to Maury and Lewis to Cockrell, April 9, 1865, *ORA*, I, 39, pt. 2, pp. 1222–23.
24. Pile to Ferguson, April 13, 1865, ibid., p. 289.
25. Scofield to Ferguson, April 11, 1865, ibid., p. 291.
26. Drew to Ferguson, April 13, Densmore and Nye to Crandal, April 12, 1865, ibid., pp. 295–96, 297–98, 299.
27. Ibid.
28. Ibid.; Andrews, *Mobile*, pp. 198–99.
29. Hawkins to Lacey, April 16, Pile to Ferguson, April 13, Scofield to Ferguson, April 11, Gilchrist to Greene, April 13, and Drew to Ferguson, April 13, 1865, see also Medal of Honor awards, all in *ORA*, I, 39, pt. 1, pp. 287, 289–90, 291–92, 293–94, 295–96, 313. Leslie Anders, *The 21st Missouri from Home Guard to Union Regiment* (Westport, Mo., 1975), pp. 229–30.
30. Anders, *21st Missouri*, p. 229.
31. Andrews to Lacey, April 10, Spicely to Monroe, April 11, Busey to Lewis, April 11, 1865, *ORA*, I, 39, pt. 1, pp. 201–2, 209–10, 211. Andrews, *Mobile*, pp. 204–05.
32. Sears to Lewis, April 10, 1864, *ORA*, I, 39, pt. 1, pp. 214–15.
33. Andrews to Lacey, April 10, Andrews to Thomas, April 13, and Moore

to Monroe, April 10, 1865, ibid., pp. 201, 205–06, 215–16. Andrews, *Mobile*, pp. 207–9.

34. Andrews to Thomas, April 13, Spicely to Monroe, April 11, Vifquain to Lewis, April 10, 1865, *ORA*, I, 39, pt. 1, pp. 206, 209–10, 212–13, 313.

35. Veatch to Emery, April 18, Dennis to Curtis, April 10 and 22, Sheetz to Kuhn, April 10, 1865, ibid., pp. 157, 171–73, 173–76. Dennis states that the order to halt came from the "commanding general," which could have been either Veatch, Granger or Canby, but probably the former.

36. Garrard to Hough, April 11, Harris to Sample, April 10, Miller to Jackson, April 10, 1865, ibid., pp. 249–50, 261–62, 266. Andrews, *Mobile*, pp. 214–15.

37. Hill, *6th Minnesota*, p. 33.

38. Gilbert to Sample, April 10, Hills to Donnan, April 11, 1865, *ORA*, I, 39, pt. 1, pp. 255–56, 258–59.

39. Eberhardt to Donnan, April 11, 1865, ibid., p. 257.

40. Rinaker to Sample, April 11, Kinney to Sawyer, April 10, Best to Simpson, October 31, 1865, ibid., pp. 251–53, 254. Anders, *21st Missouri*, pp. 228, 230. *Liddell's Record*, p. 196.

41. Howard, *124th Illinois*, p. 310.

42. Canby to War Department, June 1, 1865, *ORA*, I, 39, pt. 1, pp. 98–99.

43. Hubbard to Randall, April 12, 1865, ibid., pp. 239–40. Byron C. Bryner, *Bugle Echoes, The Story of the Illinois 47th* (Springfield, Ill., 1905), p. 153.

44. Woods, *96th Ohio*, p. 123.

45. Canby to War Department, *ORA*, I, 39, pt. 1, p. 98. Thatcher to Welles, *ORN*, I, 22:92.

46. Ibid.

47. Sperry, *33rd Iowa*, pp. 153–54.

48. Canby to Christensen, April 24, and Slough to Granger and Thatcher, April 12, 1865, *ORA*, I, 39, pt. 1, pp. 143, 144–45. Delaney, *Story of Mobile*, p. 142. Sperry, *33rd Iowa*, p. 154.

49. Gibson to Spence, April 11, 1865, *ORA*, I, 39, pt. 2, p. 1225. Delaney, *Story of Mobile*, p. 141.

50. Flowerree to Spence, April 12, 1865, *ORA*, I, 39, pt. 2, pp. 1226–27.

51. Canby's General Field Orders No. 32, April 22, 1865, ibid., pt. 1, p. 101.

Chapter 15

1. Totten to Christensen and Christensen to Totten, March 28, 1865, *ORA*, I, 39, pt. 2, p. 114.

2. Andrews, *Mobile*, p. 225.

3. Gibson to Flowerree, April 14, 1865, ibid., pt. 2, pp. 315–16. Andrews, *Mobile*, p. 166.

4. Rinaker to Sample, April 11, and Kinney to Sawyer, April 10, 1865, *ORA*, I, 39, pt. 1, pp. 252, 253, passim.

5. Taylor, *Destruction*, p. 221.

6. *Liddell's Record*, p. 195.

7. Andrews, *Mobile*, p. 225.

8. Thatcher to Welles, April 15, 1865, *ORN*, I, 22:95–96.

9. Perry, *Infernal Machines*, pp. 199–201.

10. Thatcher to Welles, *ORN*, I, 22:95–96. Perry, *Infernal Machines*, pp. 199–201.

11. Maury to Cooper, January 26 and February 3, 1865, *ORN*, I, 22:267–68, 269. Delaney, *Confederate Mobile*, p. 132.

12. Surget to Adams and Forrest, March 23, and Taylor to Lee, March 27, 1865, *ORA*, I, 39, pt. 2, pp. 1146–47, 1160–61.

13. Surget to Maury, March 28, 1865, ibid., p. 1167.

14. Canby to War Department, June 1, 1865, ibid., pt. 1, pp. 92–93.

15. Return of Federal casualties, ibid., pp. 110–15. Andrews, *Mobile*, p. 220.

16. *Liddell's Record*, p. 195.

17. Ibid., p. 196.

18. Farragut to Welles, *ORN*, I, 21:407. Farragut did not have the returns from the *Tecumseh* at the time of his report and made no subsequent report. The men drowned were taken from the list of officers and crew stated on page 492, and from a subtraction made of the men rescued on page 490.

19. Macartney, *Mr. Lincoln's Admirals*, pp. 67–68.

20. Conrad casualty report to Buchanan, and Harrison to Mallory, August 9, 1864, *ORN*, I, 21:578–79.

21. Johnston to Buchanan, August 13, 1864, ibid., p. 581.

22. General Orders No. 54, surrender terms cosigned by Canby and Taylor, May 6, 1865, *ORA*, I, 39, pt. 2, pp. 1283–84.

23. Woods, *96th Ohio*, pp. 127–28.

24. Taylor, *Destruction*, p. 222. John Wilkes Booth shot President Lincoln at Ford's Theater; he died April 15, 1865.

25. Maury's farewell address, May 7, 1865, *ORA*, I, 39, pt. 2, p. 1287.

26. Maury, *Recollections*, p. 231.

27. Canby to Rawlins, May 26, 1865, *ORA*, I, 39, pt. 1, pp. 911–12.

28. Delaney, *Story of Mobile*, pp. 145–46.

29. Lewis, *Buchanan*, pp. 246–62.

30. Lewis, *Farragut*, pp. 297–365.

31. Loyall Farragut, *The Life*, p. 403.

32. Macartney, *Mr. Lincoln's Admirals*, p. 23. At 13 years of age, Midshipman Farragut served on the United States frigate *Essex* and fought the British frigates *Cherub* and *Phoebe* off Valparaiso during the War of 1812.

Bibliography

Books

Abernethy, Byron R., ed. *Private Elisha Stockwell, Jr., Sees the Civil War*. Norman: University of Oklahoma Press, 1958.

Acker, John W. *The Eagle Regiment, 8th Wisconsin Infantry Volunteers*. Belleville, Wis.: 1890.

Alden, C. S. *George H. Perkins, USN, His Life and Letters*. Boston: Houghton Mifflin, 1914.

Ambrose, Stephen E., ed. *A Wisconsin Boy in Dixie: The Selected Letters of James K. Newton*. Madison: University of Wisconsin Press, 1961.

Anders, Leslie. *The 21st Missouri from Home Guard to Union Regiment*. Westport, Mo.: Greenwood Press, 1975.

Andrews, C. C. *History of the Campaign of Mobile*. New York: Van Nostrand, 1867.

Barnes, J. D. *What I Saw You Did*. Port Byron, Ill.: Owen and Hall, n.d.

Barnes, J. S. *Submarine Warfare*. New York: Van Nostrand, 1869.

Barnes, James. *Farragut*. Boston: Small, Maynard & Co., 1899.

Barnes, John Sanford. *Submarine Warfare, Offensive and Defensive, Including a Discussion of the Offensive Torpedo System*. New York: Van Nostrand, 1869.

Barney, Chester. *Recollections of Field Service with the Twentieth Infantry Volunteers*. Davenport, Iowa: Pub. by author, 1865.

Beauregard, Peter G. T. *Annals of the War Written by Leading Participants North and South*. Philadelphia: Philadelphia Times Pub., 1879.

Belknap, Commodore Geo. E. "Letters of Captain Geo. Hamilton Perkins, USN." Concord, NH: Ira C. Evans, 1886.

Bentley, William H. *History of the 77th Illinois Volunteer Infantry*. Peoria: E. Hine, 1883.

Black, Robert C., III. *The Railroads of the Confederacy*. Chapel Hill: University of North Carolina Press, 1952.

Boatner, Mark M., III. *The Civil War Dictionary*. New York: David McKay Co., Inc., 1959.

Bradford, Royal B. *History of Torpedo Warfare*. Newport, R.I.: U.S. Torpedo Station, 1882.

Bryner, Byron C. *Bugle Echoes, The Story of the Illinois 47th*. Springfield, Ill.: Phillips Bros., 1905.

Burdette, Robert J. *The Drums of the 47th*. Indianapolis: Bobbs, Merrill Co., 1914.

Canfield, Eugene B. *Civil War Naval Ordnance*. Washington, D.C.: U.S. Government Printing Office, 1969.

Clark, Charles E., Rear Admiral, USN. *My Fifty Years in the Navy*. Boston: Little, Brown, 1917.

Cochran, Hamilton. *Blockade Runners of the Confederacy*. New York: Bobbs-Merrill Co., 1958.

Conway's All the World's Fighting Ships, 1860–1905. Conway Maritime Press, 1979.

Corbin, Diana Fontaine Maury. *A Life of Matthew Fontaine Maury*. London: S. Low, Marston, Searle & Rivington, 1888.

Crooke, George. *The Twenty-First Regiment of Iowa Volunteer Infantry*. Milwaukee: Vang, Fowle & Co., 1891.

Delaney, Caldwell. *Confederate Mobile*. Mobile: The Haunted Book Shop, 1971.

————. *The Story of Mobile*. Mobile: The Haunted Book Shop, 1981.

Drayton, Percival. *Naval Letters from Captain Percival Drayton, 1861–1865*. New York: New York Pubic Library Bulletin No. 10 (Nov.–Dec.), 1906.

Farragut, Loyall. *The Life and Letters of David Glasgow Farragut, First Admiral of the United States Navy*. New York: Appleton, 1879.

Faust, Patricia L., ed. *Historical Times Illustrated Encyclopedia of the Civil War*. New York: Harper & Row, 1986.

Fletcher, Samuel H. *The History of Company A, Second Illinois Cavalry*. Chicago: (unknown) 1912.

Folmar, John Kent, ed. *From That Terrible Field: Civil War Letters of James M. Williams, Twenty-First Alabama Infantry Volunteers*. University, Ala.: University of Alabama Press, 1981.

Foote, Shelby. *The Civil War, a Narrative: Fredricksburg to Meridian*. New York: Random House, 1963.

Fyfe, Herbert C. *Submarine Warfare Past and Present*. London: G. Richards, 1907.

Goodrow, Esther Marie. *Mobile During the Civil War*. Mobile: Historic Mobile Preservation Society, 1950.

Hill, Alfred J. *History of Company E of the Sixth Minnesota Regiment of Volunteer Infantry*. St. Paul: Pioneer Press Co., 1899.

Howard, Richard L. *History of the 124th Regiment Illinois Infantry*. Springfield: H. W. Rokker, 1880.

Hughes, Nathaniel C., ed. *Liddell's Record: St. John Richardson Liddell, Brigadier General, CSA, Staff Offices and Brigade Commander, Army of Tennessee*. Dayton: Morningside, 1985.

Hutchinson, W. F. *The Bay Fight: A Sketch of the Battle of Mobile Bay*. Providence: 1879. Read before the Rhode Island Soldiers and Sailors Historical Society.

Ingersoll, Lurton D. *Iowa and the Rebellion*. Philadelphia: J. B. Lippincott, 1867.

Johnson, Robert U., and Clarence C. Buel, eds. *Battles and Leaders of the Civil War*. New York: Century Co., 1884–88.

Jones, Thomas B. *Complete History of the 46th Illinois Volunteer Infantry*. Freeport: W. H. Wagner & Son's, 1907.

Jones, Virgil Carrington. *The Civil War at Sea*. 3 vols. New York: Holt, Rinehart and Winston, 1962.

King, W. R. *Torpedoes: Their Invention and Use, from the First Application to the Art of War to the Present Time*. Washington, D.C.: (unknown) 1866.

Lewis, Charles Lee. *Admiral Franklin Buchanan: Fearless Man of Action*. Baltimore: Norman, Remington Company, 1929.

————. *David Glasgow Farragut, Our First Admiral*. Annapolis: Naval Institute, 1943.

Little, George, and James R. Maxwell. *History of Lumsden's Battery, C.S.A.* Tuscaloosa: n.d. (circa 1905).

Macartney, Clarence E. *Mr. Lincoln's Admirals*. New York: Funk and Wagnalls Company, 1956.

Mahan, A. T. *Admiral Farragut.* New York: D. Appleton Co., 1892.
_____. *The Gulf and Inland Waters.* New York: Charles Scribner's Sons, 1883.
Marshall, Thomas B. *History of the 83rd Ohio Volunteer Infantry, The Greyhound Regiment.* Cincinnati: 83rd Ohio Volunteer Inf. Assoc., 1912.
Maury, Dabney H. *Recollections of a Virginian in the Mexican, Indian and Civil War.* New York: Scribner, 1897.
Merrill, James M. *Battle Flags South: The Story of the Civil War Navies on Western Waters.* Rutherford, N.J.: Fairleigh Dickinson University Press, 1970.
_____. *The Rebel Shore: The Story of Union Sea Power in the Civil War.* Boston: Little, Brown & Company, 1957.
Miller, Edward G. *Captain Edward Gee Miller of the 20th Wisconsin, His War 1861–1865.* Fayetteville: Washington Coventry Hist. Soc., 1960.
Miller, F. T., and James Barnes, eds. *Photographic History of the Civil War.* Vol. 6. New York: Review of Reviews, 1911.
Morgan, James M., and John P. Marquand. *Prince and Boatswain: Sea Tales from the Recollection of Rear Admiral Charles E. Clark.* Greenfield, Mass.: A. Hall & Co., 1915.
Nash, Howard P. *A Naval History of the Civil War.* New York: A. S. Barnes and Company, Inc., 1972.
Naval Actions and History, 1799–1898. Papers of the Military History Society of Massachusetts. Vol. XII. Boston: Griffith-Stillings Press, 1902.
Nevins, Allan. *the War for the Union, The Organized War, 1863–1864.* New York: Charles Scribner's Sons, 1971.
Niven, John. *Gideon Welles: Lincoln's Secretary of War.* New York: Oxford University Press, 1973.
Owsley, Frank L. *King Cotton Diplomacy.* Chicago: University of Chicago Press, date not set.
Parker, Foxhall A. *The Battle of Mobile Bay and the Capture of Forts Powell, Gaines, and Morgan.* Boston: A. Williams and Co., 1878.
Parker, Captain William Harwar. *Confederate Military History.* Vol. XIII, *The Confederate States Navy.* Atlanta: 1899.
Perry, Milton F. *Infernal Machines.* Baton Rouge: Louisiana State University Press, 1965.
Pollard, Edward A. *The Lost Cause.* New York: E. B. Treat, 1867.
Porter, David D. *Naval History of the Civil War.* New York: Sherman Publishing, 1886.
Pratt, Fletcher. *Civil War on the Western Waters.* New York: Pratt, Rinehart and Winston, 1956.
Reed, David W. *Campaigns and Battles of the Twelfth Regiment Iowa Veteran Volunteer Infantry.* Evanston: Pub. by author, 1903.
Reed, Rowena. *Combined Operations of the Civil War.* Annapolis: Naval Institute Press, 1978.
Rich, Doris. *Fort Morgan and the Battle of Mobile Bay.* Foley, Ala.: Baldwin Times, 1972.
Robinson, William M., Jr. *The Confederate Privateers.* New Haven: Yale University Press, 1928.
Scharf, J. Thomas. *History of the Confederate States Navy.* New York: Rogers and Sherwood, 1887.
Scott, John. *Story of the Thirty-Second Iowa Infantry Volunteers.* Nevada, Iowa: Pub. by author, 1896.
Smith, C. Carter, Jr. *Mobile 1861–1865.* Chicago: Wyvern Press, n.d.

_____, ed. *Two Naval Journals: 1864. The Journal of Engineer John C. O'Connell, CSN, on the C.S.S. Tennessee and the Journal of Pvt. Charles Brother, USMC, on the U.S.S. Hartford.* Chicago: Wyvern Press, 1964.

Smith, Gustavus W. *Confederate War Papers.* New York: Atlantic Pub., 1884.

Smith, Walter George. *Life and Letters of Thomas Kilby Smith.* New York and London: Putnam's, 1897.

Soley, James R. *The Blockade and the Cruisers.* New York: Charles Scribner's Sons, 1890.

_____. *The Navy in the Civil War.* New York: Charles Scribner's Sons, 1883.

Spears, John Randolph. *David G. Farragut.* Philadelphia: George W. Jacobs and Company, 1905.

Sperry, Andrew F. *Hisotry of the 33rd Iowa Infantry Volunteer Regiment.* Des Moines: Mills & Co., 1866.

Still, William, N., Jr. *Iron Afloat: The Story of the Confederate Ironclads.* Nashville: Vanderbilt University Press, 1971.

Taylor, Richard. *Destruction and Reconstruction.* New York: D. Appleton and Co., 1879.

Tepper, Sol H. *Torpedoes? Damn!* Selma, Sol Tepper, 1979.

Thompson, R. M., and R. Wainwright, eds. *Confidential Correspondence of Gustavus Vasa Fox, Assistant Secretary of the Navy 1861–1865.* 2 vols. New York: Naval History Society, 1918–1919.

United States Navy Department. *Official Records of the Union and Confederate Navies in the War of the Rebellion.* 30 vols. Washington, D.C.: U.S. Government Printing Office, 1905.

United States War Department. *The War of the Rebellion: A Compilation of the Official Records of the Union and Confederate Armies.* 131 vols. Washington, D.C.: U.S. Government Printing Office, 1886.

Walke, Henry, Rear Admiral, U.S.N. *Naval Scenes and Reminiscences of the Civil War in the United States on the Southern and Western Waters.* New York: F. R. Reed & Co., 1877.

Way, Virgil G. *History of the Thirty-Third Regiment Illinois Veteran Volunteer Infantry.* Gibson, Ill.: 1902.

Wayland, John W. *The Pathfinder of the Seas: The Life of Matthew Fontaine Maury.* Richmond, Va.: Garrett and Massie, 1930.

Welles, Gideon. *Diary of Gideon Welles.* Vol. 1. Boston: Houghton Mifflin, 1911.

Wells, Tom H. *The Confederate Navy: A Study in Organization.* University, Ala.: University of Alabama Press, 1971.

West, Richard S., Jr. *Mr. Lincoln's Navy.* New York: Longman's, Green and Company, 1957.

Williams, John M. *The Eagle Regiment, 8th Wisconsin Infantry Volunteers.* Belleville: Recorder Printers, 1890.

Wood, Wales W. *A History of the Ninety-Fifth Regiment Illinois Infantry Volunteers.* Chicago: Tribune Co., 1865.

Woods, Joseph T. *Services of the 96th Ohio Volunteers.* Toledo: Blade Print & Paper Co., 1874.

Other Sources

Alexander, W. A. "Thrilling Chapter in the History of the Confederate States Navy. Work of the Submarine Boats." *Southern Historical Society Papers,* XXX (1902).

Baldwin, H. D. "Farragut in Mobile Bay, Recollections of One Who Took Part in the Battle." *Scribner's Monthly,* XIII, February 1877.

Brown, H. D. "The First Successful Torpedo and What It Did." *Confederate Veteran,* XVIII (1910).

Conrad, Dr. Daniel B. "Capture of the C. S. Ram *Tennessee* in Mobile Bay, August, 1864." *Southern Historical Society Papers,* XIX.

————. "What a Fleet Surgeon Saw of the Fight in Mobile Bay." *The United Service: A Monthly Review of Military and Naval Affairs.* New series, vol. VIII (September 1892).

Crowley, R. O. "The Confederate Torpedo Service." *Century Magazine,* XLVI (1898).

Davidson, Hunter. "The Electrical Submarine Mine 1861–1865." *Confederate Veteran,* XVI (1908).

————. "Electrical Torpedoes as a System of Defense." *Southern Historical Society Papers,* II (1876).

Diggins, Bartholomew. *Recollections of the War Cruise of the U.S.S.* Hartford *from January 1862 to December 24, 1864.* (Manuscript in New York Public Library).

Ford, Arthur P. "The First Submarine Boat." *Confederate Veteran,* XIV (1906).

Kinney, J. C. "An August Morning with Farragut." *Century Magazine,* May 1881. Also published in *Scribner's Monthly,* XXII, June 1881.

Kloeppel, J. E. "The Mystery Sub of Jackson Square." *Civil War Times Illustrated,* XXVIII, no. 5, September/October, 1989.

Levey, Gordon. "Torpedo Boats at Louisiana Soldier's Home." *Confederate Veteran,* XVII (1900).

Rains, Gabriel J. "Torpedoes." *Southern Historical Society Papers,* III (1877).

Stephen, Walter W. "The Brooke Guns from Selma." *Alabama Historical Quarterly,* XX (1958).

Tarrant, Edward W. "Siege and Capture of Fort Blakely." *Confederate Veteran,* XXIII (1915).

Watson, J. Crittenden. Letter dated September 6, 1880. *Scribner's Monthly,* XXII, June 1881.

Newspapers

Charleston *Mercury*
Grenada *Appeal*
Mobile *Evening News*
Mobile *Times*
Montgomery *Daily Advertiser*
Nashville *Daily American*
Richmond *Sentinel*

Manuscripts, Letters and Documents

Bernhardt-Campbell Family Papers, Carlisle Barracks
Franklin Buchanan Letterbook, Southern Historical Collection, University of North Carolina
Eugene A. Carr Papers, Carlisle Barracks Archives
Percival Drayton Letters, New York Public Library
Gustavus V. Fox Correspondence, New York Historical Society

Gustavus V. Fox Diary, New York Historical Society
Betty Herndon Maury Diary. Manuscript in Maury Papers, Manuscript Division, Library of Congress
Maury Papers, Manuscript Division, Library of Congress
John K. Mitchell Papers, Virginia Historical Society
Records from the West Blockading Squadron, United States Navy, Record Group 45, National Archives Microfilm
Records in the Bureau of Ordnance, Records Group 74, National Archives Microfilm
Records of the Confederate Engineers, Record Group 109, National Archives Microfilm
Records of the Office of Ordnance and Hydrography, Confederate States Navy, Record Group 109, National Archives Microfilm
Charles Stewart Letters, Civil War Times Illustrated Collection, Carlisle Barracks
Willis, E. "Torpedos and Torpedo Boats and Their Bold and Hazardous Expeditions." Manuscript Division, Library of Congress

Index